SELECTIONS

Virginia Museum of Fine Arts

by Anne B. Barriault

with the assistance of
Kay M. Davidson

The publication of this book

was made possible by generous support from

The Council of the Virginia Museum of Fine Arts,

through proceeds from *Fine Arts & Flowers 1995*

and a grant from *The Council Travel Fund.*

Library of Congress Cataloging-in-Publication Data
Virginia Museum of Fine Arts.
    Selections: Virgina Museum of Fine Arts/by Anne B. Barriault, with
    the assistance of Kay M. Davidson.
        p.   cm.
    Includes bibliographical references and index.
    ISBN 0-917046-47-1 (PBK)
    1. Art—Virginia—Richmond—Catalogs. 2. Virginia Museum of Fine Arts—
Catalogs. I. Barriault, Anne B. II. Davidson, Kay M. III. Title.
N716.M8A68 1997
708.155'451'074—dc21   97-24981
                                                            CIP

ISBN 0-917046-47-1
Printed in the United States of America

Produced by the Office of Publications, Virginia Museum of Fine Arts,
    2800 Grove Avenue, Richmond, Virginia 23221-2466 USA
Edited by Rosalie West and Morgen Cheshire
Book Design by Sarah Lavicka
Photography by Katherine Wetzel, Richmond, except as noted on page 123.
Composed by the designer in QuarkXpress. Type set in Adobe Stone Serif.
Printed on acid-free 80lb. Warren Lustro Enamel Dull text by Carter Printing,
    Richmond.
Binding by Bindagraphics, Baltimore, Maryland.

FRONT COVER: detail Andrea di Bartolo's *Assumption of the Virgin,* circa 1390s,
tempera on wood. Virginia Museum of Fine Arts Purchase, The Adolph D.
and Wilkins C. Williams Fund. See page 53.

BACK COVER: detail *Lhamo,* early 1400s, silk embroidery on silk ground.
Virginia Museum of Fine Arts, Gift of Berthe and John Ford. See page 26.

Contents

Foreword

The Virginia Museum of Fine Arts—born of the commitment of a handful of Virginians to art and education—has become a source of pride for people of all ages and interests throughout the Commonwealth. When the Virginia Museum of Fine Arts first opened its doors in 1936 in the wake of the Great Depression, it did so because of the energy that emerged from the newly created partnership between state government and private individuals, as participants, members, and donors of art and funds. It continues to prosper because that partnership has flourished.

From its initial holdings of fewer than 100 works of art, the Museum's collections have grown to more than 18,000 objects that represent 6,000 years of creative achievement across six continents. Although these holdings are housed in fine buildings, it has been an essential quality of this institution, with its responsibility to serve all of Virginia's citizens, to extend itself to make its collections and programs widely available. Over the years the Museum has sent its resources across the state through an ambitious network of art-lending programs and a lively mix of educational services.

The Museum's publishing program is an essential part of this effort, producing books that meet the needs of many readers, from art-lovers everywhere to specialized scholars. This is the most substantial handbook on the Museum's collections to date, and it is the first general publication on the collections in more than a decade. In selecting over 100 works to feature in this book, care has been taken to represent both the range and character of the Virginia Museum's holdings, as well as to present them in a way that is useful and interesting to readers.

With full color illustrations and a text geared to a broad audience, this book joins a series of handbooks that spotlights more focused parts of the collections. Handbooks of this type have been published on African art, the holdings of objects by Peter Carl Fabergé, and one of the world's only complete sets of British champion animals, a series by the noted American sculptor Herbert Haseltine. Others will follow in the years ahead.

Like the Museum itself, a publication of this kind can only come to fruition through the creative collaboration of many. The Council, the Museum's largest volunteer group, has long supported publications projects at the Virginia Museum of Fine Arts. It was through their encouragement that this volume was first envisioned, and they promptly sealed their commitment with proceeds from an ambitious benefit display and gala, *Fine Arts and Flowers 1995,* along with a generous grant from *The Council Travel Fund.*

Idea became reality through the concerted efforts of a talented staff: Publications Senior Editor Anne Barriault brought both her graceful prose and her extensive art-historical knowledge to bear in writing this compendium of the Museum's collections. Dr. Barriault was ably assisted by Kay Davidson. Dr. Davidson gathered and reviewed reference materials during months of research. Katherine Wetzel brilliantly produced nearly all of this book's photography, with the expert help of registrars and art handlers. Howell Perkins catalogued and made countless images available from the Museum's Photo Archives. Morgen Cheshire and Rosalie West shared the vast task of editing the entire book; Publications Manager and Editor-in-Chief Monica Rumsey thoughtfully guided the project as handbook series editor; and Sarah Lavicka, Chief Graphic Designer, arranged word and image with dedication, and artistry. Curators, educators, and volunteers alike were forthcoming and generous when polled for their wisdom, expertise, and advice along the way. We are indebted to each and every one for this beautiful and much-needed publication.

KATHARINE C. LEE
Director
Virginia Museum of Fine Arts

Preface

A picture lives a life like a living creature, undergoing changes imposed on us by our life from day to day. —PABLO PICASSO

This book—a portable Virginia Museum of Fine Arts for the visitor and reader—presents highlights that characterize the Museum's collection. Many old favorites will be found within these pages, as well as wonderful additions to the collections. We have included signature objects balanced by those that deserve to be better known because of their originality and fine quality. Still, this is by no means a comprehensive guide. The objects featured in these pages afford but a glimpse of the richness of the collections and the generosity of the donors. These selections only suggest the many cultures and periods, movements, types, and styles of art that may be explored first-hand in the galleries. This handbook acts as a kind of viewfinder, to frame objects of interest, and to refresh the memory between visits to the Museum, to see the art itself.

Part of the fun—and yes, the occasional frustration—in choosing objects for this book had to do with pure and utter wonderment, born of diverse tastes in the arts. The many voices and perspectives of our staff and volunteers helped with the difficult task of winnowing the selections to one hundred. Many a round of spirited exchanges took place as we discovered and rediscovered what makes one work of art stronger or weaker than another; what we personally like or dislike; what soothes our emotions

or stirs our intellects. We have generally selected staples from our collections, tried-and-true works of art on view in more-or-less permanent niches. It is for this reason that only a few works on paper from the Museum's collections are presented in this book.

Part of the wonder of art is its power to touch each of us individually, and so, the visitor may find personal favorites in the galleries that may not be in this book. At the same time, objects featured here may not always be found in the galleries. Works of art are rotated, they are lent to other museums or sent to storage for a much needed rest and a conservator's attention; some are taken off view from time to time so that other works of art may be shared with the public.

The purpose of this book is to provide you—viewer and reader—with what we, staff and volunteers, believe to be some of the best selections from our collections of world art. Each entry contains a careful description of the object, a color reproduction, and side paragraphs that offer additional facts. These pages present reminders of the collection, portable portions of our galleries to keep with you between Museum visits, to entice you to return. —AB

Acknowledgments

Many people deserve many thanks for their contributions to *Selections*. It was a truly collaborative effort on the part of Museum staff and volunteers. The Council has made this book possible by generously donating its proceeds from *Fine Arts and Flowers 1995,* chaired by Norma Jean Joyner and co-chaired by Charlotte Minor. Funding was also provided by The Council Travel Committee, chaired by Shirley Montz, 1996–97, and Shirley Hatcher, 1994–95, and supplemented with a Spring Council Gift, under 1996 president "B. J." Durrill.

Selections has been realized because of the vision and commitment of Katharine C. Lee, Director; Michael Smith, Associate Director, Communications and Marketing; and Monica S. Rumsey, Publications Manager, Editor-in-Chief, and series originator. Sarah Lavicka, Chief Graphic Designer, created the handsome design, infusing the book with unflagging enthusiasm from beginning to end. The beautiful new photography came from the keen eye and camera-work of Katherine Wetzel. Editors Morgen Cheshire and Rosalie West added welcome grace to the project, polishing and improving the text. An insightful and energetic editor, Morgen guided the book into print with flair. Michelle Wilson calmly corrected drafts of the manuscript with helpful good humor; always inspired, Sara Johnson-Ward skillfully managed the book's promotion and distribution.

Curators Malcolm Cormack, Margo A. Crutchfield, David Park Curry, Joseph M. Dye III, H. Ashley Kistler, Margaret Ellen Mayo, Kathleen Schrader, and Richard B. Woodward generously lent their expertise. Each recommended objects and references, consulted about photography, and reviewed sections pertinent to his or her department with lively comment and extraordinary good will. I would especially like to thank Joe Dye for sharing excerpts from his forthcoming catalogue of the Museum's permanent collection of Indian art. Elizabeth O'Leary offered thoughtful commentaries; Heather Russell, helpful references; and former curator Frederick R. Brandt, advice from experience. Mitzie Booth, Caryl Burtner, and Lulan Yu made the Collections archives readily available and facilitated research.

Registrar Jennie Runnels; Photography Assistant Susie Rock; Kathleen Schrader, Associate Director, Collections Management and Resources; and Sarah Lavicka were instrumental in orchestrating the photography sessions, directed by Katherine Wetzel. Registrars Maureen Morrisette, Mary Sullivan, and Karen Daly protected the art and the accuracy of the records, under Head Registrar Lisa Hancock, while Roy Thompson saw the task to completion, assisted by fellow art handlers, Frank Milik, Andy Kovach, and Randy Wilkinson. Photo Resources Manager Howell Perkins and his assistant, Karen Gerard, provided study photos, counsel, and chocolate.

Suzanne Freeman, Margaret Burcham, and Eliza Knox in the Museum Library patiently filled requests for reference materials. Archival essays about the Museum by Virginius Dabney and Wolf von Eckardt, and conversations with Deputy Director Carol Amato, Special Projects Coordinator Kristi Pipes Lane, and Evaluation Specialist Maria Spencer-Etienne provided focus for the book's *Introduction.*

Sandra Rusak, Associate Director of Education and Outreach, graciously offered an educator's expertise, helping to compile initial lists of objects and to review proofs. Staff and volunteers from many departments deserve thanks for joining Publications, Collections, and the Director's Office in the process of selecting objects for the book: Dana Conte and Anita Holloway, Tour Services Coordinators, with Docents Arlene DeConti, Carol Dunham, and Alex McGrath; Carolyn Adams, Community Affairs Director, and Teresa Dayrit; Kate Clary and the Visitor Services volunteers; and Museum Shop volunteers Nancy Clements, Emily Elmore, Lucille Briere, and Margo Natvig. Brenda Parker and the Shop's book department also deserve thanks. Natalie Crichigno, community volunteer, offered fresh perspective on art in the Museum's galleries and in the book, while fulfilling many fact-checking missions; Ruth Twiggs, Media Production Manager, prompted dialogue about the presentation of the collections, and Virgie Foster, Kenneth Farrow, and Marjorie Maybush, Housekeeping staff, gave sound evening advice to go home.

I would like to thank consultants for their advice about specific works of art: James Farmer, Virginia Commonwealth University; Loretta Cooper, Anderson Gallery, Virginia Commonwealth University; Stephen Addiss, University of Richmond; Marion Roberts, University of Virginia; Paul Barolsky, University of Virginia; John Seidensticker, The National Zoological Parks; and Nicholas Rumsey, cabinetmaker and furniture conservator. Heartfelt appreciation goes to Bruce Young, Arthur M. Sackler Gallery, and Catherine Ritter, two outside readers with infinite knowledge about the Museum's collections and its history.

Susan M. Glasser, the Museum's former Coordinator of Statewide Educational Resources, introduced Kay M. Davidson to Publications in 1996. With her research skills, docent experience, and perceptiveness, Kay ensured the project's successful completion. She brought wisdom and watchfulness to the book, worthy of Buddhist guardian figures Tara and Lhamo.

Finally, I am grateful for my understanding family and friends, and for Randall Henniker, my patient artist, critic, and project enthusiast in residence.

—AB

Introduction

The Museum

World art makes the Virginia Museum of Fine Arts one of the largest and liveliest visual arts institutions in the southeastern United States. Here, collections have been gathered from all corners of the earth—Africa, Asia, Europe, Central, South, and North America—and range in date over a 6,000 year period. The vast array of visual delights in the galleries often surprises first-time visitors; many newcomers become long-standing supporters, returning to view old favorites, new acquisitions, and special exhibitions.

The Collections

The Virginia Museum's collection began in 1919, when Judge John Barton Payne—a Virginian, U.S. Cabinet member, and head of the American Red Cross—donated approximately 100 works of art to the people of the Commonwealth. Enhanced through the years by countless donations of art, funds, and bequests from generous individuals, the Museum's collection now consists of more than 18,000 objects.

Among the holdings are Lillian Thomas Pratt's 1947 bequest of imperial eggs and other objects from the House of Fabergé; the T. Catesby Jones Collection of early twentieth-century European paintings; and a growing collection of European painting and sculpture from 1300 to 1900, first established in the 1950s through the bequests and endowments of Adolph D. and Wilkins C. Williams, and Margaret and Arthur Glasgow.

The Museum houses one of the six finest and most comprehensive collections of Indian art in the nation, founded upon the Nasli Heeramaneck collection acquired through funds given by Mr. Paul Mellon in 1968. The early 1990s acquisition of mystical Nepalese and Tibetan objects from the notable collections of the Zimmerman family, and Berthe and John Ford, was made possible in part by the E. Rhodes and Leona B. Carpenter Foundation. The Museum's ancient Egyptian artifacts, South Italian and Greek vases, and Roman sculpture and painting form one of the few ancient Mediterranean collections in the mid-Atlantic region; its collection of African art represents a wide range of diverse continental cultures, including the Dan, Akan, Yoruba, Kuba, and Hemba. The collection of Ancient American art comprises objects from many cultures, among them Peruvian, Columbian, Panamanian, and Mexican.

The J. Harwood and Louise B. Cochrane Fund has greatly strengthened the collection of American painting, sculpture, and decorative arts. The Museum's collections of Art Nouveau and Art Deco jewelry, furnishings, and sculpture, as well as its collection of contemporary art have been given magnanimously by Sydney and Frances Lewis, who have also supported the Museum through funds and endowments. The generous 1997 gift from Rita Gans—her collection assembled with her husband, the late Jerome Gans—brought fine English silver by such masters as Paul de Lamerie and Paul Storr to the galleries. Extensive holdings in French Impressionist and Post-Impressionist painting, Degas' bronze and wax sculpture of ballerinas and thoroughbred horses, and British sporting art are the generous gifts of Mr. and Mrs. Paul Mellon.

The commitment from private sources to support the growth of collections is a fundamental part of the Museum's well-being. The sources of that support, through gracious gifts and endowed funds, are listed for each object in this book.

The Building

Because of Judge Payne's initial gift, the collection existed long before the Museum itself became a reality. In 1932, the Virginia General Assembly authorized

Governor John Garland Pollard to accept a gift of $100,000 from Judge Payne, in order to erect a suitable building for the collection and exhibition of works of art. It was in 1934, fifteen years after Judge Payne donated his collection to the Commonwealth, that a further act of the General Assembly established the Virginia Museum of Fine Arts as a state agency. That act described the Museum's primary mandate: "to promote throughout the Commonwealth education in the realm of art."

Governor Pollard issued a challenge to Virginians to help raise funds to build the Museum, and they responded with characteristic enthusiasm. The funds were raised, a site was selected in Richmond's burgeoning West End and, with the help of master craftsmen working under the Depression-era's Works Progress Administration, the new building was opened in 1936. Since then, the Museum has expanded wing by wing to keep pace with the steady growth of its collections and variety of programs. Its many facades— a blend of classical and modern styles, mortared red brick and chiseled limestone, curved walls and plate glass— hint at the many facets of art inside.

Today, a visitor approaching the Museum sees three distinct styles of architecture, reflecting the changing look of museums in this century. Facing the Boulevard, off-white limestone and red brick define the original 1936 building, designed in the Georgian style. Named for the succession of Kings who ruled England between 1713 and 1820, the style—also known as English Renaissance—consists of classicizing elements based on ancient Roman and Italian Renaissance architecture. The august style, using pediments and pilasters, garlands and volutes, had come to define European and American fine-arts museums built during the late 1800s and early 1900s

in Berlin, London, Philadelphia, and Washington, DC. It was the preferred style of Peebles and Ferguson, Norfolk, the architectural firm chosen to design the Museum in Richmond.

Limestone and brick were used to carry the design of the original building through the flanking northern addition of 1954–55 and the southern addition of 1970. The familiar materials reappeared in a second North Wing, which opened in 1976. Its windows and curved surfaces, however, represented a new age in museum architecture. The architect, David Warren Hardwicke, described the North Wing as "fluid space." Indeed, the exterior shapes fluid interior spaces that open onto views of galleries and gardens across bridges, landings, and stairwells. The circular North Lobby now serves as the Museum's main entrance.

In 1985, the West Wing opened and "turned the entire museum into a unified, communal experience," in the words of architectural historian Wolf von Eckardt. Designed by Malcolm Holzman of the New York firm of Hardy Holzman Pfeiffer Associates, the wing is made entirely of off-white stone—no brick this time, in contrast to the earlier architectural campaigns. Faint echoes of the classical structure and the curvilinear one are present in small details: the heavily rusticated limestone base contrasts the smooth-stone base of the 1936 building; the rounded stone molding ("bull-nose") plays upon the curves of the 1976 addition; a ground-level ribbon of pink-and-black speckled granite wraps the entire West Wing with a touch of color, the opposite of the older red brick editions trimmed in weathered off-white stone. Two large glass bays, housing stairwells inside and trimmed outside with the architects' signature blue paint, serve as colorful brackets on the "facade" overlooking the Museum's campus to the west.

The Galleries

Three-dimensional objects of exceptionally high quality make up a large part of the collections in the galleries: Asian, Ancient Mediterranean, African, Art Nouveau and Art Deco, Ancient American, Later European and American, and Fabergé. From sculpture to textiles, gold jewelry to silver vessels, fine furniture to stained-glass lamps, the objects are spiritual, decorative, or utilitarian by turn, or sometimes in combination.

Paintings in the galleries offer insights into collectors' and donors' tastes over many generations, as well as curatorial vision. Fine works by less well-known artists and unusual works by famous names contribute to the collections' distinctiveness and appeal. A glance at the European galleries reveals a predilection for portraits, landscapes, and histories— especially French, Dutch, and Flemish— and a collection of Italian pictures from Siena, Rome, Naples, and Venice. West Wing galleries reflect a taste for French Impressionist works, British landscapes and sporting art—many intimate in scale—as well as huge, boldly painted contemporary works. Every unique object attests to art's infinite richness and variety, as well as to the collections' diversity.

Throughout the galleries, exceptions prove the rule in works by well-known artists. Frank Lloyd Wright may be famous for his neutral-colored glass with natural motifs (do not miss the *Tree of Life* window in the galleries), but he also designed an unusual set of windows in primary colors and geometric patterns (see pp. 102–103). Mary Cassatt achieved her reputation through strong drawing (the *Banjo Lesson* is on view in the galleries), yet she also painted in the Impressionist style (see p. 90). Eileen Gray—renowned for clean lines in lacquered screens and metal tables (in the galleries)—experimented with lavish styles that she eventually renounced (p. 104). Today, Fragonard's paintings may seem to contain the essence of 18th-century France (p. 64); at the time, however, Carle Van Loo better personified that age of art academies (p. 63). Salvator Rosa aspired to be a history painter (p. 55), though he became better known for his figured landscapes. A panel by Altichiero is a rare example of a small picture by a large-scale fresco painter (p. 52).

Art sometimes defies boundaries and categories. The symmetry of a gold necklace from Africa's west coast accentuates, by its uniqueness and cross-cultural influences, the asymmetry that usually characterizes the Akan culture's gold jewelry. One of the finest Tibetan images on cloth *(thankas)* in the Museum was embroidered in silk, not painted as usual, and probably comes from China. The Museum also houses examples of *thankas* painted by Tibetan artists in the Nepalese style for Nepalese merchants living in Tibet. The collection of Japanese screens reveals complex cross-currents between schools of painting in China and Japan. One by one, objects show us that no matter how much we know about an artist, and no matter how familiar or how foreign the work of art may be, it will always offer something new to see and understand. Like a jewel box, the Museum is filled with treasures meant to enhance life's experiences.

Art and The Viewer

Seeing the magic of color, light, and form; being elated by the beautiful or perplexed by the puzzling; experiencing joy or tranquility, or even feeling sad or uneasy—such sensations can be inspired by art, to provoke a thought and enrich a life. For the viewer willing to look, to learn, to question, and to have fun, the appreciation of art is but a blink of an eye, a frown, a laugh, and a new discovery away. Curiosity is all it takes to begin to make the world of art unfold. This book presents some of the best of the Virginia Museum of Fine Arts; there is much more, waiting to be seen.

Architects: The Original Building

The firm of Peebles and Ferguson, architects of the Museum's original building on Boulevard and Grove Avenue, also contributed classical-style designs for additions to the Virginia State Capitol, Richmond, and the University of Virginia, Charlottesville.

Architects: The West Wing

Architects of the Museum's West Wing— Hardy Holzman Pfeiffer Associates—have participated in designs for the Brooklyn Children's Museum; the new wing of the Los Angeles County Museum of Art; and the St. Louis and Toledo Museums of Art.

Architects: The North Wing and Lobby

Designs for the Museum's North Wing reflect the influence of earlier plans by Leslie Cheek (Director 1948–1968) and his architect Robert Welton Stewart.

The Marble Hall

The West Wing's Marble Hall is named for its walls, lined with shiny, soft-red, dappled stone. The marble, from Carrara, Italy, surrounds a space supported by columns of fossilized Texas limestone.

TheatreVirginia

The Virginia Museum also houses a 500-seat theater, home of TheatreVirginia, one of Richmond's many cultural offerings, and main stage for Fast/Forward, the Museum's performance arts series.

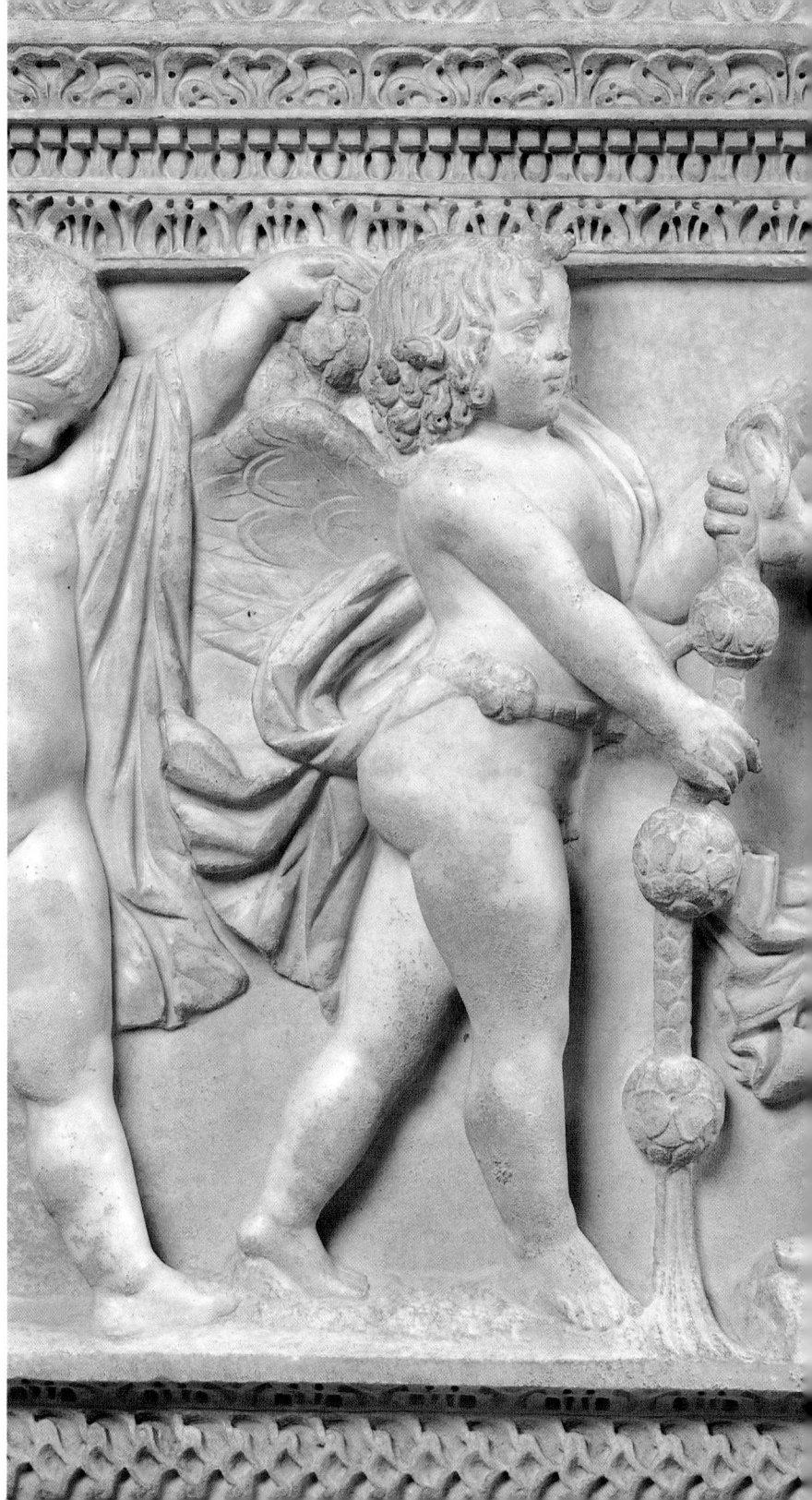

Figure of a Woman

"Self-contained" is one phrase that comes to mind to describe this figure. She has a face without features, and she folds her arms tightly across her body. Though she was carved more than 4000 years ago, her simple contours—lyre-shaped head; long, cylindrical neck; broad, sloping shoulders; and hips that narrow to slightly bent legs—might at first remind us of the clean geometry of contemporary sculpture. Contemplate her, however, and her symmetry softens as her sculptor's distinctive hand is revealed. She displays a slight unevenness of nose, breasts, arms, and knees; a foot was shortened and toes reworked when the marble cracked under the pressure of the carving tool. She could be held in the hand but, with angled feet, she was never intended to stand. The figure was meant to recline. The longer we look at her, the more she discloses about her nature, hand-made from marble washed by the sea or broken from the hillsides of her island home.

The figure comes from the Cyclades, a group of small islands in the Aegean Sea east of Greece and north of Crete. Known to the ancient Greeks as "the Circling Ones," this chain of mountainous islands supported pre-Greek, non-literate people who farmed, fished, and traded with fellow seafarers between 3200 and 1100 B.C. Clusters of families lived together on these islands, in tiny communities scattered where fresh water could be found. They built homes of unmortared stone, buried their dead in cemeteries of shallow stone graves, and carved stone figures and vessels of timeless, mysterious beauty.

The precise meaning of Cycladic sculpture is unknown. Looted from the earth before archaeologists could study their exact placement, many figures laid to rest with the dead may once have offered information now lost to us. Perhaps they were created for religious purposes, blessings of fertility in this life, or companionship in the hereafter. We know that the figures were originally less abstract in appearance than they are today. Traces of paint, such as the faded lines on this figure's chest, tell us that artists added eyes, hair, and adornments in reds and blues. The complex meaning of these figures is as elusive as the ancient Cycladic communities themselves, whose own golden age vanished when trade with the Minoans in Crete and the Myceneans on the Greek mainland increased, and new golden ages were born.

Tradition in Cycladic Art

Most Cycladic figures take the form of reclining females with folded arms. For a thousand years, generation after generation, figures such as this one were carved, usually with U- or lyre-shaped heads, prominent noses, and left arms folded above right. Faces were sometimes painted, and fingers, toes, and pubic triangles were incised. Artisans of the Cyclades also fashioned seated and standing figures, sometimes male, as well as marble bowls, beakers, and boxes. Between 3200 and 2200 B.C., the tradition of Cycladic marble carving continued unbroken, altered only by an artist's personal nuances and refinements.

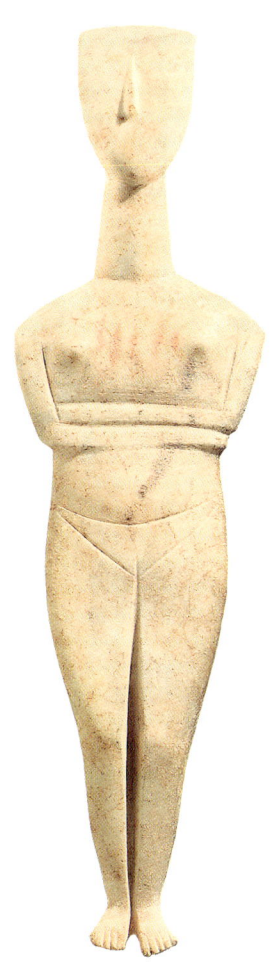

Figure of a Woman
Cycladic Islands, circa 2400 B.C.
Marble; 14¾ inches high
Virginia Museum of Fine Arts Purchase, The Adolph D. and Wilkins C. Williams Fund, 83.73

Tomb Relief

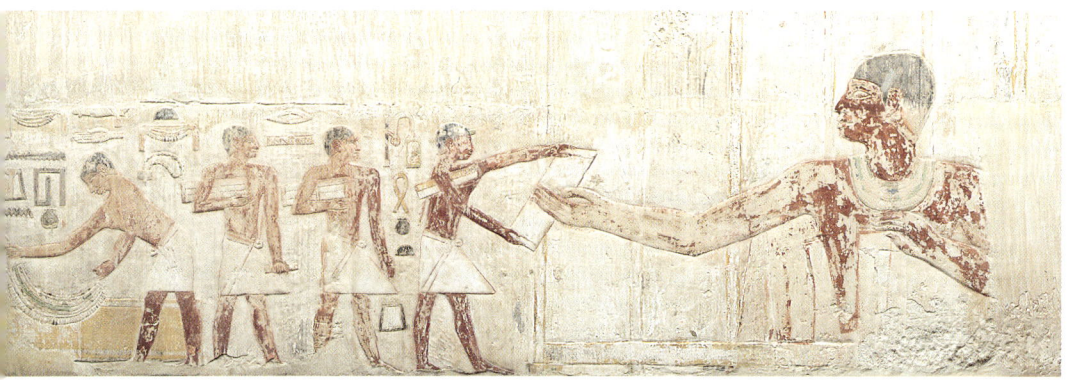

The Nobleman's Identity

The large figure may be Methethy, a nobleman of Saqqara who lived around 2345 B.C., during the 5th and early 6th Dynasties. He left records of his life, and he is depicted in several wooden statues, now in the Brooklyn Museum of Art; The Museum of Fine Arts, Boston; and the Nelson-Atkins Museum, Kansas City. This relief may have come from his tomb.

Old Kingdom Egypt, land of pyramids and papyrus, is evoked in this relief. Egyptian funerary art honored patricians and rulers, who were believed to be divine. Here, the artist uses form and scale to make the hierarchies clear: a large nobleman (right) gestures from his chair to smaller subordinate figures. The first attendant (center) unfurls a papyrus roll, thought to be an account of the estate. Two assistants carry other rolls—the books of ancient Egypt—tucked beneath their arms. The fourth attendant (left) turns from the group to withdraw a wide, beaded necklace, called a *menat*, from the treasure chest behind him. This jewelry will be added to the inventory for the master of the household. He has a taste for finery: traces of blue and green paint suggest strands of gemstones around his neck.

These male figures—large and small, nobles and workers—are painted reddish-brown, according to tradition in Egyptian art. Women are often painted yellow or white (see the Greek *Symposium Vessels*, pp. 4–5). Bodies are rendered by accepted custom, too, so that the human form may be clearly seen. Profiles of eyes, nose, arms, and legs give way to frontal views of broad shoulders and narrow waists. Figures of high social status strike static poses that lend an air of permanence; those of lower social rank appear to move in a more transitory world. Here, attendants turn to grasp the corners of scroll or necklace; as they walk, their kilts fan out against a wall of hieroglyphs.

Perhaps two artists, a sculptor and a painter, made this raised relief. On plaster-coated limestone, the painter sketched his composition in black or red. He first made preparatory drawings, then transferred the design to the wall by means of a grid. The sculptor then chiseled around the sketched-in design, so that the figures emerged from their background. Finally, the painting could begin. Single scenes such as this nobleman's inventory were usually displayed side by side, or one above the other, around the walls of the tomb. Figures often stand on a common groundline in very shallow space.

Ancient Egyptians immortalized the richness of life—dancing, dining, fishing, harvesting, hunting—with art that filled their tombs. Raised reliefs painted in fresh, bright colors—blues, reds, yellows, whites, greens, blacks—enlivened dark chambers. The images were intended to be seen only by immortal eyes in the afterlife. As timeless offerings to accompany the dead, tomb reliefs were designed to nourish the spirit (Ka) and to last for all eternity.

Old Kingdom Saqqara

The city of Saqqara on the Nile was steeped in the art of Old Kingdom Egypt (from the 3rd to the 6th Dynasties, around 2600 to 2100 B.C.). It is the home of the earliest known colossal pyramid, King Zoser's step pyramid of 2750 B.C. It was the home of the royal architect and sculptor Imhotep—one of the first known names in ancient art—who designed Zoser's funerary complex of courtyards, temples, and sculpture. A limestone relief from Saqqara, now in the Egyptian Museum, Cairo, dates from the same period as this relief. It depicts sculptors at work, carved by similar techniques, and suggests that the Virginia Museum's relief may too come from Saqqara.

Tomb Relief

Egyptian, 2475–2195 B.C.

Limestone and traces of pigment; 22⅜ by 58½ inches, including frame

Virginia Museum of Fine Arts Purchase, The Adolph D. and Wilkins C. Williams Fund, 55.6.2

Bes

This funny little creature masks the power and the status that he once held in a world of exquisite beauty. He is Bes, the Egyptian god of marriage, protector during childbirth, and guardian of children, hearth, and home. His roly-poly body served as a cosmetic jar to house kohl to paint the eyes, rouge to color cheeks, or perfumes to anoint the body. He dates from Late Period Egypt and is regarded as one of the finest examples of his kind.

With infectious enthusiasm, Bes squats on his haunches, both fists originally resting on his knees, breasts tapering toward his belly, belly settling to the ground. Human and animal features form his affable face. He gazes beneath eyebrows that arch like goat's horns, set against a furrowed forehead with ridges of wrinkles. His wide nose and smile-lines give way to even wider cheekbones. His thick mustache drapes along each side of his mouth into a beard of carefully curled locks. As he grins, or laughs, he sticks out his tongue and shows a solid row of upper teeth. Leonine ears protrude from his mane of hair, which falls down his back into a single curl. Like a lion's, his ears have an inner fringe of fur.

He wears a leopard skin, cut with a hole to pull over his head. Feline paws wrap around his shoulders; a feline head falls between his breasts. Though the spotted beast's hindquarters and tail trail down and around the portly god's back, the fur fails to conceal his pudgy buttocks.

Molded of faience, a type of glazed Egyptian ware made from powdered quartz, his features could at once amuse his owners and ward off evil. His jolly expression and lust for life would have cheered a mother-to-be; his ferocious aspects were meant to chase away the dangers and the pangs of childbirth. In his left hand he once held a brush or rod for dipping in the jar; and a plumed headdress once topped him as a stopper.

Although his glassy blue-green surface has now faded to soft green, one look at eager Bes reveals how vital a protector and companion he would have been.

Bes's Place in History

This figure of Bes probably comes from the 26th Dynasty of ancient Egypt's Late Period (700–332 B.C.). Even before the 1st Dynasty, around 3100 B.C., Bes held a place in Egyptian religion and art. His image evolved differently, however, from the thin, regal comeliness of his fellow deities, even those with the head of a dog, falcon, or ibis. Love, luck, music, and dance are Bes's realms; his popularity spread throughout the Mediterranean basin until around A.D. 300. Though still uncertain, Bes's origins may lie in sub-Saharan Africa; he is sometimes associated with Silenus, the jolly-but-wise companion of Dionysos, Greek god of wine, and with the Phoenician god, Patechus.

Egyptian Faience

The ancient Egyptians were unsurpassed in their art of faience, a material that is neither glass, nor ceramic, nor related to European earthenware by that name. Artisans molded small objects from ground quartz that fused into shape when fired. The blue, green, or bluish-green color of Egyptian faience derives from the use of alkaline glazes, made from plant ash. Molds for faience beads, scarabs, amulets, and small vessels survive from at least the 18th Dynasty, around 1600 B.C. (see the ancient mold for an amulet of Isis with the Infant Horus *in the Virginia Museum's galleries).*

Vessel in the Form of the God Bes
Egyptian, Late Period, circa 600 B.C.
Faience; 5⅝ by 3¾ by 3⅜ inches
Virginia Museum of Fine Arts Purchase, The Adolph D. and Wilkins C. Williams Fund in Memory of Bernard V. Bothmer, 93.110

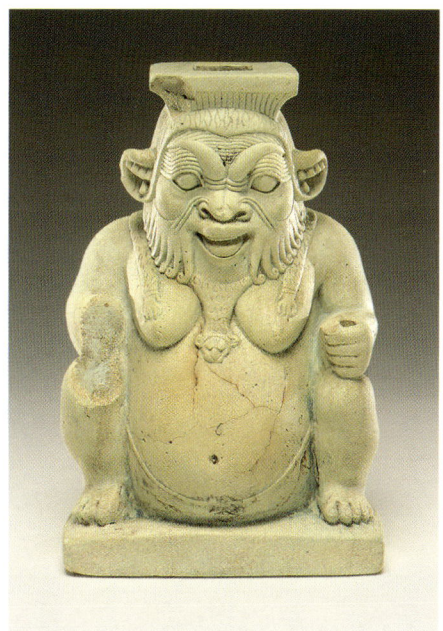

Symposium Vessels

These vessels were born of wine-drinking, song-singing celebration—the ancient Greek symposium. A hymn to the gods would begin the evening, and the ratio for diluting wine with water would be chosen. Drinking songs would sound from singer to singer around the room, and wine-dregs would be tossed at a target (*kottabos*).

Such lighthearted fellowship had a serious side: Dionysos, the god of wine, was also a revealer of truth. Symposia originally honored heroes and ancestors; participants sought to become *entheos,* at one with the deity through intoxication and ecstasy. Vessels, too, have deep meaning: they held elixirs for the living and served in tombs at banquets for the dead. They show us early moments when ancient Greek myth first stepped out of the realm of Homer's poetry (around 800 B.C.) and assumed a painted form.

The *Black-figured Amphora* (left), from around 540 B.C., shows the newborn goddess Athena springing from the head of Zeus. This amphora—made by Group E, a circle of unidentified potters and painters—once held wine. "Amphora" means "carried on both sides," and refers to the two handles; the elongated, swollen form ("belly") allowed a prominent place for a painted scene. The decorations mimic the vessel's shape: shoulders of the figures align with the shoulder of the vase. Slick black glaze on baked red clay creates a scene of strong silhouettes. Lines etched into the glaze define the figures' forms—an eye, a knee, a calf muscle, a fabric pattern. Ancient Greek artistic traditions help us to identify women, painted white with almond eyes. Men are glazed black with rounded eyes; here, central protagonists—Zeus and Athena—are shown frontally. Greek vase painting reduces imagery to its essentials: one moment tells a story; one gesture indicates emotion.

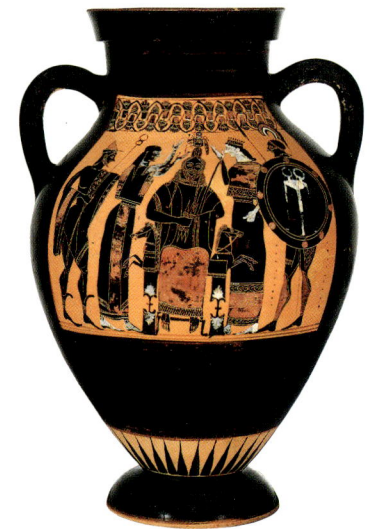

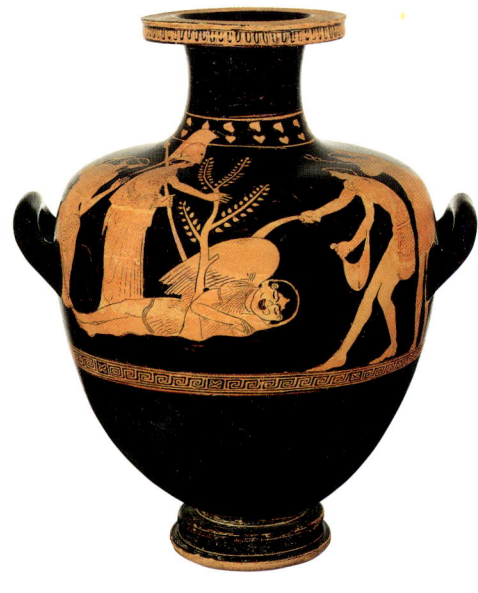

Made around 450 B.C. by the so-called Nausikaa Painter, the *Red-figured Hydria* (second from left)—a water jar with one handle at the back for pouring and two handles on the sides for lifting—reverses the vase-painting technique. The fired red clay surface is reserved for the figures, outlined and surrounded by black glaze. The technique presented new opportunities: brushes dipped in black glazes could investigate details of anatomy, drapery, and expression on red figures (see the *Red-figured Lekythos,* p. 7). Painted scenes expand around vessels, as painters no longer adjusted their designs to fit the vessel shape. Instead, they copied the complex illusions of distance and height seen in large-scale murals. Here, in a pared-down setting, figures occupy different spatial planes. Perseus slays Medusa, a Gorgon. Because the Gorgon's stare could turn a beholder into stone, the hero attacks her as she sleeps. Guided by Athena, Perseus lowers his sword to sever Medusa's head and place it in his bag.

The low-handled *Red-figured Calyx-Crater* (opposite page, left) is formed like its namesake, the cup-shaped base of a flower (*kalyx,* from which the word

"chalice" derives). In it, wine and water would have been mixed. On the outside, the Nikias Painter shows how the red-figure technique had evolved by 400 B.C. Ge, goddess of the Earth, gives the baby Erichthonios, future king of Athens, to Athena, one of the city's protectors. Olympian deities sit and stand on different levels of an invisible landscape. Rich details animate the red ground: a checkered helmet and short cloak, black ribbons, ringlets, and plumes. White is reserved for precious things—the infant king, jewelry, and berries on a poet's laurel wreath, borne by Athena's owl.

On the outside of a *Black-figured Cup* (opposite page, center), made around 520 B.C., huge eyes watch from a field of lotuses and palmettes. Two handles bracket the cup, which is supported by a pedestal. Inside, at the bottom of the wide, shallow basin, a Gorgon stares from dizzying concentric circles. As wine was swallowed, the Gorgon's head would appear, as though the power of the creature and the drink might transform the imbiber. The outside eyes at once warn the cup's beholder to beware and give the object its name: "Eye Cup."

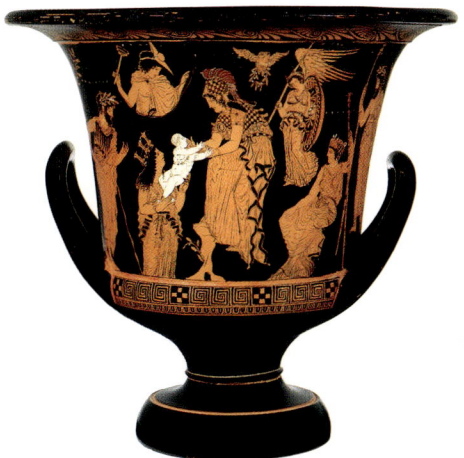

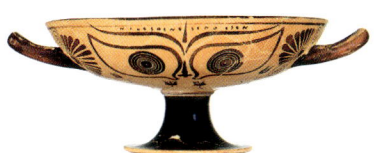

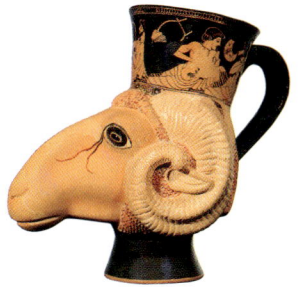

The potter Nikosthenes signed this cup, followed by the word "epoiesen" (made).

Some vase-makers signed their work "so-and-so made me" or "painted me," as if the vase were speaking. "Charinos made me," the *Red-figured Ram's-Head Rhyton* (far right) declares in writing, down the bridge of its gently sloping muzzle. This rhyton belongs to a popular type of drinking vessel (480–450 B.C.) made in the form of animal heads— rams, mules, cows, hounds, lions. The ram's massive horns spiral inward to a small ear; their bony ridges contrast with a fleecy crown. Black glaze outlines the eye. Painted around the top, mythical Athenian kings recline on couches and raise their wine-filled cups. Drawn by the Triptolemos Painter, their symposium illustrates the purpose of the five vessels pictured here.

A Contained History of Greek Vases

Archaic potters and painters often signed their ceramics; they were sometimes one and the same person. With roots in a group of anonymous artists, called Group E, Exekias (active from about 545–530 B.C.) is thought to have perfected the forms of the

Amphora and the Calyx-Crater and to have first placed the eyes on the Eye Cup. His influence may be seen in the vases pictured here. Exekias raised black-figure vase painting to the level of poetry, by depicting poignant moments: a dog greets its long-awaited master, warriors distract them-selves with board games on a battle's eve (Vatican Museums). Exekias taught the Andokides Painter (active 530–515 B.C.), who may have invented red-figure vase painting, and he, in turn, taught Euphronios (active 520–470 B.C.). Euphronios potted a vase for the Triptolemos Painter and painted in the Pioneer Group. These mas-ters of the red-figure technique were sensi-tive to small, meaningful details: an eye-lash, a fingernail, an arched foot. (See also the work of the Berlin Painter among the ancient Greek vessels in the Virginia Museum's collection).

**Black-figured Amphora,
attributed to Group E**

Greek (Attic), circa 540 B.C.
Terra-cotta; 16¾ by 11¼ (diameter) inches
Virginia Museum of Fine Arts Purchase, The Arthur
  and Margaret Glasgow Fund, 60.23

**Red-figured Hydria,
attributed to the Nausikaa Painter**

Greek (Attic), circa 450 B.C.
Terra-cotta; 18 by 13 (diameter) inches
Virginia Museum of Fine Arts Purchase, The Arthur
  and Margaret Glasgow Fund, 62.1.1

**Red-figured Calyx-Crater,
attributed to the Nikias Painter**

Greek (Attic), circa 400 B.C.
Terra-cotta; 14¾ by 16⅛ (diameter) inches
Virginia Museum of Fine Arts Purchase, The Arthur
  and Margaret Glasgow Fund, 81.70

**Black-figured Cup,
signed by Nikosthenes as potter**

Greek (Attic), circa 520 B.C.
Terra-cotta; 4⅛ by 9⅛ (diameter) inches
Virginia Museum of Fine Arts Purchase, The Adolph D.
  and Wilkins C. Williams Fund, 62.1.11

**Red-figured Ram's-Head Rhyton,
attributed to the Triptolemos Painter,
signed by Charinos as potter**

Greek (Attic), circa 480 B.C.
Terra-cotta; 8⅞ by 5½ by 10½ (diameter) inches
Virginia Museum of Fine Arts Purchase, The Adolph D.
  and Wilkins C. Williams Fund, 79.100

Olive Wreath

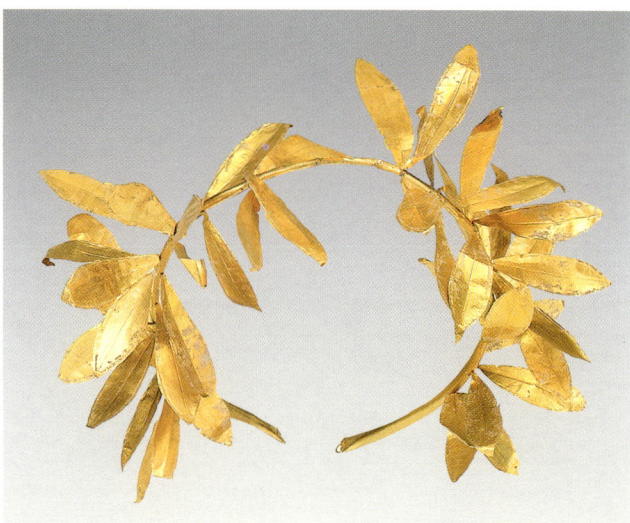

Ancient Greek Jewelers

Artisans of ancient Greece fashioned gold jewelry by building up their forms from hammered sheets of gold. Greek designs derived from nature—buds, palmettes, blossoms, and leaves—and took the form of earrings, pendants and necklaces, hooped bracelets, and seal or signet rings (see the Late Roman-Byzantine Openwork Armbands, *p. 46). Jewelers' names are recorded only rarely. The orator Demosthenes (384–322 B.C.) writes of one: Pammenes of Athens, who made wreaths for him to wear for a festival of Dionysos.*

A History of Greek Gold

The Myceneans learned to make gold jewelry—using the techniques of granulation (applying tiny "grains" of gold), filigree (delicate openwork), and repoussé (raised designs) from Egypt and the Near East before 1000 B.C. Very little gold jewelry survives from the Archaic period (630–480 B.C.) on the Greek mainland, in the Greek colonies south of Italy, or in the Hellenized East (Turkey). Following the defeat of the Persian invaders in 480 B.C., the opening of gold and silver mines brought prosperity to Greece and great demand for gold adornment. As the eastward advances of Philip II of Macedon and his son Alexander the Great opened new opportunities in trade, both gold and gemstones became more plentiful in the Hellenistic era (332–30 B.C.).

Wreath

Greek (Amphipolis), 400–200 B.C.

Gold; 12 inches diameter

Virginia Museum of Fine Arts Purchase, The Adolph D. and Wilkins C. Williams Fund, 65.43.2

A wreath of olive leaves seems to have been showered in gold to last forever: paper-thin leaves spray from a circular base. An ancient Greek jeweler fashioned this fragile foliage from finely hammered sheets of gold, arranging the delicate leaves in groups of three and grafting them to a golden stem.

The olive wreath belongs to a tomb treasure found perhaps in the ancient Greek city of Amphipolis, a northeastern crossroad for the ancient gold trade in Macedonia. The treasure (in the Virginia Museum's galleries) also comprises a gold myrtle wreath with garnet berries, a pair of gold earrings with garnet ducks, a gold chain necklace with a garnet clasp carved as the head of a gazelle, a serpent-shaped ring of hammered gold, and an Isis Crown brooch. The precious objects, many of them tiny, may have been buried in the family tomb at different times between 400 and 100 B.C., or collected as heirlooms over many generations and then buried at one time.

Wreaths of gold often honored ancient Greeks. "They bind their hair with bay leaves of gold, they feast and are glad," writes the poet Pindar (518–438 B.C.). Officials crowned athletes, poets, and statesmen with them; men, women, and children dedicated them to deities in temples; worshipers wore them in religious festivals and processions; the dead took them to their graves. Gold signified worldly beauty and wealth; both men and women wore jewelry. Of all the personal ornaments that they made—rings, earrings, necklaces, and bracelets—jewelers lavished particular attention on headdresses: wreaths, diadems, and even golden hairnets.

Lasting and alluring, gold connected the mundane world with the divine. Many believed that it enhanced communication with gods and goddesses and that the precious metal imparted divine qualities to the deceased. Oak leaves were sacred to Zeus, olive leaves to Athena, ivy to Dionysos, laurel to Apollo, and myrtle to Aphrodite. Each type of leaf inspired golden wreaths. The most fragile crowns were saved for the dead, to rest in their hands or adorn their heads.

Red-figured Lekythos

Eos, goddess of dawn, spirits away the handsome hunter Kephalos in her four-horse chariot. On this large vase, the Underworld Painter depicts an amorous abduction while he celebrates the art of vase painting. Patterns dance across the surface of this *Lekythos* (one-handled jug—with a narrow neck and mouth, and a well-defined shoulder—for oils). Using black glaze, red washes, white and yellow highlights, and the natural red color of baked clay (called painting in "reserve"), the painter presents a broad repertory of ornamentation. Garlands, palmettes, rosettes, and buds, as well as "bead-and-reel," "egg-and-dart," and "diamond" motifs fill wide and narrow bands from mouth to shoulder. Two gorgon faces, painted white with red curls, guard the handle. Around the belly, vines, tendrils, birds, and hares spring from unexpected places.

In the upper tier, deities welcome the mortal Kephalos into Eos's immortal realm. Eos covers the object of her affection with a nimbus (radiant encircling cloud) as a winged little Eros, one of three little loves, blesses the couple with a garland. Aphrodite, goddess of love, holds a magic wheel for love spells; Hermes, the messenger god, has slipped off his traveler's cloak and hat, tied around his neck, while he examines his snake-entwined wand. From below, bewildered companions—nude except for panther skins—reach in vain for their abducted friend, while loyal dogs leap after their master. The white-bearded *Paidagogos* ("pedagogue" or teacher) reaches too, but fails to save his young companion. Around the vase, on the right side of the scene, elegant women grace the occasion with flowers and musical instruments, while a faun and a fawn—one human with goat horns and hooves, the other a young woodland deer—straddle this world of myth and reality.

South Italian Vases
This Lekythos *comes from Magna Graecia (Great Greece), the Greek colonies of South Italy and Sicily that became portals between the ancient Greek and Roman cultures. Vase-painters there established an independent, highly decorative style that flourished between 400 and 200 B.C. Smaller, oil-filled lekythoi were common grave gifts. This large vase, made with a hole in the bottom and painted with grave-guarding gorgons and a story of loss, was undoubtedly made for a funerary purpose.*

The Back of the Vessel
A trellis-like display of thin palm leaves (palmettes) fills the back surface of the vase. These fan-shaped sprays surround the head of Medusa, the staring Gorgon whose black locks turn to writhing white snakes before our eyes (see the Symposium Vessels, *pp. 4–5).*

Greek Culture in the Colonies
Like black- and red-figured vases from Athens (see the Symposium Vessels, *pp. 4–5), vessels from the Greek colonies of South Italy and Sicily depict Greek gods and goddesses, athletes, banqueters, and warriors. They also feature Greek tragedies, particularly those by Euripides. These Greek colonies are said to have been the home of the poet Theocritus and the mathematicians Pythagorus and Archimedes. The playwright Aeschylus, the philosopher Plato, and the sculptor Lycippus also worked there.*

The Underworld Painter
The painter of this vase worked in Apulia (now southwestern Italy), one of five regional centers of South Italian and Sicilian vase-painting. Another of his vases is in the Virginia Museum's collections (see the Apulian Lekythos *with Castor and Polydeuces, and the Daughters of Leucippus in the galleries.)*

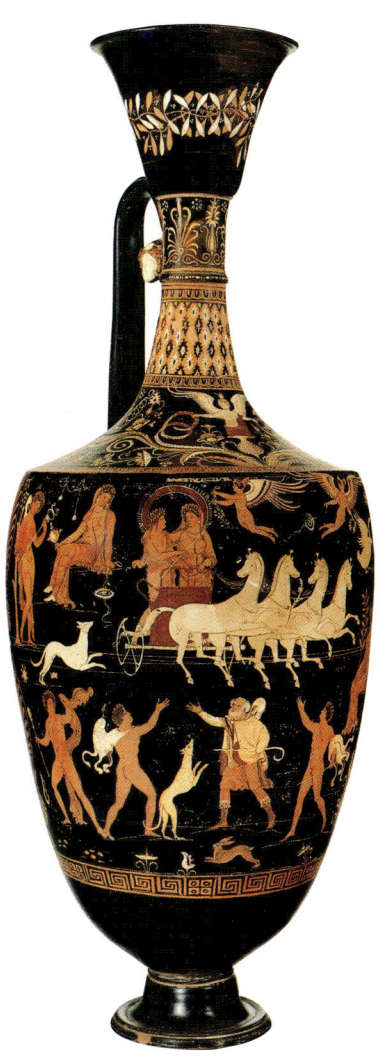

Red-figured Lekythos
Greek (South Italian, Apulian), 350–340 B.C.
Attributed to the Underworld Painter
Terra-cotta; 37¼ by 13½ (diameter) inches
Virginia Museum of Fine Arts Purchase, The Adolph D. and Wilkins C. Williams Fund, 81.55

Statue of a Young Boy

A tender young boy, carved of flecked and sparkling marble, stands before us. His sweet features capture the essence of childhood—delicate eyes, small ears and nose, rounded lips, soft cheeks. As he lowers his head, his dreamy expression captivates us. One long lock of hair, gathered into a braid, emerges from the crown of his head; a mantle gently shrouds his compact little body. He may be three or four years old, and he has survived for two thousand years.

He was carved in Hellenistic times (332–30 B.C.), after Alexander the Great's conquests (356–323 B.C.) had spread Greek culture to trade centers in Egypt,

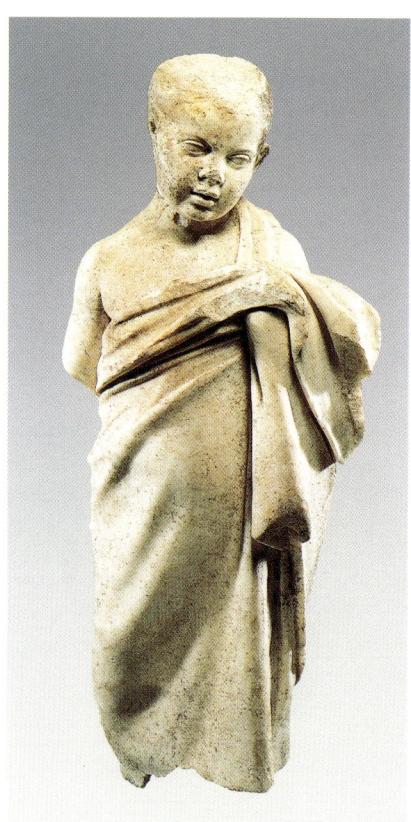

across Syria, and east to India. The statue may have come from Alexandria, where the Nile meets the Mediterranean Sea.

He once stood at a grave or an altar in memory of a deceased child. The figure poignantly embodies unrealized hope. Dressed as a little philosopher, he wears the himation of an adult scholar and probably once held writing implements. In his day, young girls and boys learned to read and write, but further education, then a male prerogative, would have awaited this child had he lived.

The statue's "Isis" braid descends from the cult of the Egyptian goddess of women, mothers, and children; Isis's son, Horus, wore such a braid. By 200 B.C., the divine mother and son both had followings that extended through Greece and Rome, Northwestern Africa, and Eastern Europe. In the Greco-Roman world, a child grew the protective braid to be sacrificed to the goddess if illness or death threatened; the lock would eventually be severed to mark the end of childhood. Here, the braid sadly remains, and childhood lasts forever. The sculptor graces the lament with a touch of serenity, a child's innocence preserved in stone.

Museum Marbles

Carved from a block of Pentelic marble, quarried northeast of Athens, the head and body of this Young Boy *may have been made separately and pieced together— a common practice at the time to avoid veins and flaws in stone. He may have been placed in a niche as part of a family grouping; he now joins other fine examples of Ancient Mediterranean marbles in the Virginia Museum's collection (see the* Cycladic *Figure of a Woman, p. 1; and two Roman examples:* Sarcophagus, *p. 10, and* Caligula, *opposite).*

Hellenistic Art

Hellenistic Greek art witnessed the relaxation of Classical Greece's sculptural tradition. Carved figures became more dynamic, restlessly expanding in all directions; drapery began to swirl with a life of its own; diverse subjects often took the form of satyrs, erotes (little loves), children, aged men and women, and less-than-beautiful boxers as well as beautiful gods.

The Young Boy and Other Children

Children in Hellenistic sculpture are usually represented nude or in children's clothing; they often hold pets or games. Other marble heads of little boys with Isis braids have been found in northern Algeria; in Rome; and in Athens. A full-length bronze of a little scholar in a himation may be found in the Musée du Louvre, Paris.

The Library and Museum of Alexandria

During the Hellenistic era, diverse cultures— centered in such cities as Antioch, Ephesos, and Pergamon—thrived under diverse monarchs within the Greek sphere of influence. Alexandria, Egypt's new "Greek" capital from which the Ptolemies ruled, became a center of learning. A great scholarly library and museum (called the "Birdcage of the Muses") harbored papyrus rolls containing lyric and elegiac poetry, Euclidean mathematics, and Greek translations of the Hebrew Bible.

Statue of a Young Boy

Greek, Late Hellenistic Period, 100 B.C.–A.D. 100
  Pentelic marble; 34⅜ inches high
Virginia Museum of Fine Arts Purchase, The Adolph D.
  and Wilkins C. Williams Fund, 89.24a/b

Statue of Caligula

Caligula means "little boot" (from the Latin *caliga*, a soldier's boot). Roman soldiers gave the nickname to Gaius Julius Caesar Germanicus (A.D. 12–41) when he traveled as a child on his father's military campaigns. Today the name *Caligula* conjures images of the Roman emperor's reign: despotism, corruption, lasciviousness, and madness. Historians are still sorting fact from fantasy. Meanwhile, this idealized full-length portrait of Caligula bears no trace of his notorious reputation.

This statue of the "young emperor," one of four portrait types that chronicle Caligula's brief career, dates to his short reign (A.D. 37–41). His head is turned slightly; his gaze is direct. His counterpoised stance—one straight leg bearing his weight, the other relaxed and bent at the knee—imitates ancient Greek statuary that Romans admired and copied. The sculptor has depicted the emperor in the dignified style for which the Augustan age was known: the youthful Caligula strikes the conventional pose of a distinguished orator about to address his public. Yet touches of Roman realism temper Greek idealism. Family resemblance links Caligula to the Julio-Claudian line: broad forehead, deep-set eyes, thin but protruding upper lip, small chin. His likeness in surviving portrait busts and on coins enables us to identify him here. He wears a high-born citizen's toga, which may once have had a purple border, to denote the wearer's status. His patrician shoes—the laced, soft leather boots rolled over the feet and folded at the ankles—subtly indicate his position of authority. One hand may well have held a scroll; one heel rests against a block, possibly a box *(scrinium)* of papyrus rolls, while the other is upraised.

Studies indicate that the sculpture was probably cut from a single block of marble. The head, however, was separated and has been reattached to the body.

Ancient Romans deliberately altered images of disfavored politicians *(damnatio memoriae)*. Sculptured heads of the disgraced were often removed from full-length statues and replaced with new portrait heads of those in favor. After Caligula's assassination, the emperor Claudius decreed that overturning statues, rather than severing their heads, would be sufficient. Damage to the face, hands, and foot of this sculpture indicates that it may have fallen forward at some point. Chisel marks on its neck also indicate the deliberate detachment of its head. Today, the sculptor's spirited carving reminds us of the perilous politics of Caligula's ancient Roman court.

Caligula in Art

This portrait of Caligula, catalogued in 1880 from Rome's Palazzo Colonna and said to have been found in the Theater of Marcellus, is one of two standing figures of the emperor. The other depicts Caligula as a boy and was discovered in Gortyn on the island of Crete. About twenty-four busts of Caligula also survive, as well as numerous images on coins.

Roman Art

The Roman Empire contributed to the visual arts in at least four great areas: portraiture in bronze and marble, reliefs and paintings of mythical and historical subjects, carved marble sarcophagi, and copies of ancient Greek statuary, which preserved Greek advances in the art of sculpture. Through its political and spiritual messages, Roman sculpture served emperors. In ancient Roman homes, complex schemes of painting—pure ornament and colorful mythologies—integrated art and architecture and foreshadowed modern sensibilities (see the Roman Wall Painting *in the Virginia Museum's galleries, as well as* Herter Brothers, p. 89, Guimard, p. 98, *and* Gray, p. 104).

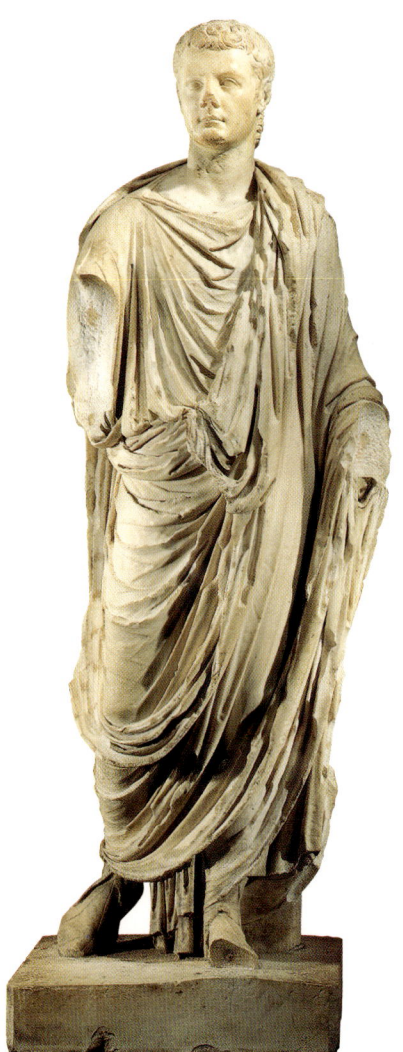

Statue of Caligula
Roman, A.D. 38–41
Marble; 80 by 26½ by 19½ inches
Virginia Museum of Fine Arts Purchase, The Arthur and Margaret Glasgow Fund, 71.20

Sarcophagus

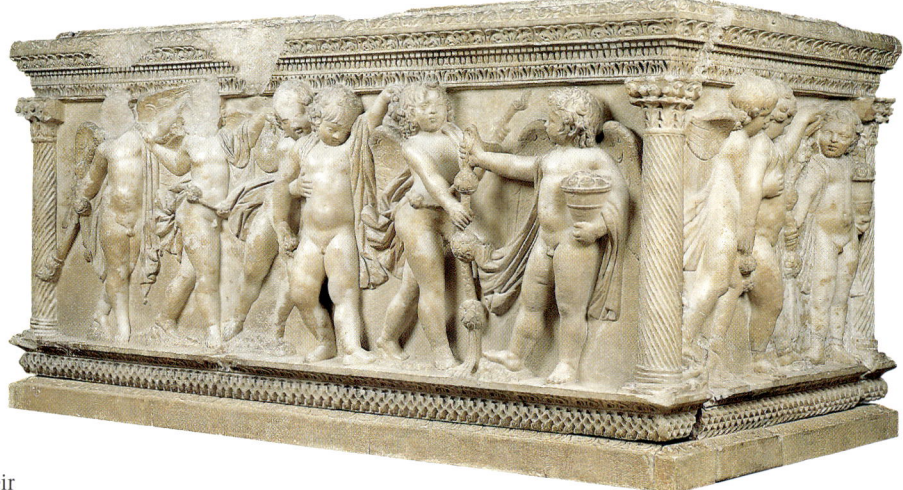

Little winged boys (called *erotes,* related to Eros, the God of Love) strut across four sides of this stone coffin. Their lighthearted antics imitate the followers of Dionysos, the Greek god of wine. Known as Bacchus by the Romans, Dionysos was also a god of vegetation, ecstasy, death, and rebirth. Although religious mysteries underlie this relief, playfulness describes these little cupid-like actors. Garlands of flowers—looped around shoulders and tucked around tummies—link one tousled boy to another. Wings expand and drapery flutters. In mock drunkenness, one boy leans and swoons into the arms of another (center), while their torch- and tambourine-bearing companions proceed toward a jaunty little fellow on the right. He cradles a fruit basket in one arm, steadies himself with one turned-out foot, and accepts the garland that they offer.

Ancient cultures intermingle in this coffin, reflecting trade and travel throughout the Mediterranean. A Greek sculptor carved the sarcophagus in Asia Minor for a Roman patron. Marble trade had increased with the opening of quarries and the growing practice of entombment during the first and second centuries A.D. Certain myths became popular as coffin decorations, to memorialize the deceased rather than to ensure an afterlife. Here, a Greek and Roman subject is carved in high relief with ornate architectural detail. The interweaving garlands and the framing columns, with fluted spirals and stylized capitals, came from Asia Minor. Molding carved into registers of ivy, lotuses, and egg-and-dart motifs frames the coffin. The lid, now lost, was probably roof-shaped, with pediments at each short end. Accustomed though we are to seeing the natural tones of antique marble, the background of this sarcophagus would have once been painted, as were so many marble carvings of ancient Greece and Rome. Color would have brightened this setting, where imaginary winged boys celebrate the mysteries of life and death.

Seeing the Sarcophagus in the Galleries

Rounding the corner of the coffin on the viewer's right, the pair of "drunken" playmates from the front is repeated on one short end. Still more erotes "dress-up" on the other long side—piping songs, cradling a bird, and holding grapes. There a boy imitates Herakles wielding his club. The other short end, apparently carved by a second, lesser sculptor, depicts erotes in a wrestling contest. On the front, faint traces of paint may be seen in the space between one little Eros's cloak and knee (far right).

History of Sarcophagi

Marble is a form of granular limestone. The Greek word sarkophagos, *which means "flesh-eating stone," refers to the properties of limestone from which coffins were made, as early as 700 B.C. During the Hellenistic and Roman periods, sculptors working in Greece, Rome, and Asia Minor produced large numbers of marble sarcophagi, primarily for wealthy patrons. Subjects range from the Dionysian mysteries to the labors of Herakles, the four seasons, and "victory" portraits of the deceased, flanked by erotes. Playful parodies evolved as winged boys—dressing up as gods or heroes—acted out myths (see the* Roman Mosaic *in the Virginia Museum's galleries). Early Christians borrowed the sarcophagus form, transforming the reliefs to represent the Christian triumph over death.*

Sarcophagus

Roman (Asia Minor), circa A.D. 150

Marble; 3 feet 6¾ inches by 3 feet 10½ inches by 7 feet 6³⁄₁₆ inches

Virginia Museum of Fine Arts Purchase, The Adolph D. and Wilkins C. Williams Fund, 60.1

Funerary Image of a Woman

The image of this young woman, with large dark eyes and dark curls, is arresting in its freshness and immediacy. Rapid brushwork catches highlights: the glint in her eyes, the bridge of her nose, the reflections in her jewels, the folds of her garment. Gemstones adorn her hooped earrings and her double-strand necklace; black bands of fabric trim her plum-pink dress.

Her portrait, painted 1700 years ago, was placed within wrappings over her face on her mummified body. She comes to us from Roman-occupied Egypt— a cosmopolitan center where Roman, Greek, Macedonian, and Egyptian cultures intermingled for several centuries after the birth of Christ. Her image reflects the artistic cultures of her era: Roman realism, Hellenistic naturalism, and Egyptian timelessness resonate in her features.

This portrait preserved an image of the deceased for the afterlife. Evolving from the Egyptian tradition of idealized portrait masks made of gold or stucco, this picture belongs to a type of portrait painted on wood panels or linen in encaustic (wax and pigment) or tempera (egg and pigment). Mummy portraits were produced by anonymous artists in Egypt from Julius Caesar's era (100–44 B.C.) to the Emperor Constantine's (A.D. 285–337). The sitters are lifelike; their faces vary (Pliny the Elder, writing before A.D. 79, noted that for generations, realistic portraiture had been "the highest ambition of art"). Still, each portrait conforms to simple conventions: a direct and immediate study of the head, or head and shoulders, of a young woman or man, turned just slightly.

The type is often called a Fayum portrait, named for the site, just south of Cairo on the Nile, where many panels were found. Though memories of the deceased have vanished, their palpable presence lingers in their portraits, the earliest painted likenesses on panel to survive from antiquity.

Encaustic Mummy Portraits

Artists mixed their powdered pigments with melted beeswax, then applied it to a wood panel with either a brush or a blade. The surface could then be reheated, allowing the image to be reworked over the course of several days. Egypt's hot, dry climate preserved these portraits, the only surviving examples of the ancient Greco-Roman tradition of painting on panel in wax or tempera. Of 1000 or so portraits that still exist today, around 700 came from Fayum.

The Sitter's Cultural Heritage

The people depicted in these portraits are thought to have descended from Alexander the Great's soldiers (around 332 B.C.) and the Ptolemies, the last Greek rulers of Egypt (323–30 B.C.).

Schools of Thought: Made from Life or after Death?

A recent study of eight mummified bodies with portraits at the British Museum, London, found a close correspondence between the approximate age at death and the apparent age in the likeness, based on CAT scans. An average life expectancy of 30 years may explain the youthful appearance of the subjects. Many scholars believe that the portraits were painted after death. Another school of thought argues that patrons commissioned the likenesses during the "prime" of their lives, to be placed with family group portraits in homes. After the death of the sitter, the portrait was removed to adorn the mummy.

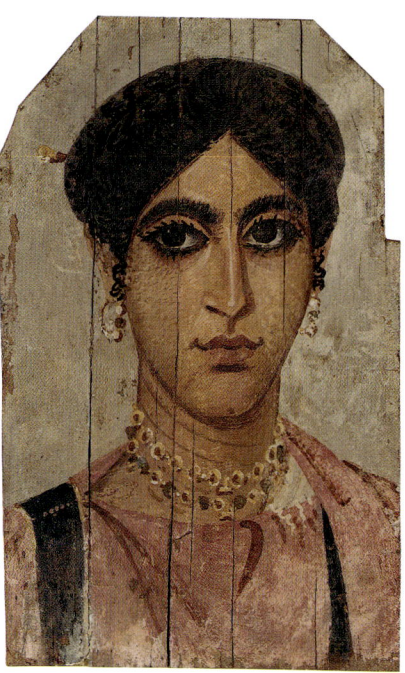

Funerary Image of a Woman
Egyptian, Roman Period, A.D. late 200s–early 300s
Beeswax and pigment on wood panel; 13 by 8¼ inches
Virginia Museum of Fine Arts Purchase, The Adolph D. and Wilkins C. Williams Fund, 55.4

CHAPTER 2

Ancient American Art

Moche

Olmec

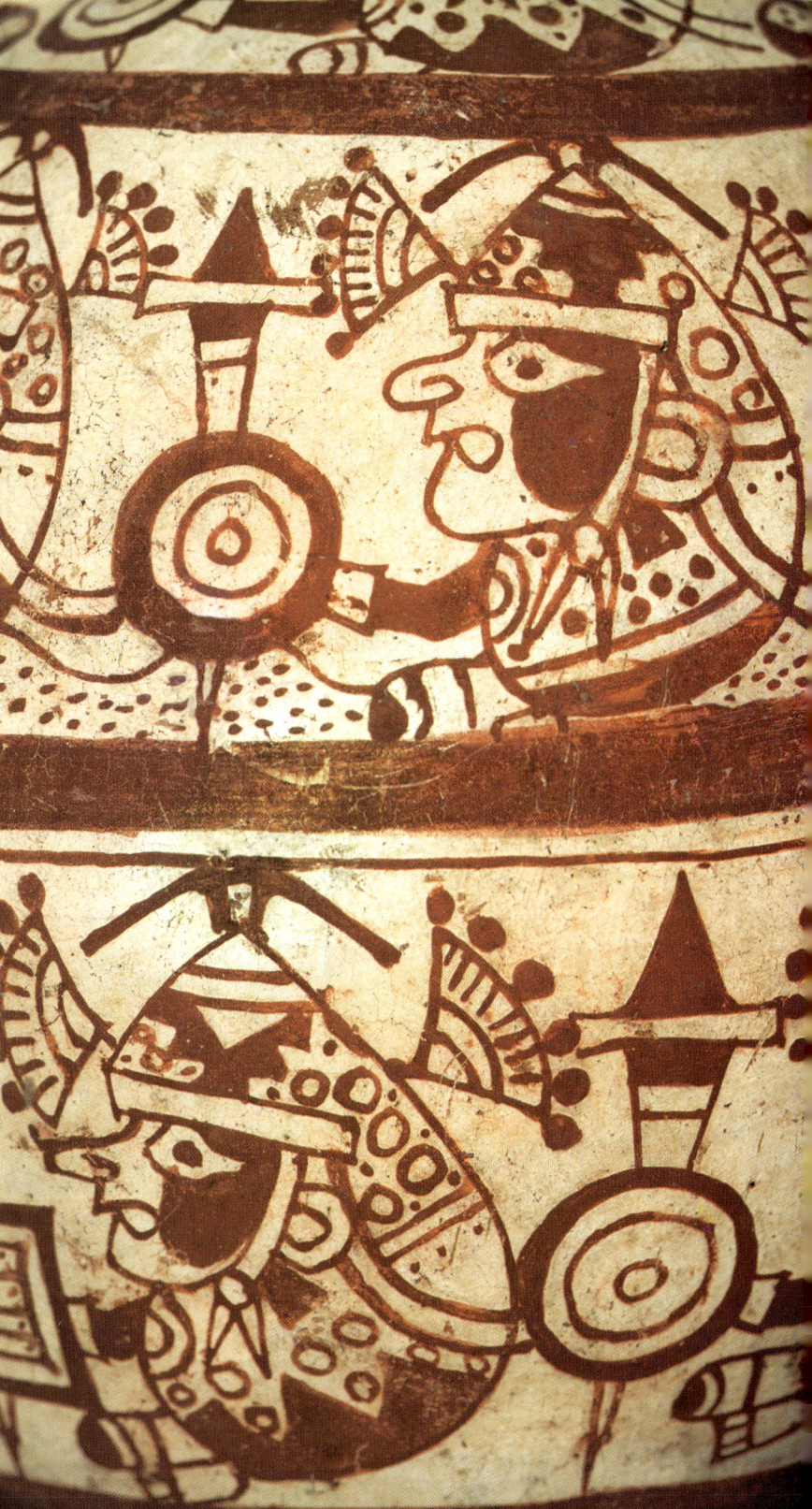

Jaguar

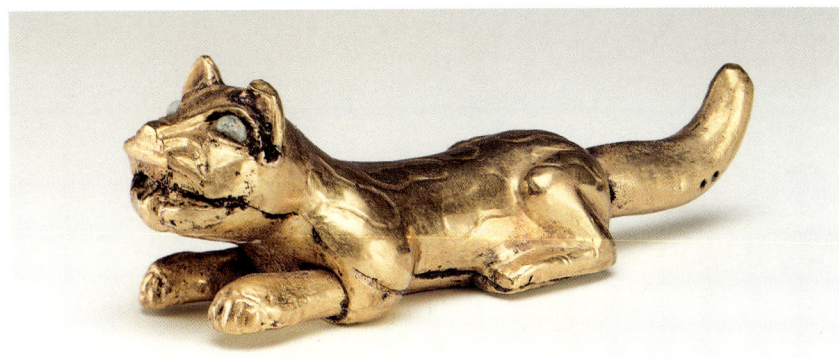

One of seven related gold cats now in museum captivity, this hollow gold *Jaguar* comes from the coastland of northern Peru. Primed to pounce, its tiny form is packed with power.

From the early Moche period, this jaguar provides a glimmer of what goldsmithing looked like just before the dawn of an artistic golden age. The gold jaguar may have served to transmit ancient traditions in religion and art from the Chavin (pre-Moche) culture in the highlands to the Moche culture in the valley, around 300 B.C.

Six other small gold jaguars are believed to have come from the same workshop as ours, along Peru's Lambayeque River. The cats may have been made by different artisans, who formed hammered sheets of gold around a master model. Inscribed patterns *(intaglio)* simulate a coat of spotted fur. This jaguar's eyes shine green, though the stones are later insets; the other jaguars' eye sockets now lack gems. Pairs of holes, on each side of the tail and beneath each shoulder, suggest that these jaguars may once have been attached to a headdress, shirt, or belt, or strung together as a necklace. The Museum's jaguar is one of two that contain a pebble, as though this golden cluster of cats may have been meant to rattle when it was worn.

The largest and strongest cat in the Americas, the jaguar inspired images of Andes Mountain deities, who assumed its features and its prowess. Although the jaguar is pervasive in Andean art, its meaning today remains mysterious. The Chavin—one of the earliest of the great cultures of ancient Peru—believed that the essence of their creator-god was the jaguar. Images depict him with a feline mouth and fangs, wearing a headdress that radiates like the Sun. Perhaps related to this Chavin god, a Moche deity with feline mouth and headdress is associated with the Moon. Images on Moche vessels depict jaguars and owls as companions of gods and priests (see the *Stirrup-handled Vessels*, p. 14); the jaguar often participates in scenes depicting the sacrifice of captives. A nocturnal predator like the owl, the jaguar prowled the valley waterways—rivers and irrigation canals essential to Moche existence. This small gold copy of the great cat remains as secretive as its model in real life.

Gold Jaguars in Museums

This hollow gold jaguar is one of seven related pieces preserved in museums around the world. The other six may be found in the Art Institute of Chicago; the Milwaukee Public Museum; the Montreal Museum of Art; the Museum für Völkerkunde, Hamburg; the Staatliches Museum für Völkerkunde, Munich; and the Mujica Gallo Museo "Oro del Peru," Lima. As solitary animals, real jaguars would rarely be found together as these gold ones may originally have been.

Making Hollow Gold Jaguars

Our jaguar, like the other six of its kind, consists of twelve parts. The upper and the lower body, including the hindquarters, are joined at a seam, which may be traced from the abdomen, across the shoulders, and around the mouth. The ears, front legs, and tail are formed separately; each has two symmetrical halves. This technique— the building of metal forms by assembling pre-shaped pieces from hammered sheets— *characterizes the arts of Peruvian metallurgy since the Chavin (pre-Moche) period.*

Jaguars and Pumas

Jaguars—great, roaring, stocky cats with tawny coats and black spots (rosettes)— generally inhabit Central and South America. Large, purring cats of a single, tawny color (concolor) are known as pumas, cougars, or mountain lions, and are found in North and South America, from the South Yukon to Patagonia. This hollow gold cat, sometimes called a puma, is closer to a jaguar— given its markings, Peruvian provenance, and the role played by the jaguar in Andean mythology. Jaguar derives from Tupi, the native language of neighboring Brazil, across the Andes. The word Jaguara originally referred to a broad class of powerful, carnivorous beasts, from jaguars to dogs.

Jaguar

Moche (Peru), 400–100 B.C.
Gold with green stones; 1½ by 4¼ inches
Virginia Museum of Fine Arts Purchase, The Arthur and Margaret Glasgow Fund, 59.28.9

Stirrup-handled Vessels

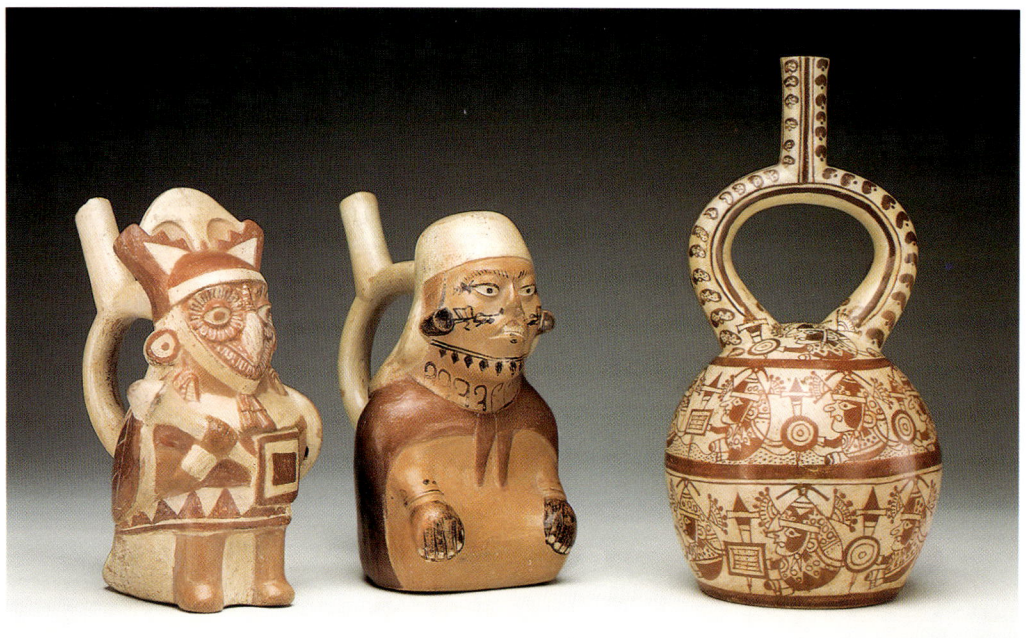

An "owl-masked" man, a decorated figure, and painted bands of "bean" warriors shield and preserve the ancient realm of Moche culture. Only art and artifacts survive to tell the history of the Moche people in northern Peru—no written records exist. Yet these vessels—created almost two thousand years ago—overflow with fact, fancy, signs, and symbols. In effect, they stand as sentinels of their culture; they do not readily reveal information. Recovering the meanings of their now-lost world requires care, as we attempt to "read" Moche images today.

Here, in clay, plant and animal kingdoms merge with human experience and imagination. We glimpse the Moche ceramists' golden age—of lustrous orange- and buff-colored wares, painted with red and cream slips (water-diluted clay) and teeming with scenes of myth and daily life. The natural and supernatural combine in wondrous ways. In the vessels shown here on the left and in the center, potters have transformed clay into two "effigy" vases, so-called because they mimic human forms. The owl-masked figure wears a crested helmet, wields a domed club, and holds a square shield. His are warriors' weapons, also painted on Moche pots that depict a people battling for seas to fish and territory to farm, taking prisoners to sacrifice, and appeasing deities and demons in order to survive. This warrior, however, watches from behind a red and cream colored "mask," with a hooked beak and wide, round eyes encircled by feathers. Owls—sharp-sighted creatures of the night—appear on Moche ceramics as guardians of deities, war, darkness, and spirits of the dead; they also oversee wisdom, healing, and agriculture. Warriors, too, defended these essential realms of Moche society. This figure—masked owl-warrior or mythical owl-like being—takes on the form of both human and spiritual protectors, guarding his still-secret meanings.

The center vessel—a man with a disfigured nose and upper lip—holds other mysteries. Motifs in a dark glaze extend across his cheeks to spools that adorn his ears; painted patterns of diamonds and hooks tattoo his chin and neck. A red cloak, tied at the neck, covers his shoulders as he kneels and places his hands on his knees. The significance of his dress, demeanor, and decoration is disguised; his meaning remains puzzling. Deformity, disease, and disfigurement often appear in effigy vessels; the Moche, it is said, believed that gods touched human beings with afflictions to bring them closer to their own supernatural realms.

Around the vessel on the right, "bean" warriors clutch "weapons bundles" as they race across sandy landscapes in three separate bands called "registers." Named for the looped handle that rises from its rounded body to a central spout, this stirrup vessel abounds with both natural and supernatural life. Eyes peer, noses and chins protrude, and hands and feet emerge from bean-shaped bodies, in glazes that now range from brown to red. These hulls resemble lima beans *(pallares)*, decorated with dots and stripes and animated by human profiles. Like the owl-masked figure, the bean warriors carry clubs and wear helmets with ax-shaped crests. From their vanquished enemies they have gathered daggers, clubs, and shields, both round and square, and they have bound them as booty for ceremonial display. Above this army of imaginative pods, naturalistic beans march around the handle. These beans, whether speckled or silhouetted, may hold unknown meaning. Their numbers and markings may have conveyed messages. On vase-paintings, priests "read" beans, and runners transport them in bags; ancient graves have yielded buried bean-filled pouches. While ceramic vessels reproduce the forms of maize, squash, potatoes, and peanuts cultivated by the Moche, only beans—traditionally the oldest crop—take human form as painted warriors. These vessels contain the spirit of the Moche; we see amazing things and ponder even more.

Moche Geography

The Moche looked west to the Pacific Ocean and east to the Andes Mountains. From this wedge of desert scrub and irrigated fields, women and men—fishermen, farmers, healers, priests, and warriors—faced extremes of geography and climate that ranged from hot, sea-level sands to freezing mountain ranges that dwarf rainbows.

Moche Imagery

Images of native animals, birds, and vegetables from Peru's northern coast enliven Moche pottery. Pots may take the form of squash, potatoes, and peanuts. They display paintings of owls, jaguars, frogs, foxes, and llamas, as well as hunting scenes for deer, seal, and sea lion.

History of Moche Ceramics

Moche history, from about 300 B.C. to A.D. 800, divides into five phases. Vessels modeled in naturalistic forms and painted with expressive line-drawing characterized the Moche's golden age, between 150 B.C. and A.D. 200. During this phase, Moche potters refined their techniques of forming vessels from clay slabs, by firing them under an oxidation process to create lustrous black or orange wares, and by painting them with red, cream, and orange slips.

Themes of Painted Pottery

Moche vessels depict a variety of subjects: hunters, warriors, and runners; ceremonies, rituals, and presentations; prisoner-takings and blood-lettings. Women appear occasionally: in scenes of weaving, healing, and nurturing, and in erotic acts evoking life's vitality and death's inevitability.

Stirrup-handled Vessel
in the Form of a Warrior with Owl Mask
Moche (Peru), 150 B.C.–A.D. 200
Orange ware with red and cream slip; 8¾ by 5 by 6⅞ inches, 84.87

Stirrup-handled Vessel
in the Form of a Painted Warrior
Moche (Peru), 150 B.C.–A.D. 600
Orange ware with red, cream, and orange slip; 8¾ by 5¼ by 7¾ inches, 84.88

Stirrup-handled Vessel
Moche (Peru), circa A.D. 500
Buff terra-cotta with brown, red, and cream slips; 11½ by 5⅝ (diameter) inches, 82.193

Virginia Museum of Fine Arts, Gifts of Mr. and Mrs. Sandford G. Etherington

Seated Figure

A fierce face rivets our attention on the Olmec culture of MesoAmerica, which originated along the Gulf Coast of Mexico and spread to Honduras, Guatemala, and Costa Rica. This figure comes from the ancient city-states of tropical Olman (meaning "rubber country," named for the trees). Although the Olmec have been known since the 1862 discovery of a colossal stone head with rounded helmet and forceful features, archaeological sites have only been studied and excavated since 1938. Like the ancient Moche and Chavin (pre-Moche) cultures of Peru (see pp. 13–15), the Olmec did not leave written records. Instead, cities of earthen buildings, stone sculpture, white-clay ceramics, and jade carvings tell the history of the Olmec, called the "ancient ones" by Central American residents today.

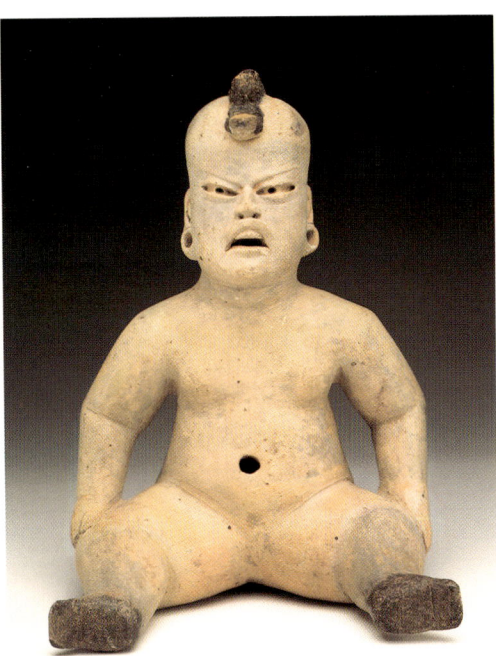

One of many baffling and genderless ceramic "babies," this hand-modeled figure sits squarely before us. Its body looks soft: puffed cheeks and plump torso, thick neck and round shoulders, chubby arms and pudgy legs. Weighty "earplugs" distend the lobes, and a jagged crest forms the headdress. The head's elongated form is thought to reflect the Olmec practice of shaping an infant's soft skull as a mark of distinction. The figure stares through upturned eyes, narrowed beneath severely angled brows that slice across the forehead. A down-turned mouth opens to reveal zigzagged teeth, deliberately filed into points for spiritual reasons.

Olmec ceramic babies come in a variety of styles and postures—bared heads, helmeted heads, solid forms, and hollow ones. Some sit or recline; others raise their arms or suck their thumbs. Some, like this one, have hollowed-out pupils, mouths, and navels.

From a culture that regarded infants—the most recent arrivals on Earth—as still close to the supernatural world, these clay sculptures served a special, though now shrouded, purpose. One figure was found in a household context: it had been discarded as refuse, as though cast away after use. We wonder: did it attend a healing ceremony, to absorb an actual child's illness? Did it accompany or replace a child, to be sacrificed to gods?

Harpy Eagles and Jaguars
This figure's rare crest, called a "harpy eagle" headdress, resembles that worn by a tiny Olmec Jaguar-Baby—part human, part feline, and carved of jadeite—in the American Museum of Natural History, New York. Images of Olmec deities have attributes of jaguars, symbols of spiritual power and life force (see the Peruvian Jaguar, p. 13). The harpy eagle—a Central and South American bird of prey—may too have lent its strength to Olmec sculpture.

Before and After the Olmec
The Olmec descended from Asian hunter-gatherers who crossed the Bering Strait—a strip of land that once linked Asia to North America—and migrated southward throughout the Americas 12,000 years ago. Olmec chiefdoms evolved from farms to village cultures to class-based cities, among them San Lorenzo and La Venta (in what is now Mexico), which flourished between 1200 and 300 B.C. Olmec-style art influenced the Maya 1000 years later, and the Aztecs, 500 years after the Maya.

Olmec, Chavin, and Moche Cultures
The Olmec culture in Mexico is as old as the Chavin (pre-Moche) in Peru (see p. 13). Each is considered the first great culture of its region. Native flora and fauna frequently appear in Olmec, Chavin, and Moche art; hybrid images—godlike, human, and feline—exist in all three artistic traditions.

*Olmec Seated Figure
with Harpy Eagle Crest*
Olmec (Mexico), circa 500 B.C.
Terra-cotta with black pigment; 12¾ by 9⅛ by 7 inches
Virginia Museum of Fine Arts Purchase, The Adolph D. and Wilkins C. Williams Fund, 80.327

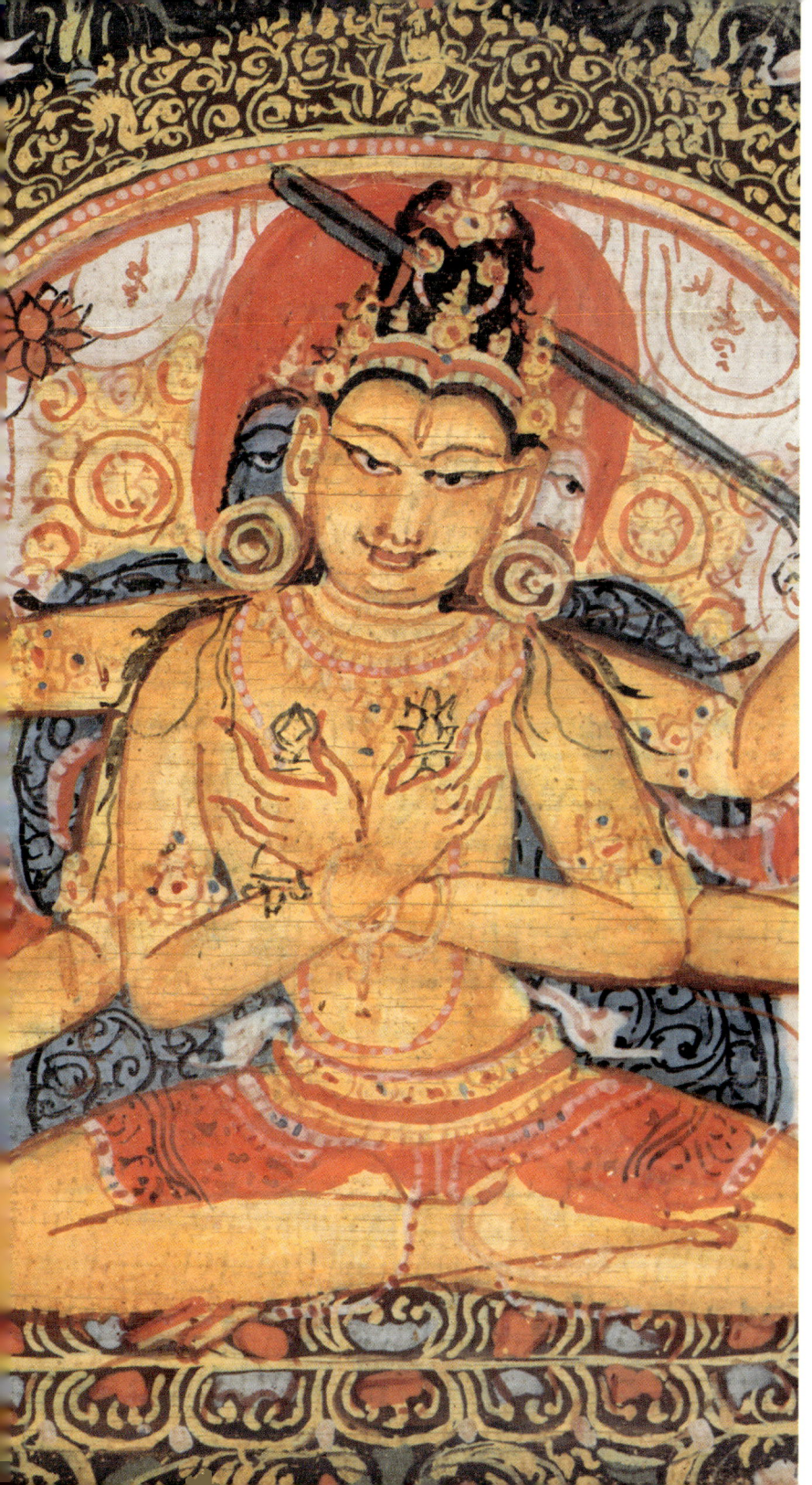

CHAPTER 3

Asian Art

Indian

Nepalese

Tibetan

Chinese

Japanese

Gautama Buddha

Buddha (the Enlightened One) sits serenely, feet crossed to rest upon thighs, eyes fixed in contemplation. Centered and floating like the lotus petals that support him, he emanates tranquility. From head to toe, silken surfaces of polished bronze unify smooth skin and gliding garment into one ethereal vision. Delicate lines of curved brows and straight nose frame large eyes, set in silver. Sensuous lips, inlaid with copper, form a quiet half-smile. The style—a figure of full face, mouth, chin, and limbs, its satiny finish heightened by colorful metal inlays—is characteristic of eighth- and ninth-century bronze sculpture from Kashmir, a center for Buddhist prayer and learning, north of India, west of Tibet.

The sculptor defines Buddha's form with several of the thirty-two physical

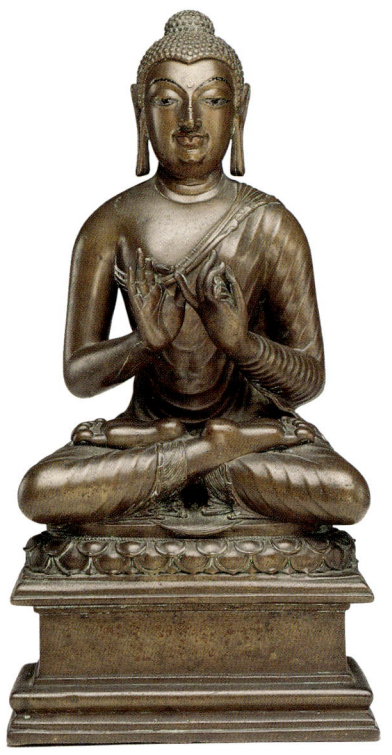

traits said to reveal the Enlightened One's spiritual perfection. His body is harmoniously proportioned; his limbs are supple, his fingers slender. His topknot (the *ushnisha*), under a beaded crown of tight curls, symbolizes the Buddha's superhuman wisdom; he has attained a higher state of being, above all others. The silver whorl (the *urna*, a lock of hair that lies between his brows), signals his pure, insightful nature. His unadorned earlobes, elongated by the heavy weight of princely earrings that he once wore, show that he has renounced a life of luxury for salvation.

Buddha's gesture (*mudra*) is that of teaching (see *Green Tara*, p. 25). He turns his hands to "set the Wheel of Law" in motion, as he reviews essential elements of Buddhism for his followers. He preaches ethical conduct and meditation as a way to spiritual enlightenment.

Sometimes known by his given name, Siddhartha Gautama, Buddha set an example for others by his compassion for suffering and his quest for Nirvana (a state of stillness, released from earthly cares). Fourteen hundred years later, a Kashmiri sculptor captured Buddha's clarity of mind and calmness of being— a moment of perfected insight detached from life's clutter—for those who seek to follow his path. Though the content of the sculpture is complex, its beauty rests in the quiet simplicity of its form. This elegant image evokes a perfect calm that approaches the nature of Buddha himself.

Kashmir

Kashmir was a center of Buddhism by A.D. 200 and the chosen home of Hindu poets and holy men. Hindu temples, Buddhist monasteries, universities, and artists enjoyed generous patronage. Charm and inventiveness characterize its medieval metal sculpture.

The Life of the Buddha

Born on the border between present-day northern India and Nepal, the historic Buddha (circa 563–483 B.C.) prescribed the "middle path" as a way of physical and spiritual life, avoiding sensual self-indulgence on the one hand, and ascetic self-denial on the other. So compelled was he that he left a wife, a son, and a princely life of comfort to pursue his difficult, life-long spiritual journey.

Medieval Art of the Indian Subcontinent

Between A.D. 550 and 1300, Indian sculpture evolved in many regional schools represented in the Virginia Museum's collection. These pages present sculpture from three regions: from Kashmir in the north, the Gautama Buddha; from Karnataka in the Deccan, Ganesha (see p. 20); and from Tamil Nadu in the south, Shiva, King of Dancers (opposite). Images of Hindu gods are thought to invite deities to dwell temporarily in a physical form; sculpture of Buddhist divinities remind the faithful of the limitless aspects of enlightened beings.

Lost-Wax Metal-Casting

The art of metal-casting in the Indian subcontinent dates as far back as 2500 B.C. To cast a figure in bronze, copper, brass, and other metal alloys by the "lost wax" process, a wax model is made, often around a central core, and a clay mold is formed around it. The wax is then melted away, and the mold is filled instead with molten metal. When the metal has cooled, the clay mold is removed, and a cast metal image emerges, ready for burnishing, engraving, or inlay.

Shiva, King of Dancers

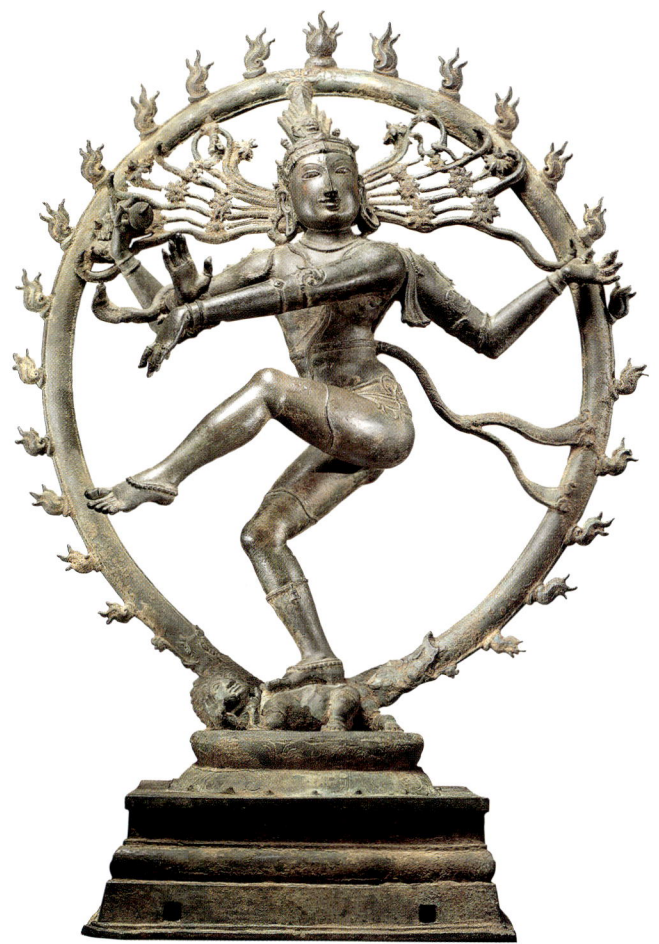

Shiva, Hindu King of Dancers, pauses momentarily to face the viewer before he begins to twirl again. With a flex of the wrist, bend of the knee, and point of the toe, he forms the picture of harmony, balance, and counterpoint.

Shiva's is a cosmic dance. He is Lord of Existence, the one who creates, sustains, and destroys. Encircled by a ring of fire, he surrounds himself with symbols of how creation came to be—flames, flowing rivers, flowers. In two hands he once held objects of sound and light—a drum recalling the beat of the beginning of time and a flame, now lost, foretelling the fire that will cause time's end. His third hand gestures to deliver the faithful from fear; a fourth points to the path of release from the limited world of human understanding.

Shiva's spellbinding beauty conflates male and female. Delicate features define a gentle face; broad shoulders, thin waist, and full hips create a sinuous silhouette; earrings, necklaces, and bracelets encircle nearly every divine inch of arm, wrist, and ankle. An imperial crown rests on his head, covering a topknot worn by holy men to bind their matted locks. As he dances, however, Shiva's locks have broken free; they fly out in all directions, echoing the movement of his many arms and swirling sashes. Flowers sprout from Shiva's hair, and from his crown a crescent moon emerges to mark the waxing and the waning of time: days and nights, seasons and cycles.

Looking closely, viewers will discover that Shiva has three eyes. The third one, centered in his forehead, sees the mysteries of enlightenment...or death. From this window, Shiva watches. Viewers are reminded that ultimate enlightenment is Shiva's message. The small creature at the base of the sculpture, crushed by the god as he dances, is said to be the demon of ignorance and forgetfulness. This demon must be overcome so that the faithful may join the King of Dancers and accept his forces: life and death, male and female, movement and rest, frenzy and calm, comfort and fright, procreation and destruction, light and dark. At once alluring and a little alarming, Shiva dances these cosmic paradoxes before our very eyes.

Sculpture of Hindu Gods

Shiva was cast in bronze long ago by the Tamil sculptors of medieval India. Once kept in a temple and carried in religious processions, the sculpture was believed to be a vessel that could house the god's spirit. In his true state, perfect and immortal, Shiva is formless and cannot be perceived by mortal eyes.

Shiva Nataraja (King of Dancers)
Indian, Tamil Nadu, late 1100s–early 1200s
Bronze; 38⅝ by 28 by 12 inches
Virginia Museum of Fine Arts Purchase, The Adolph D. and Wilkins C. Williams Fund, 69.46

Ganesha

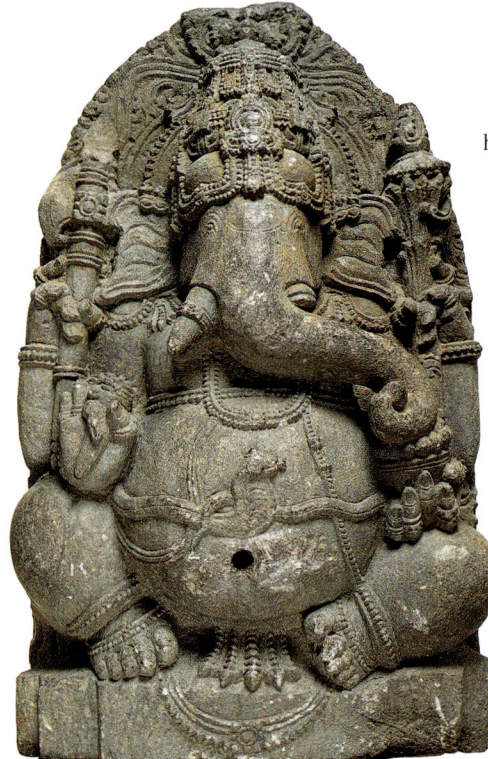

Ganesha, the chubby, childlike son of Shiva and Parvati and one of the most beloved Hindu gods, sits regally before us. He has an elephant's head; his trunk curls in search of the sweets that he loves and cradles in his hand. Meanwhile a serpent girds the god's potbelly, so it will not burst again. Legend tells us that once upon a time it did split open, spilling the sweets Ganesha had eaten. When the Moon laughed at the sight, the embarrassed Ganesha hurled one of his tusks and darkened the orb, thereby originating its phases. He now holds his tusk in his hand. A second legend says that a rival chopped off the tusk when Ganesha denied him access to Shiva and Parvati; the guardian son now wields an ax in another hand.

Framed by his throne and crowned with jewels, Ganesha is carved in the elaborate style of the Hoyshala Dynasty. Fashioned from stone, he appears as devotional songs describe him. Diamonds adorn his crown, and strings of pearls his neck; layered rings surround his fingers and toes; and beaded anklets seem poised to jingle when he dances (see *Shiva, King of Dancers,* p. 19, and *Dancing Ganesha* in the Virginia Museum's galleries).

We are charmed by Ganesha's whimsy, yet he has a truer, deeper nature. Like the Moon, he waxes and wanes: as Shiva creates and destroys, so Ganesha can bless or dismiss. He holds the power to grant devotees safe and successful undertakings in life. He is the Lord of Beginnings, to be worshipped first, before all others. If neglected, he withdraws support; if honored, he bestows earthly prosperity. As the Lord of Obstacles, he removes obstacles or places them in our path; he affects the outcome of events, regulates the universe's flow of power, and thus keeps order in the Cosmos.

As he straddles the threshold between sacred and profane, benevolent and malevolent, Ganesha rewards the faithful and punishes the faithless. In temples, which are decorated with such figures, Ganesha sits on the outermost wall of the innermost sanctum.

Perhaps we find him comforting because he had once been vulnerable. One myth explains that Ganesha's mother created him, but his father nearly destroyed him. Shiva beheaded his son when Ganesha denied him entrance to Parvati's bath; he then restored Ganesha at Parvati's pleading by replacing the child's lost head with that of an elephant. Such tales of Ganesha's ambiguous aspects—animal but divine, pleasant but painful, playful but wise, clumsy but clever, greedy but generous—shed light on the human heart. Once hurt but now healed, Ganesha offers encouragement to each sweet-bearing follower who asks

his help. Proof of his popularity lies in this sculpture's navel, the center of Ganesha's goodness, worn smooth by the touch of devotees beseeching his blessings over eight hundred years.

Ganesha in India

Images of Ganesha may be found on altars in many Indian homes; over doorways to shops or offices; at cross-roads and city limits; within temple walls. Devotees honor the god with processions, celebrations, and sculptured images at his annual festival in August.

Ganesha's Sweets: Modaka Cakes

Ganesha possesses an insatiable appetite for modaka cakes, made of sweetmeats of rice or wheat. It is said that anyone who breathes the aroma of modaka cakes will become learned, will be clever at weapons, will write and paint, and will acquire divine knowledge and immortality. Ganesha is the patron of literature and education.

Ganesha's Form and Nature

Jolly in appearance and mischievous in nature, Ganesha is as strong and authoritative as an elephant who can clear a jungle or transport a king on his back, yet as clever as a rat who can always find stored grain. The rat is traditionally regarded as Ganesha's mount or vehicle, companion or attribute.

Ganesha

Indian, Southern Deccan, Karnataka, Hoyshala Dynasty, early 1100s
Schist; 33 by 20¼ by 10 inches
Virginia Museum of Fine Arts, The Nasli and Alice Heeramaneck Collection, Gift of Paul Mellon, 68.8.18

The Perfection of Wisdom in Eight Thousand Verses

Three enchanting figures keep watch over an ancient Indian manuscript of sacred writings about the ways of Buddha. Their skin glows in pure, vibrant colors—bright red, yellow, and white—and a closer look reveals their extraordinary arms, heads, and hands. They are not mere mortals; they inhabit other worlds.

Called "Cosmic Buddhas," these beings are aspects of the Supreme Buddha, and divinities themselves. Their jewel-like skin, sacred poses and gestures, and symbolic objects—lotus blossoms, wheels, bells, swords—indicate who they are: the white teaching Buddha of the East, the red meditating Buddha of the West, the yellow gift-giving Buddha of the South. Bracelets and armbands encircle their graceful limbs; their hair is piled high and fastened with crowns of gold and jewels. Each one—as a kind of spiritual mentor seated on an ornate throne of swirling flowers, birds, and animals—reveals to the worshiper a different aspect of the universe. They share serene smiles, upraised swords, and the fervor of a purpose, however: to guard the holy book they decorate and to keep its reader from harm. These colorful holy beings animate the manuscript; by painting them, the artist hoped to invoke their magical, spiritual powers of protection.

Manuscript Illumination in India
One of the oldest traditions in Indian painting is the art of manuscript illumination. The oldest illuminations survive from the age of the Pala kings (between A.D. 1000 and 1200). Pictures, like these three images, decorated books of scripture based on Buddhist writings, which began to appear soon after the Buddha's death in 483 B.C., much earlier than Buddhist paintings.

Painted Palm Leaves
Pala manuscripts were made from the treated leaves of palms that grow along the coasts of India. Words were written in ink and pictures painted in watercolor. The leaves were then bound with wooden covers to make a book. These three long and narrow leaves (less than three inches wide) came from a book that probably consisted of 200 such pages, filled with paintings surrounded by columns of Sanskrit writing. The book journeyed during the course of centuries from eastern India north to Nepal, before its leaves were scattered into North American collections. Six leaves are fortunately now preserved in the Virginia Museum of Fine Arts.

Painting in India
The art of painting has always been valued in India as an expression of human spirit and religious faith. Although inspirational painting is practiced by many people as part of daily life, professional artists—such as the painter of these lively gods—tend to come from long lines of families who pass the secrets of their art down from generation to generation.

The Perfection of Wisdom in Eight Thousand Verses
Three of six pages from the manuscript of the
Ashtasahasrika Prajnaparamita
East India (Bengal or Bihar), 1150–1200
Opaque watercolor and ink on palm leaf; 2½ by 17½ inches
Virginia Museum of Fine Arts, The Nasli and Alice Heeramaneck Collection, Gift of Paul Mellon, 68.8.114a,f,c

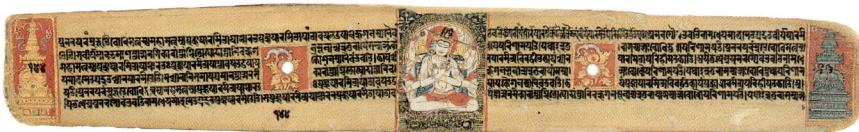

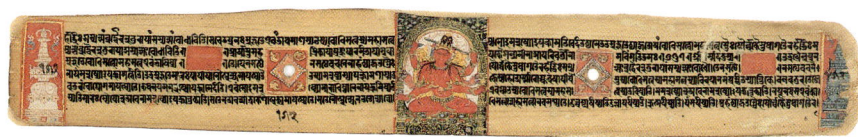

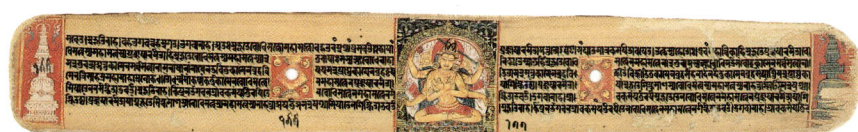

Krishna and Balarama Arrive in Brindaban

The Indian village of Brindaban and its surrounding rocky countryside provide the setting for this scene from the life of the Hindu god, Krishna. The god embodies *bhakti*, passionate devotion to the divine, as a way of salvation, and is often associated with love and nature.

As this picture reveals, nature thrives under the watch of Krishna, who enchants all creatures—horses and cows, cowherds and maidens. The scene illustrates part of the manuscript that describes a charming land of good fruit and green grass. Cows graze (center), bulls uproot trees (upper left), calves cavort inside corrals (middle left). Women, their hair laced with flowers and their bodies draped in colorful fabrics and jewels, balance water jugs on their heads (middle right).

Into this poetic landscape—where children play as the aroma of warming milk wafts through the air (lower right and left)—the young Krishna enters (lower right). His skin is blue (he is not of this Earth as human beings perceive it); he wears his hair in a topknot and is adorned with ear pendants, necklaces, armlets, and bracelets that befit a god. He rides a horse-drawn carriage and is seated next to his older white-skinned brother Balarama. Their guardian, the cowherd Nanda in a white turban and a beard, sits behind the two brothers. Their father has placed the boys under Nanda's loving protection, so that they might grow up in a beautiful land, hidden from the dangers of the demon King Kamsa. Krishna's incarnation led to the defeat of the evil that Kamsa represented. Here, Nanda gestures to the welcoming villagers who offer the young Krishna and Balarama refreshments and a safe home.

The Life of Krishna in the Harivamsa Manuscript

Krishna is considered an incarnation of the god Vishnu, the champion of goodness and order and one of the four great Hindu deities (including Brahma, Shiva, and Devi). Vishnu's and Krishna's lives are recorded in the Harivamsa, *a sequel to the* Mahabharata, *the great Sanskrit epic that tells of early Hinduism, written between 300 B.C. and A.D. 300.*

Mughal Manuscript Painting

Descending from Genghis Khan and Tamerlane in Central Asia, the Mughal emperors ruled India between 1526 and the 1850s. Under the Mughal dynasty, a culture of combined Muslim, indigenous Indian, and European influences flourished. Libraries, artistic workshops, and manuscript painting thrived. About 1585, the great Mughal emperor Akbar, who held a strong interest in diverse religions, asked that the Harivamsa *be translated from Sanskrit into Persian, his native language. This scene from the* Harivamsa *is one of only twenty-eight leaves that survive from the large illuminated Persian edition, painted by an unknown artist between 1585 and 1590. In the Virginia Museum's galleries it is framed by a flowered border.*

Krishna and Balarama Arrive in Brindaban

Page from a manuscript of the *Harivamsa*
Mughal, circa 1585
Opaque watercolor on paper; 11⅞ by 7⅜ inches
Virginia Museum of Fine Arts, The Nasli and Alice
  Heeramaneck Collection, Gift of Paul Mellon,
  68.8.50

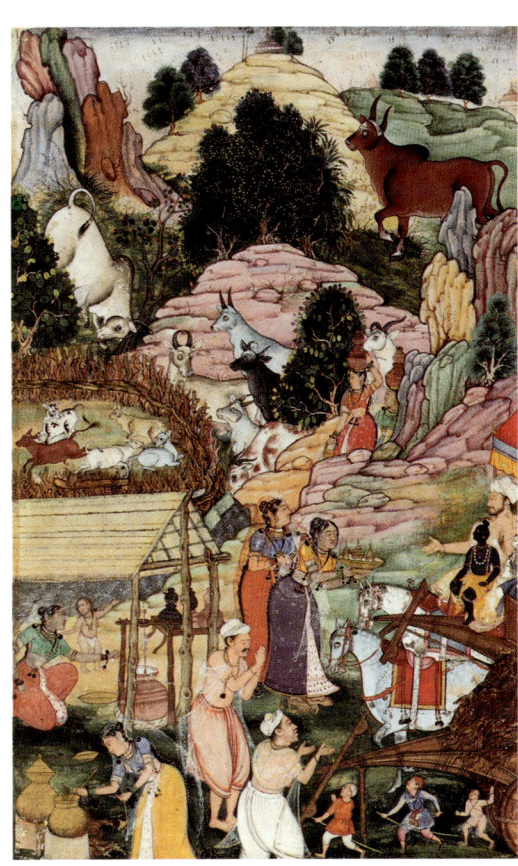

Ritual Crown

The sheer opulence of this rare Buddhist *Ritual Crown* engages the viewer at first sight. A second look, however, brings intricate details into focus. Tucked within its shimmering surfaces, the crown harbors spiritual meanings.

Made of hammered copper and embellished by gilding and gemstones, the crown hints of the ancient mystical beauty of Vajrayana Buddhism—a sect devoted to the pursuit of enlightenment through a personal god—in the Kathmandu Valley of Nepal. Small cast metal figures of the five Cosmic Buddhas—emanations of the supreme Buddha—adorn the triple tiers of its conical form. Through a tour-de-force of miniature metalwork, the meticulous artistry that formed these figures enhances our sense of their divine nature. Hundreds of years ago, Buddhist priests wore this crown during religious ceremonies to bring their own beings into harmony with the Buddha's divine essence. Today, the crown reminds us of the fine art of medieval Nepalese metalwork, known for its elegant finishes, elaborate decoration, and gemstone inlays.

At the crown's peak, a *vajra* rises from a lotus as an emblem of the Vajrayana sect's "diamond-path" or "thunderbolt." The *vajra*—commanding gold prongs that meet at a delicate central point—signifies the authority of the priest who, by donning the crown, becomes the "Master of the Thunderbolt" imbued with mystical power. Encircling the crown beneath this symbol, two tiers of gilded, flowerlike forms display ornate inlays of glass and gemstones the color of garnets, rubies, emeralds, and jade. The jewels in turn are offset by stones of turquoise and lapis lazuli.

In the main tier, just above the serpentine band of diamond-patterned lapis lazuli, surface ornament enhances the spiritual message. Gold-framed petals of deep-blue lapis radiate around the Central Buddha. Representing supreme wisdom, he cups the fingers of one hand around the index finger of the other, to symbolize the five elements (earth, water, air, fire, and ether) that surround the flame of knowledge. A lotus supports him; its symmetrical blossoms converge into a lion's head, the auspicious "face of glory" *(kirtimukha)* that, in turn, confronts us.

To the Central Buddha's left (counter-clockwise), the Buddha of the West sits in a meditative posture; to his right (clockwise), the Buddha of the North gestures to dispel fear. Lost during the course of centuries, the Buddhas of the East (earth-touching) and South (gift-giving) once decorated the back of the crown, probably couched in flourishes of metal and stone. Representing the four cardinal directions, plus the center, the Cosmic Buddhas took their places on the crown to guide its wearer toward spiritual enlightenment.

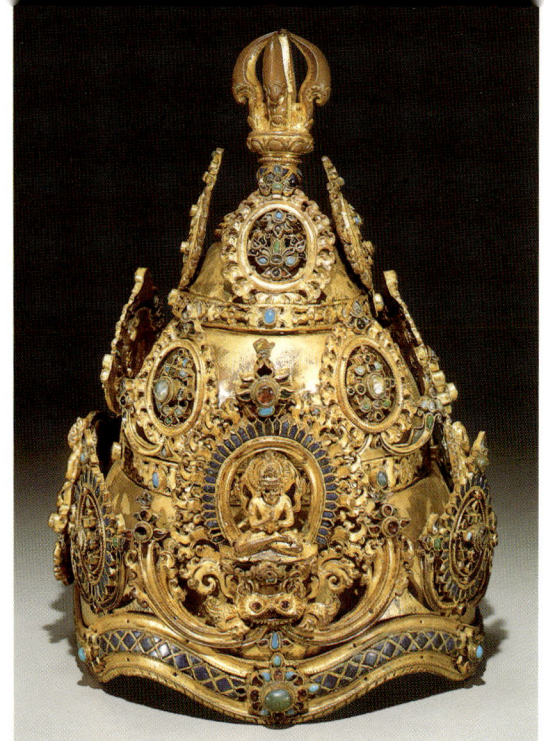

Repoussé Metalwork

This crown is an example of the art of repoussé, a French word meaning "pushed back." The term refers to the painstaking process of hammering a sheet of metal from the back into desired forms. Artists first inscribe the shapes on a metal sheet with a sharp, pointed tool. Then, using various hammers and shaping tools, they carefully work the metal, bit by bit, bracing the work against a pre-shaped mold. Once common in Asia and Europe, and still practiced today in Nepal, the art of hand-worked repoussé is now somewhat rare in modern metalsmithing.

Nepalese Metalworking

Born of royal and religious patronage, cast-metal sculpture in Nepal dates at least to the late 500s; the oldest surviving Nepalese objects in repoussé were made in the early 600s. Jewelers and metalsmiths created this crown during the golden age of their art, which lasted from the mid 1100s to around 1482, when the Kathmandu Valley was divided into three kingdoms (see additional Nepalese metal sculpture in the Virginia Museum's galleries). This crown is considered among the finest of its kind in any museum.

Ritual Crown

Nepalese, Patan, Kathmandu Valley, 1100s–1200s

Gilded copper alloy, glass, gemstones; 11½ by 8¾ by 7¾ inches

Virginia Museum of Fine Arts Purchase, The Arthur and Margaret Glasgow Fund, 84.41

Sacred Diagram of the Universe: Mandala

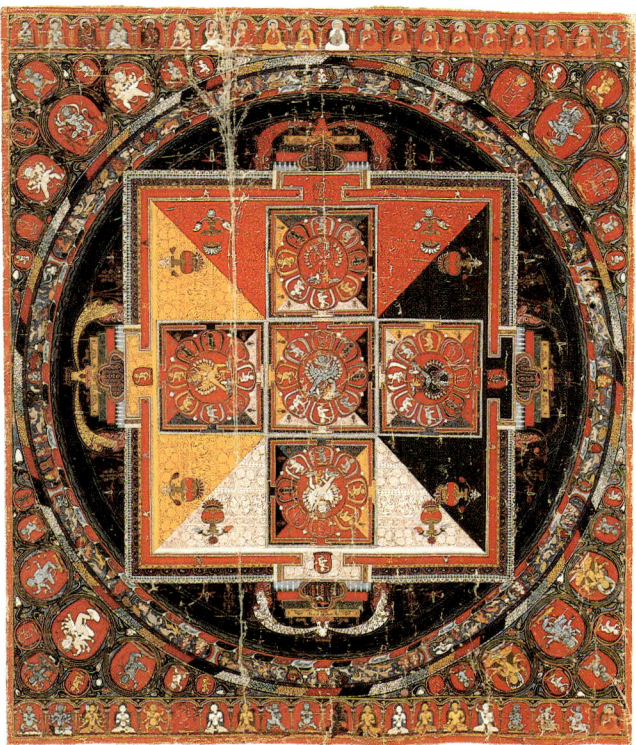

Spinning with images, this diagram captures the mystery of the universe as seen through the eyes of Tibetan Buddhist monks. A magical Cosmos expands through a pantheon of gods, spirits, saints, and religious teachers in this geometric painting on cloth, called a *mandala*. Decorative lines trace kaleidoscopic color—reds, blacks, yellows, whites, and blues—in which Buddhas, bodhisattvas, and other holy beings invite contemplation of the path to enlightenment (the word *bodhisattva,* in Sanskrit, means an enlightened being). Striking a variety of symbolic poses within their spheres, these holy beings offer instruction in the complex precepts of Buddhism, the center of life in a land where monasteries are said to outnumber cities.

In Tibet, perched high in the Himalayas above the rest of the world, the practice of Buddhism revolves around meditation, worship, and instruction. Sacred diagrams of the Cosmos serve as a focus for the faithful. This painted universe seems infinite. Sewn to a blue silk field to make a hanging scroll, it comprises layers of images of life and death: blossoming trees, human bodies, birds of prey. A solid red rectangle contains a large black circle; inside the circle, triangles of color and pattern meet to form the central square. This square stands for the celestial palace, the center of enlightenment guarded by four gateways. Inside it, smaller squares may be seen, and inside these, tiny triangles, more color, and more pattern. Then, like newly opened

flowers, five circles—small *mandalas* themselves—unfold to reveal Buddhist gods and goddesses framed by petal-like arches. At the center of each circle, Hevajra, one of many Buddhist deities, embraces his consort, Nairatmya. Together these loving gods—a "father/mother" (*yabyum* in Tibetan)—embody the state of enlightenment that the faithful seek and may attain through the union of wisdom (considered in this universe to be a female quality) and compassion (assigned to the male).

The Art of Tibet
The history of Himalayan art—from Tibet and neighboring regions of Nepal, India, and China—is one of itinerant painters, sculptors, tradespeople, and patrons who spread religious philosophies and artistic styles to villages and monasteries. Buddhism had been brought to Tibet from India around A.D. 650, and the Tibetans added to the Indian Buddhist pantheon of gods their own spirits, demons, and religious leaders (see Yamantaka, *p. 27, and* Green Tara, *opposite). While reflecting influences from bordering cultures, Tibetan art has its own distinctive character, visible in its precious metal sculpture and painted hanging scrolls—thankas of individual holy figures and* mandalas *of the universe (see* Lhamo, *p. 26).*

Sacred Diagram of the Universe (Mandala of Hevajra)
Tibetan, 1400–1600
Opaque watercolor on cloth; 32 by 28½ inches (image)
From the Berthe and John Ford Collection
Virginia Museum of Fine Arts Purchase, with funds provided by The Arthur and Margaret Glasgow Fund, The Kathleen Boone Samuels Fund, and The Robert A. and Ruth Fisher Fund, 91.509

Green Tara Attended by White Tara, Bodhisattvas, and Nagas

One of the most widely worshipped divinities of Tibetan Buddhism, Green Tara gracefully emerges from layers of lotus blossoms. Tara means the "one who saves." She comforts her followers and bestows gifts of abundance, goodness, and prosperity. Her identity, importance, and closeness to Buddha find expression in the embellishment that surrounds her slender, silver form: at her shoulders, two silver lotuses; at her sides, two gilt-bronze bodhisattvas (enlightened beings who choose to remain on Earth to help others). Below them, two copper Nagas (serpent deities) offer wish-granting gems to her, and between them, at the center, a small White Tara meditates within an ornate brass base of flowering vines. Surrounded by a mandorla (halo), she is cast in silver as a smaller complement to the larger Green Tara above her.

Green Tara sits in a posture of ease that expresses both readiness for action and a state of contemplation: she extends her right leg and folds her left leg close to her. She raises one hand, holding a lotus stem, to offer sanctuary in her power and in Buddhist teachings; she lowers the other in a gesture of gift-giving to the faithful. She wears gold wire necklaces, armlets, bracelets, and anklets; a golden crown rests on her head; a gold-and-silver sash encircles her hips, and a delicately patterned skirt clings to her hips and legs. A silver shawl is draped over her shoulders, and a garland of flowers cascades down her left side, front and back.

Tara's green and white forms, here represented in silver, personify divine compassion, born when the Bodhisattva of Compassion cried over the suffering on Earth. He shed two tears, one green and one white, from which the Taras sprang to strengthen him

as he comforted others. Tara's green color signifies fierceness to convert hate-filled envy, first into wisdom and then into compassion, the expression of wisdom. Her white color stands for peacefulness, to convert passions of ignorance into calmness.

The first Dalai Lama (1391–1474), spiritual leader of Tibet, favored Green Tara among the other Buddhist deities. In his poem about the goddess, Green Tara frees her followers from fear, rescues them from suffering, and invites "the wise to a feast of supreme accomplishments." Here, in sculpture, she appears as the poet's lovely "goddess of action . . . the union of wisdom and art."

Mudras

Images of Hindu and Buddhist deities are usually depicted in symbolic postures and hand gestures, called mudras, *which represent aspects of their faiths: meditating, teaching and explaining, releasing from fear, gift-giving, touching the Earth for spiritual affirmation (see* Gautama Buddha, *p. 18, and* Shiva, King of Dancers, *p. 19).*

Eight Perils

Tara's green and white aspects are her most popular forms (she has at least twenty-one manifestations). Green Tara protects her followers and wards off the "eight perils" (earthly beings and the temptations they represent) that prevent enlightenment: 1) lions and pride, 2) wild elephants and delusions, 3) forest fires and hatred, 4) snakes and envy, 5) robbers and fanaticism, 6) prisons and avarice, 7) floods and lust, 8) demons and doubts. "You save us from these dangers the instant of our prayer," writes the first Dalai Lama in his fifteenth-century hymn to the kind and wise goddess.

Buddhist Icons

Sculptures such as the Green Tara *are often hollow, not solid. They sometimes contain paper inscriptions with prayers to the god and invocations of power. The sacredness of the object remains intact so long as the seal to its interior is unbroken.*

Green Tara Attended by White Tara, Bodhisattvas, and Nagas
Tibetan, 1300s–1600s
Silver, brass, copper alloy, gold, gilded copper, gilded silver; 8¾ by 6 by 4 inches
Virginia Museum of Fine Arts Purchase, The Adolph D. and Wilkins C. Williams Fund, 84.74

Lhamo

The most terrifying of Tibetan deities, the fierce goddess Lhamo rides her mule through a stylized sea of blood, shed by the faithless. As Defender of Buddhist Law, she wields a trident, her three-pronged spear of authority, while she grasps a writhing snake and readies a chopper (a curved blade) to cut through veils of ignorance. Wearing a crown of staring skulls and a garland of severed heads, she flashes her red eyes, red palms, and red grimace as she bares her teeth.

Frightening in appearance, horrifying in deed, the macabre Lhamo may at first seem a stark contrast to the beauty of the hanging scroll, or *thanka*, that bears her image. Lhamo is one of eight Tibetan Protectors of the Faith, and the only female deity among them. She is the guardian of the Dalai Lama, earthly Defender of Buddhist Law, and of Lhasa, Tibet's capital city. As such she is cast in elegant and refined embroidery worthy of a goddess, though the *thanka* is at once as brilliant and as shadowy as the divinity it honors. Simple, embroidered forms create broad contrasts of color—deep bluish black and pale blue set against a coral background. Yet the hues are elusive. As silken threads catch the light, silvery colors slip and shift across the shimmering surface. Details of gold patterns begin to appear as infinite as they are intricate.

Texture and highlight emerge from forms traced with raised strands of couched and wrapped gold cords, laid along the surface and stitched neatly to the background cloth. Subtle sheen and shading result from satin-stitching, the dense and tireless needlework that fills large areas with color. The black silk mounts that border Lhamo's image bear embroidery as well: on top, a royal canopy with sun and moon; at the bottom, the guardians of the Four Directions (see *Lokapala*, p. 30). To the left,

a crocodile-headed Dakini (celestial being) leads Lhamo. The Dakini is stitched in greenish-gold threads to evoke her reptilian aspects. Above her, in the upper corner, a serene monk in red robes quietly contemplates the blood-curdling image below. His black hat and his undisturbed presence may indicate that he is a member of the Black-Hat Buddhist sect and the patron who commissioned the image. Opposite him, in the upper right, a figure dances triumphantly; her identity is mysterious.

Lhamo does not fear to show us what we fear—pain and suffering, violence and death, enormous tests of faith. Evils are not unknown to her; nor are horrors. She will resort to violence to safeguard

her religion. She has sacrificed her own disbelieving son, stretching his flayed skin into the red riding blanket on which she sits. More gruesome tales are told of her, as if by magic to strengthen her protective power by scaring those around her. Yet we must not confuse her ferocity with evil itself; it is a guise she assumes to combat negative forces—at all costs—as the guardian of Buddhism (see *Yamantaka*, opposite).

Chinese Embroidery

Embroidery probably originated in China some four thousand years ago. Chinese textiles in general, and the art of embroidery in particular, flourished during the Ming dynasty (1368–1644), when this Lhamo thanka was made. Its silk speaks of China. Although most Tibetan and Nepalese thankas are painted on cloth (see the Sacred Diagram of the Universe, *p. 24), those embroidered on silk grounds can be traced to Chinese monasteries practicing Tibetan Buddhism. Both Ming and later Qing (1644–1911) dynasties shared close connections with that religion: artistic influences, imperial Chinese gifts, and tributes from Tibetan locales—often in the form of Buddhist relics—were exchanged between the cultures, as this thanka may have been.*

Lhamo
Sino-Tibetan, early 1400s
Silk embroidery on silk ground; 32 by 18¼ inches
From the Berthe and John Ford Collection
Virginia Museum of Fine Arts, Gift of Berthe and
 John Ford, 91.505

Yamantaka

Yamantaka is the Terminator of Death: in Sanskrit, *Yama* means Lord of Death, *Antaka* means Slayer. From a land of harsh weather, forbidding terrain, and magical beauty, the ferocious Yamantaka stands triumphant and ready to instruct the faithful in Tibetan Buddhism.

He is actually Manjushri, the Bodhisattva of Wisdom (one who attains the highest state of spirituality on Earth); he has taken this fearsome form, with the head of an Asian water buffalo, to conquer the Lord of Death. He once did so, it is said, to protect his own village from persecutions and slayings. He scowls, flares his nostrils, and prepares to roar. His eyes flash as they focus on unseen malevolent forces to be vanquished. In his many hands, he wields daggers, bells, *vajras* (implements with curved prongs at each end), and other weapons used to attain spiritual victory. His feet trample the forces of evil and suffering, symbolized by gods, demons, birds, and animals. The thirty-four arms, sixteen feet, and six faces that peer from the sides and back of his head symbolize facets of supreme enlightenment and power. His crown of five skulls represents the five wisdoms; his garland of severed heads refers to the quelling of selfish egos that remain self-absorbed and thus vulnerable to death. Ready to shred any obstacle to enlightenment, he raises a chopper (a curved blade with handle). Able to change life's blood into the elixir of immortality, he holds a skull-shaped cup. He grasps the four-faced head of Brahma, the Hindu creator god, as a warning against the temptation to assume godlike power. His temple gong will awaken the soul, and his noose will gather up stray thoughts that interfere with clear thinking.

Devout contemplation of the figure's many aspects, one after another, can lead to comprehensive spiritual wisdom (see the *Sacred Diagram of the Universe*, p. 24, and the *Green Tara*, p. 25). Search and you will find the bodhisattva's holy face, small but blissful, radiating goodness at the top of Yamantaka's head.

Yamantaka's Origins

This Yamantaka may have been carved in China as a gift from an imperial Chinese court to a Tibetan Buddhist monastery of the Gelupka order. Gelupka monks, the largest and most powerful sect of Tibetan Buddhism, especially revere Yamantaka for the battle he fights against negative forces and the energy he harnesses toward spiritual transformation. This rare Yamantaka shares similarities with different types of Chinese sculpture: gilded metals, polychromed wood, and polychromed terra-cotta (see Lokapala, *p. 30). It now ranks among the finest large-scale wooden carvings of a Tibetan Buddhist deity outside of Asia.*

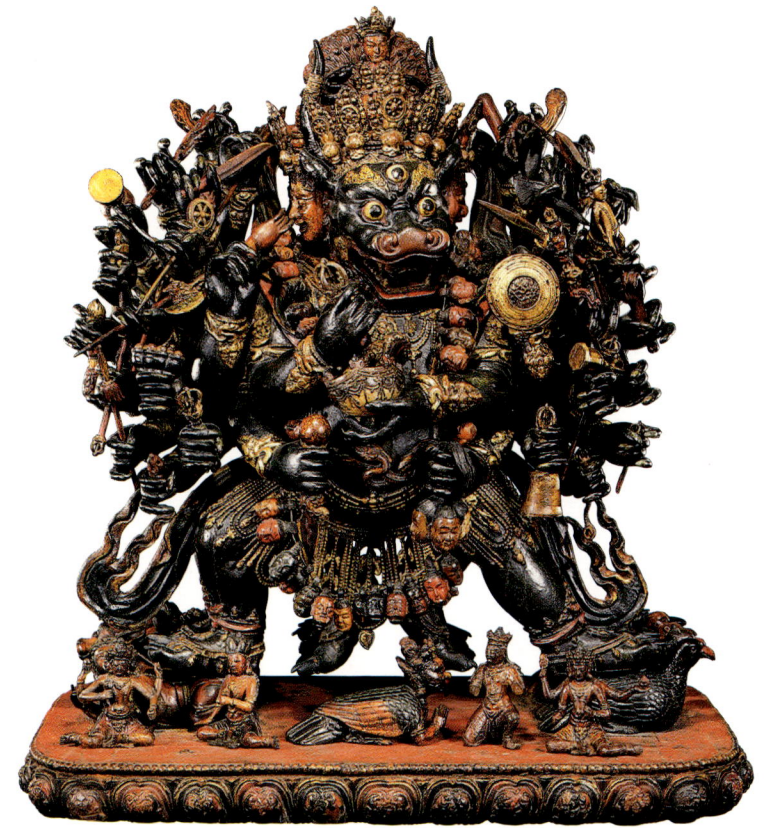

Yamantaka
Sino-Tibetan, circa 1700s
Polychromed wood; 53¼ by 50¾ by 30¾ inches
Virginia Museum of Fine Arts Purchase, with funds provided by The E. Rhodes and Leona B. Carpenter Foundation and The Arthur and Margaret Glasgow Fund, 93.13

Ritual Vessels

At first sight, it is hard to imagine the dimensions of time and space, age and history that these vessels so quietly embody. Cast more than 3,500 years ago—between the Bronze Age and the Age of Confucius—these bronzes rank among the oldest objects in the Virginia Museum's collection. "Respect ghosts and spirits but keep them at a distance," counseled Confucius. Yet to spend time with these bronzes—studying their intricate patterns, green patina, and worn surfaces—is indeed to summon forth spirits of the vanished kingdoms of ancient China, one of the oldest civilizations on Earth.

Created in the artisans' workshops and bronze foundries of the Shang and the Zhou dynasties (around 1600–1100 and 1100–221 B.C., respectively), these vessels once held food and drink for sacred rituals. They offered grains and wine to the spirits of ancestors, who were worshipped as intercessors between the gods and the living. During the early Shang dynasty, families made such offerings to appease and supplicate the spirits of the dead, sustaining them with extensions of earthly existence so that they might help to bestow blessings and good fortune upon their descendants. By the late Zhou dynasty, clans continued to

revere their ancestors as part of their heritage, but more often they made offerings to commemorate their daily successes—in military, social, economic, and political spheres—as though reporting the family's accomplishments to both the living and the dead.

The bronzes illustrated here represent four of at least twenty types of vessels, each type designed and named for a particular ceremonial function. The youngest vessel in the collection (left)—a three-legged, pot-bellied cooking cauldron called a *ding* from the Late Zhou period—may actually be cast in one of the oldest forms. Vessel forms passed from one dynasty to another, generation to generation: "May sons and grandsons cherish this vessel forever and ever," reads a wish inscribed on a late Zhou-dynasty vessel, made 2000 years after its type was first cast. Of the vessels pictured on the opposite page from left to right, the *fang yi*, a small rectangular box with roof-shaped lid, stored food or wine during the Shang period. The *gu,* a wide-mouthed goblet, flares dramatically outward from stem to lip so that it could contain liquids. The Shang *zun* once held ceremonial wines in its expansive body, which narrows to elegant shoulders and stout neck before broadening again to form a wide lip.

Symmetry defines these vessels, although occasional lop-sidedness reminds us of their hand-crafted origins. Their decoration, divided into registers of ornate geometric shapes, rarely changed. Lively tigers, elephants, ox- and ram-heads, perched on the *zun's* shoulders, animate the registers. Creatures born of the imagination teach about the unseen world of spirits. A dragon mask *(taotie)* peers from each side of the *zun* and the *fang yi*. Trace the eyes (two rivet-like dots), snout

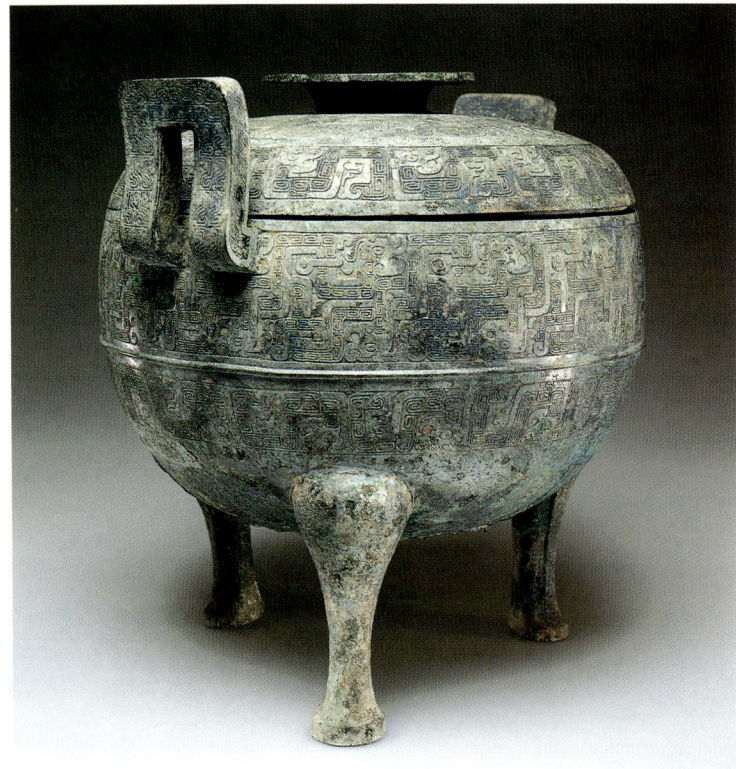

(the central join between segments), and fangs within intricate spiral patterns handed down through the ages.

The Art of Piece-Mold Casting

These bronzes belong to the Virginia Museum's much larger collection of Chinese vessels, that span more than three thousand years, from 1600 B.C. to A.D. 1600. To make a vessel by piece-mold casting, an artisan would first model a clay core in the form of the vessel and then make an outer mold by fitting together slabs of clay. Decorative patterns could be incised on either the inner core or on the inside surfaces of the outer mold segments. The outer mold segments were pressed around the inner core, and molten bronze would then be poured in between. Once the bronze had cooled and become solid again, the clay segments would be removed, and a single-piece cast vessel emerged. Though this casting method limited the vessel bodies to symmetrical forms, it allowed unlimited possibilities for surface ornamentation. Over time, artisans even incorporated the seams, where the outer mold segments met, into the design of the finished bronze.

Bronze-Casting Dynasties

The Shang dynasty, one of the oldest cultures in China from the lower reaches of the Yellow River in Hebei province, dates between the ancient Hsia and Zhou dynasties. The history of the Shang tells of a slave-supported society based on agriculture and silkworms, as well as mining, workshops, and foundries for casting bronze weapons and vessels.

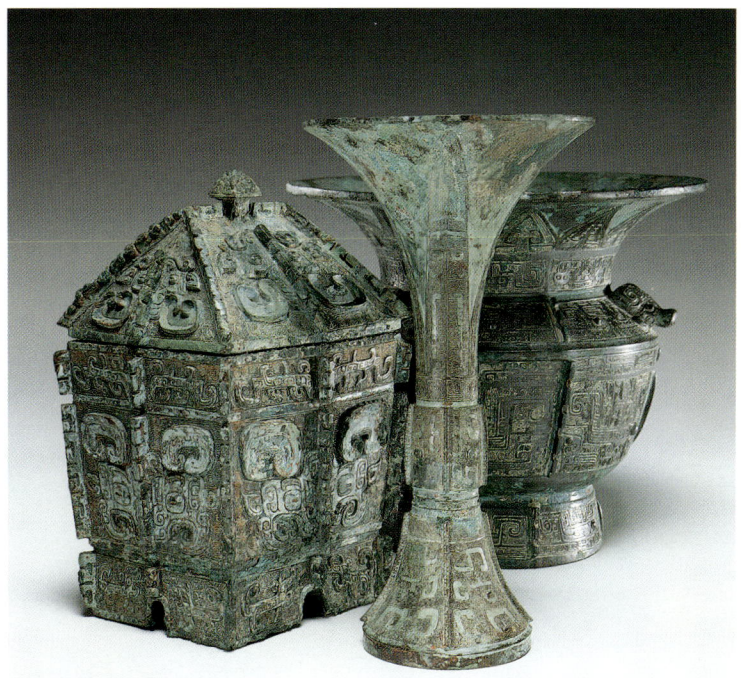

Chinese Bronzes and Burials

During the past fifty years, archaeologists have uncovered the tombs of kings and nobles in which bronze vessels and other furnishings accompanied the dead, often after a lifetime of use in ceremonies and rituals (see the Greek Symposium Vessels, pp. 4–5). Still, much of the history of Chinese bronzes remains a mystery. Chinese legend does explain the origin of the Late Zhou ding in the Virginia Museum's collection. In the days of the Hsia dynasty, around 2200 B.C. and long before Chinese history was recorded, King Yu divided his land into nine provinces and ordered the casting of a cauldron (ding) for each province as a symbol of state authority and power.

Chinese Ritual Vessels

Virginia Museum of Fine Arts Purchase, The Adolph D. and Wilkins C. Williams Fund

Covered Ding

Late Zhou, 770–256 B.C.
Bronze; 13¼ by 14⅛ by 12 (diameter) inches, 57.45.7a

Fang Yi

Shang, circa 1300–circa 1100 B.C.
Bronze; 9½ by 6 by 5 inches, 57.45.5a/b

Gu

Shang, circa 1300–circa 1100 B.C.
Bronze; 10¼ by 6 (diameter) inches, 57.45.17

Zun

Shang, circa 1300–circa 1100 B.C.
Bronze; 10 by 9½ (diameter) inches, 57.45.11

Lokapala

An indomitable will galvanizes this windswept warrior, charging him with energy. Armor-clad from head to toe, he is a Chinese Lokapala who stands guard at Buddhist sanctuaries, defends the world against evil spirits, and accompanies the dead in the afterlife. Created for a burial, never to be seen again, he joined a lively entourage of figures in a Tang-dynasty tomb. Suppressing a struggling demon underfoot and brandishing a now-lost spear, he once protected the chambers of the deceased. His mighty arm is still upraised; his broad features swell as he glowers at threatening forces.

A plumed phoenix (a mythological bird based, in part, on the Asian pheasant) rises from the crest of his helmet. A breastplate encases his chest, curling at the shoulders into daunting dragon wings and reptilian scales. Gauntlets sheathe his arms, then broaden at the elbows into protective cuffs; greaves shield his legs. So armed, he is one of the four Lokapalas of Buddhism, the guardians of the Four Cardinal Points—East, West, North, and South (see the *Ritual Crown,* p. 23, and *Lhamo,* p. 26).

This Lokapala is made of fired earthenware (terra-cotta). A thin coating (slip) of fine white clay (kaolin) mixed with water covers the sculpture, while added detail decorates its surface. Gilding highlights both his breastplate and his gauntlets; beneath them, black and reddish floral patterns swirl about his sleeves and tunic. Bold strokes of pigment emphasize helmet feathers, tunic folds, and the painted flanges of his belly-binding armor.

He seems to draw his vehemence from an inner spirit. Such vitality is, in fact, characteristic of Tang-dynasty sculpture (around A.D. 618–976), which proclaims the confidence and splendor of a people who enjoyed foreign trade in silks and

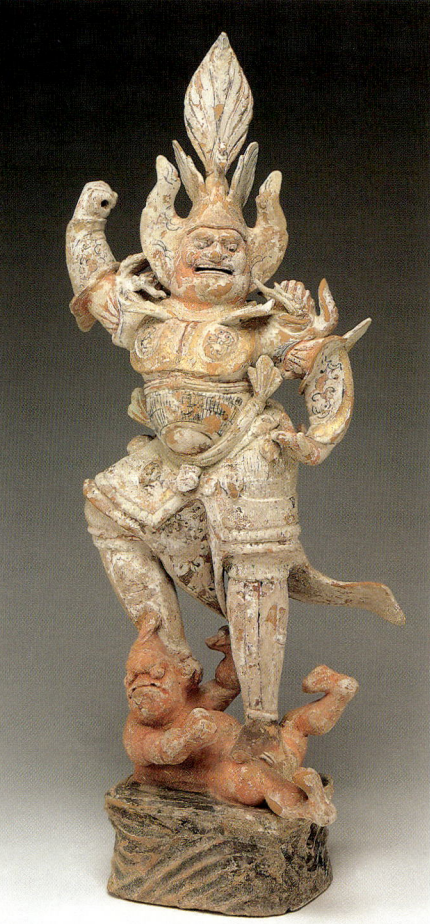

spices, prosperity for certain upper classes, military might, and intellectual and artistic freedom. Colorful tomb sculptures offered lasting versions of life's pleasures and necessities, to enhance the spiritual afterlife. Ceremonial horses, camels, and chariots; servants, musicians, and dancers; architectural models and guardian figures such as the Lokapala rank among the finest gifts from the Tang dynasty to the history of Chinese art.

Sculpture created for noble burials by generations of Chinese artists shows a reverence for traditional forms and age-old principles (see the *Ritual Vessels,*

pp. 28–29). Individual beauty and power, like the Lokapala's, rested in each artist's ability to convey inner spirit through outer form, embellished with glazes or paints, in celebration of a visually bountiful world.

Art of the Tang Dynasty

The golden age of Tang-dynasty art displays the richness of its culture and its natural surroundings. Chinese culture enjoyed a cosmopolitan period of centralized power and religious acceptance, for the many faiths that traveled the trade routes east and west between Chang'an, China's capital (modern Xi'an), and Byzantium's Constantinople (modern Istanbul). The natural world—human, plant, or animal—was observed through the eyes of artists from this flourishing civilization and translated into engaging landscape painting and tomb sculpture.

Lokapala
Chinese (Tang Dynasty), 600s
Painted and gilded earthenware; 26¾ by 9⅞ by
6⅝ inches
Virginia Museum of Fine Arts Purchase, with
funds provided by Floyd D. and Elisabeth S.
Gottwald, 90.219

Lacquered Ewer

The simple silhouette and brilliant red color of this Japanese ewer attract the eye. Clear, clean contours may be traced around the elegant handle, over the easy undulations of knob and lid, across wide shoulders, down the generous body and foot—echoed in the lines of the handle—and along the curved spout. A closer look reveals that layers of red lacquer have been applied over a base coat of black lacquer. The hues have softened through the ages by human handling. Here and there, touches of black undercoat emerge through the red. Whispers of worn elegance enhance the beauty of the ewer in the eyes of many, making it more worthy of esteem and veneration. Form and function become one: the ewer's lovely lacquered surface confides its long history of respect and use.

This ewer belongs to a type of Japanese art with red-lacquer coating and black undercoating called *negoro* ware. The technique originated in the region around the Negoro Temple in Kii Province (modern Wakayama Prefecture) and was practiced primarily between the 1300s and 1500s. According to tradition, monks and artisans fashioned these objects for ceremonies in the temple, but they also sold them to pilgrims and other travelers for daily use in households. This ewer may have held water for making tea, or perhaps it contained sake, to be served at formal banquets.

Its lustrous surface attests to the unsurpassed talents of Japanese artisans, who first developed lacquerwork as a technique to protect and decorate porous wood, and later refined it to serve religious ritual and social ceremony. The art of *negoro* ware evolved into one of understated elegance, clarity of form, and pleasing finish. In its simple beauty, this ewer embodies the Japanese concept of *wabi* ("quiet taste"): plain, humble, but eloquently expressed.

The Tea Ceremony

The Japanese tea ceremony became part of Zen monastic life in the late 1100s. The custom was influenced in part by the use of treasured ceramics for drinking tea in China. In Japan, the monks' ceremony was adopted during the following centuries by shoguns and warriors, who elevated their gatherings into rituals, accompanied by the formalities of preparing and presenting tea using highly valued objects and utensils.

Negoro Ewer

Japanese, 1300s
Lacquer on wood; 12¾ by 10 (diameter) inches
Virginia Museum of Fine Arts Purchase, The Arthur
  and Margaret Glasgow Fund, 73.41a/b

The Art of Lacquer

Lacquer is a resinous varnish made from the sap of certain Asian trees. Known for its excellent finish and durability, lacquer is expensive and the process time-consuming when applied in layers in the Asian tradition. A tree annually yields only a few ounces of sap, which is toxic in its raw state; each coat of lacquer may take weeks to dry, and each object may have up to fifty coats. This ewer of porous wood has been lacquered both inside and out (see the Japanned High Chest, *p. 79, and* Canoe Sofa, *p. 104).*

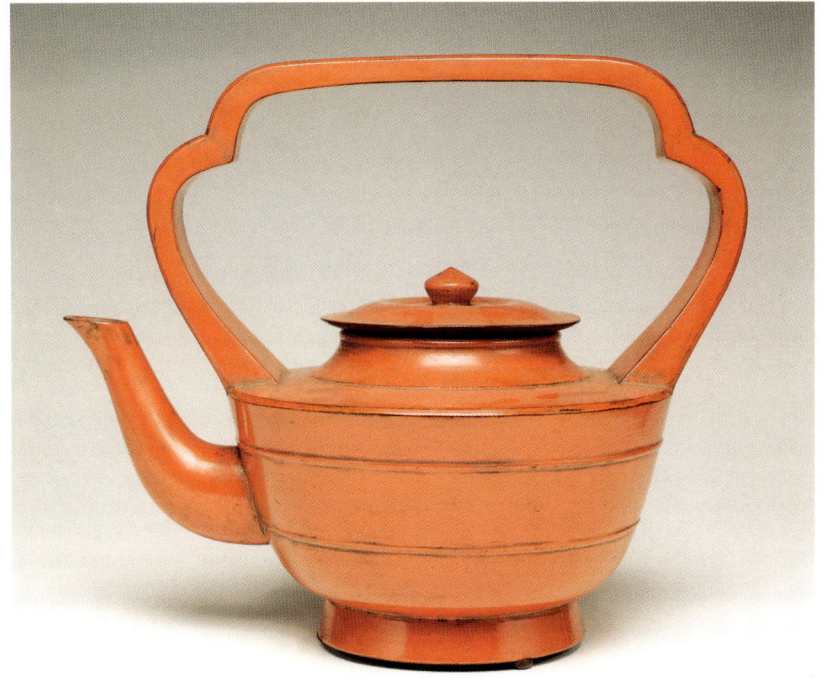

Pair of Sixfold Screens

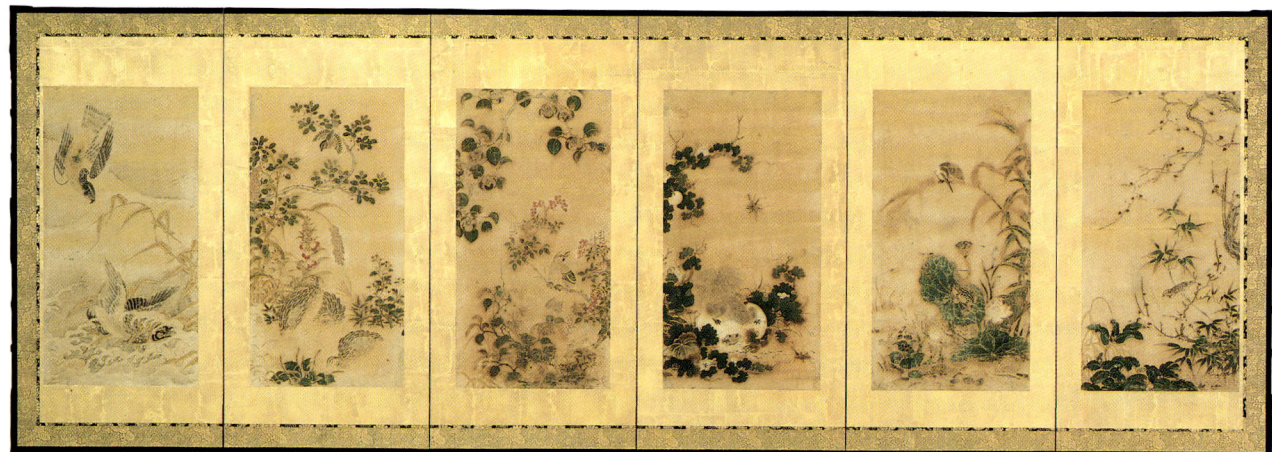

Colorful birds, animals, and flowers—busy and blossoming against a gold-washed sky—fill these Japanese painted screens, to enfold and delight the viewer with an intimate vision of nature. When the panels are seen as they were intended—from a comfortable seated position on the floor—an animated world beckons the viewer to draw closer to share its array of pleasures. Rich color and subtle brushwork depict nature's lively mysteries: cats, quails, butterflies, wasps, frog, and worm.

From the word *byobu*, meaning "protection against the wind," Japanese folding screens served both as partitions to define interior spaces and as painted decorations to create moods. Made in the early 1500s, the Virginia Museum's pair of screens foreshadows by one generation the dawning of Japan's golden age of screen-painting. Here begins an artful blend of Japanese and Chinese painting traditions, when the secrets of re-creating nature through gold leaf and color are mastered, to be kept alive by Japan's greatest artists for at least two hundred years.

It is said that Tosa Mitsunobu (active 1469–1523), the superintendent of Imperial court painting in Japan, created the images on these screens. For two generations he led the Tosa school of Japanese painting, known for *yamato-e*. Beginning around the 1100s, this traditional style was characterized by colorful depictions of birds and animals, the four seasons, scenic views, and poetic subjects set into shallow, almost flat, pictorial spaces. These screens are rare examples, however, of Tosa Mitsunobu's ability to borrow elements from Chinese painting in order to please Japanese patrons who favored the Chinese style *(kara-e)*.

The artist draws the viewer into nature, alternating tranquil scenes with predatory ones, subjects that would become popular in ink paintings of the late 1500s.

Poems written at that time have been inscribed on the back of the panels: reflections about a world of dreams, realities, and appearances; changing seasons; aging bodies; passing time. Without precisely corresponding from text to picture, the poetic imagery evokes the visual images. These paintings suggest the four seasons, and with them, change: wild hawks on a cold winter evening, the spring return of songbirds and red camellias, a squirrel's summer meal of muskmelon, a monkey's delight in autumn-frosted chestnut burrs. Life cycles transpire—a weasel catches a bird in its mouth, a monkey cradles her young—against tall grasses, graceful branches, and skies bathed in gold.

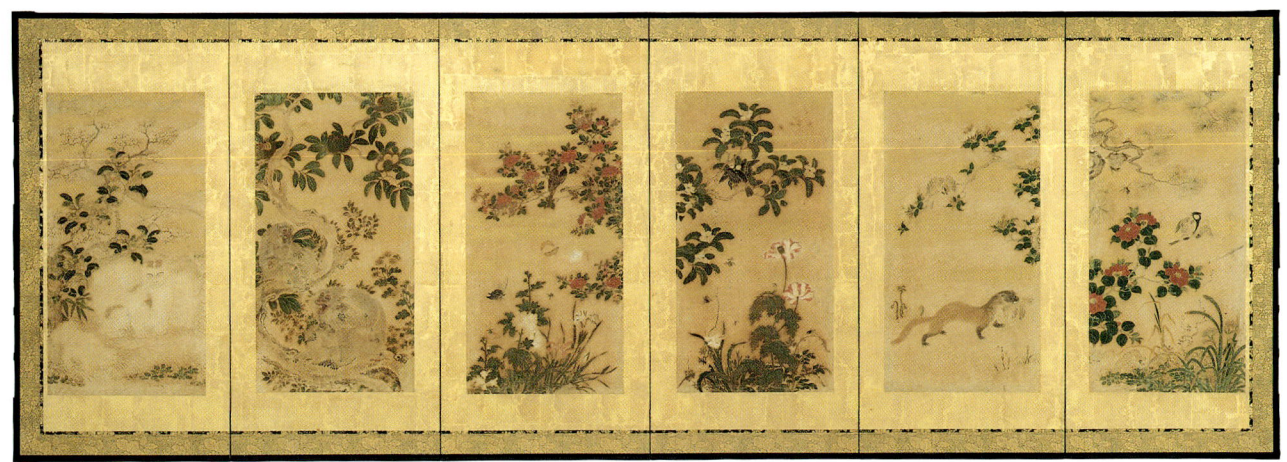

Making Painted Folding Screens

Japanese folding screens of the 1500s and 1600s are usually painted in pairs of two to six panels. The artist applies pigments and gold leaf to a surface of paper or silk. The support consists of underlying layers of paper and a wooden latticework frame. The freestanding screens are meant to be appreciated at the eye-level of a seated viewer, and were displayed during both formal ceremonies and informal gatherings.

Styles and Schools

Complex crossovers between Japanese (yamato-e) and Chinese (kara-e) schools of painting occurred between 1500 and 1650. National schools had been evolving; in Japan, local schools of painter-families worked in styles from both cultures, often selected to please imperial or middle-class patrons. These interwoven histories have yet to be fully written, and research into the interaction between styles and schools is ongoing. Some say that gold backgrounds and strong colors—for which another school of family painters, called the Kano, is known—actually originated with Tosa Mitsunobu and the Tosa school. Tosa Mitsunobu's son-in-law, Kano Motonobu (1476–1559), is said to have perfected the art of gold-screen painting in the Kano school, by combining lessons from Mitsunobu, from his own father's Chinese-style painting, and from the Ming dynasty's bird-and-flower images of the 1400s. By doing so, Kano established a strong style of Japanese painting—of cranes, pines, bamboo, birds, and flowers—foretold by the Virginia Museum's panels.

Pair of Sixfold Screens with Birds, Flowers, Grasses, Insects, and Animals
Attributed to Tosa Mitsunobu (Japanese, 1435–1525)
Japan, Muromachi Period (before 1523)
Pigments and ink on paper; 38¾ by 110½ inches
Virginia Museum of Fine Arts Purchase, The Arthur
 and Margaret Glasgow Fund, 66.72.1/2

Kano Gyokuraku
Three Hanging Scrolls: Hotei, Winter, and Summer

One of Japan's Seven Gods of Good Fortune, Hotei looks up and laughs from the center of three scrolls. His image, at once ancient and immediate, transcends time and space. Simple lines and light washes capture Hotei's appearance—rounded head, rounded shoulders, rounded stomach. The surrounding stillness evokes his inner nature and his austere life. A wandering disciple of Buddha (called a *lohan* in Chinese and an *arhat* in Sanskrit) who became a popular protector of Japanese households, Hotei himself is homeless, with nothing but a cloak, walking stick, and sack. He travels equally elusive terrain. Seen from high vantage points in the two flanking scrolls, the land of his journeys reaches vast distances only to disappear into mists of emptiness.

Hotei is based on the life of a tenth-century Chinese priest named Pu Tai. He was sometimes regarded as a holy fool; his name may be humorously translated as "Big Belly" and "Cloth Sack." Soft brushstrokes outline his eyes and ears, beard and belly, hand and hemp bag. A blush of color graces his forehead and cheeks. Jagged lines define his cloak. The barest brushwork that suggests the monk also brings forth each landscape: summer unfolds on the viewer's right and winter on the left. Craggy cliffs and gnarled evergreens hold the corners, while nature's immensity dwarfs figure, bridge, boat, and temple. In their dramatic grandeur, the vistas recall Chinese landscape paintings and the monk's native land; in their mood and simplicity, the art and faith of Japanese Zen Buddhism.

Kano Gyokuraku painted these three hanging scrolls in the late 1500s, the golden years of the Zen painting tradition, which had flourished since the 1300s in the Buddhist monasteries and artistic workshops of Japan (see the Tibetan *Sacred Diagram of the Universe*, p. 24). Fleeting and understated, each brushstroke is carefully considered, measured to echo the essence of its subject as simply and clearly as possible. Artists like Gyokuraku sought the subtlety and richness of monochromatic painting and explored how seemingly limited one-color ink gives way to infinite ranges of expressive tones, from light gray to deep black. As the brush moved across the paper, the artist captured nature's vastness and variety as keenly in a tiny pine needle as in the broad expanse of sky. Brushwork—broad and narrow contours, nuances of light and shadow—outlines physical form, but more profoundly expresses the spiritual vitality of monk and mountain. Seasons change; ageless rocks vanish into nothingness. Still, an aged man, wrinkled and bent, casts a twinkling eye toward us and laughs. So did the Buddha, some say, to reveal the nature of Zen.

The Art of Ink Painting

In the art of suiboku-ga, *meaning "water-ink painting," a brush is dipped in dark ink and then applied to silk or paper. Hints of quiet, delicate color may be added occasionally here and there. The artist controls form through thick or thin strokes, texture from the angle of the bristles on the paper, and light and dark through proportions of ink to water. The art of ink painting is sometimes called* sumi-e, *after the carbon ink itself (*sumi*). The technique is unforgiving: mistakes cannot be corrected. A stroke that appears to be completely spontaneous must in fact be applied with thoughtful concentration and deliberate control. Meditation helps the artist to attain the peace and purity of mind, purged of all emotions, necessary to depict life's transience in a permanent medium.*

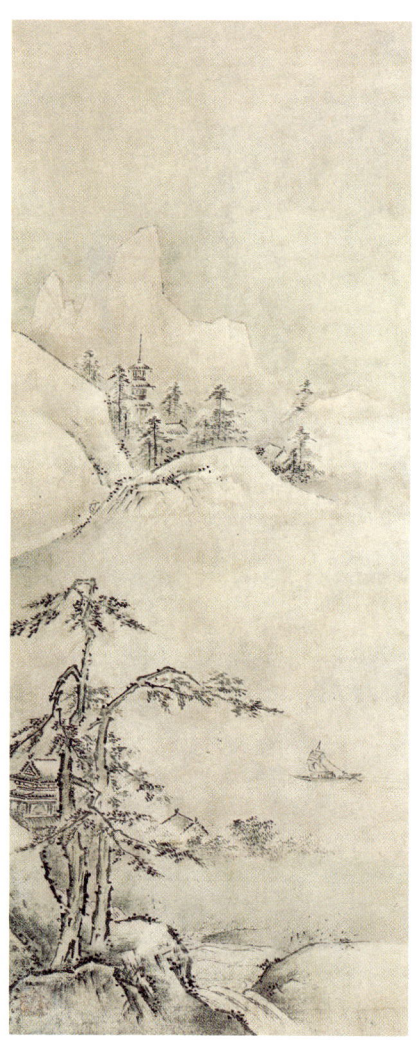

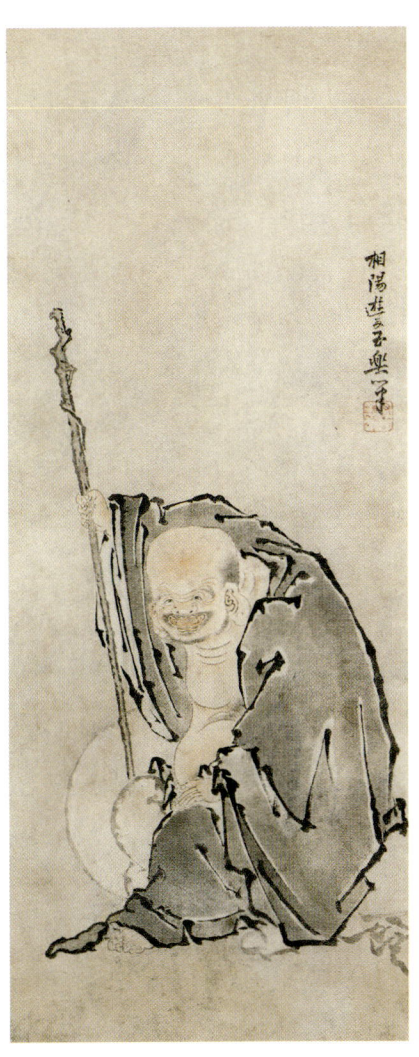

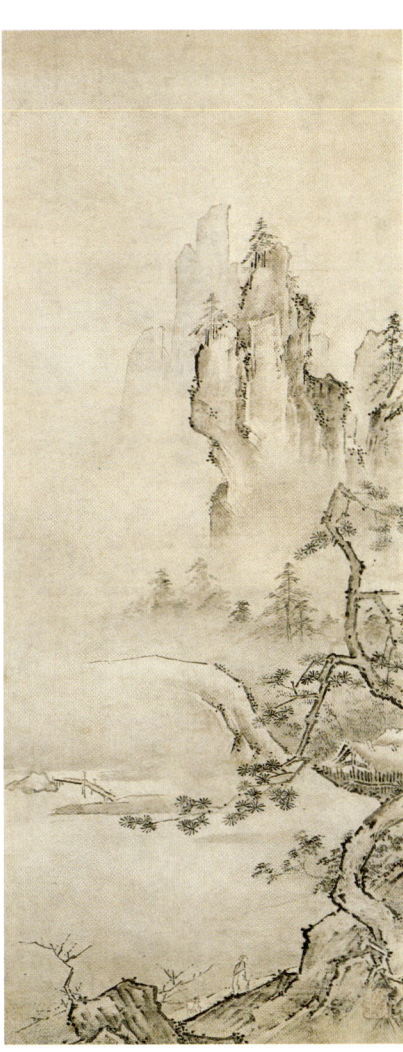

Japanese Ink Painting

Although ink drawing was known in Japan during the 700s, the art of monochromatic painting flourished in the 1300s, influenced by Zen Buddhism and ink brush techniques developed in China during the 1200s.

Hanging Scrolls

The hanging scroll (kakemono) *was often designed for public display, or for a niche* (tokonoma) *in a home or tea room, where its quiet beauty would invite leisurely contemplation.*

Kano Gyokuraku

Kano Gyokuraku may have been the nephew (some say niece) of Kano Motonobu, the master of Japanese screen-painting who established the Kano school as the official school of the shogunate (see also Pair of Sixfold Screens, *pp. 32–33). Gyokuraku's style blends elements of Motonobu's softer, more romantic work with the intellectual rigor and visual austerity of Zen Buddhist painters. Gyokuraku created these scroll paintings of Hotei even as Japanese society was growing more secular, and as power was shifting from monks to feudal shoguns.*

Three Hanging Scrolls:
Hotei, Winter, and Summer Landscapes
Kano Gyokuraku (Japanese, active 1550–1590)
Japan, Momoyama Period, circa 1575
Ink and pigments on paper; 73 by 23½ inches
Virginia Museum of Fine Arts Purchase, The Adolph D.
  and Wilkins C. Williams Fund, 66.70.1/3

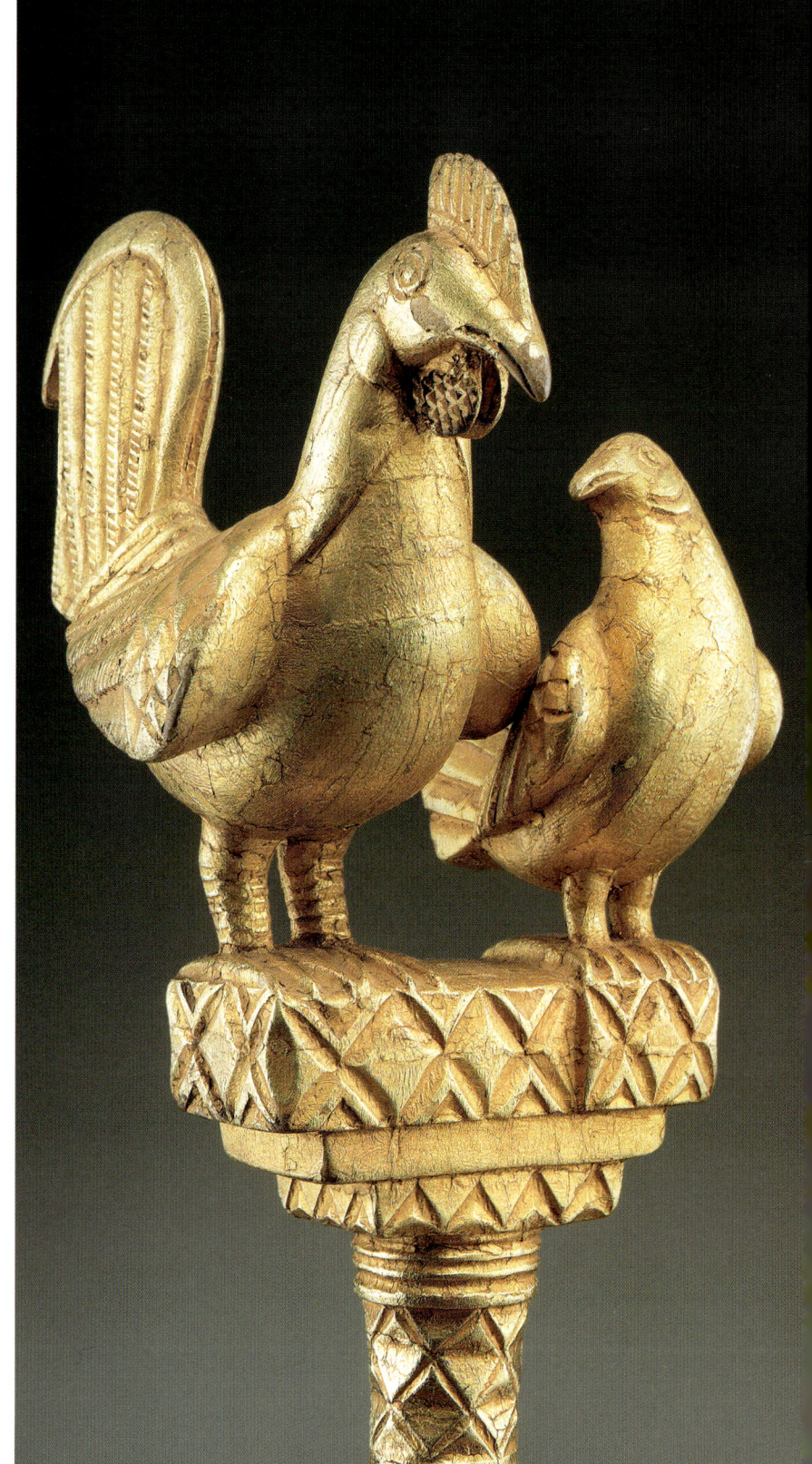

CHAPTER 4

African Art

Akan

Yoruba

Cameroon Grasslands

Kuba

Memorial Portrait Head

Her face expresses peacefulness—smoothed brow, closed eyes, serene lips. Her elegant coiffure of spiraling curls indicates her high social status; her broad forehead displays refined standards of beauty; her graceful neck of soft folds reveals her prosperity. She belonged to a royal family. She has "gone elsewhere"—as it is sometimes said of the deceased in the Akan culture of present-day Ghana—although memories of her reside in her terra-cotta portrait. A symbol of continuity, this portrait served to house her spirit within the larger spirit *(kra)* of her community.

Clay slips (mixtures of clay and water) or paint may once have added color to the surface, now roughened and weathered through the ages. As a combination of earth, a feminine component in the Akan culture, and water, a masculine one, white clay slips especially are said to symbolize the indivisibility and endlessness of the divine *(Nyame)*. Because Akan myth assigns women the task of working with earth, the ceramist who made this image of clay would have been female.

Individual traits characterize Akan memorial portraits—features, coiffure, scarification, crowns, jewelry. Still, recent studies have identified a number of idealized types to which they conform. Whether general or specific, these clay images of lost loved ones hold the magic of remembrance in their legacy. Legends even say that some portraitists "retrieve" the reflection—a memory—of the dying one's face by gazing into palm oil or water. Here, a quiet countenance must have emerged, for this royal portrait emanates tranquility.

Fashioned from such a memory, a portrait head would then be carried in procession for the funeral and farewells. Later, the portrait head would sometimes be placed in the home or the cemetery ("thickets of ghosts") where the deceased would be entombed, but more often it would be set at a distance from the cemetery in a mausoleum or sacred grove of trees ("place of pots"). Fragile yet enduring, the clay portrait would then become a calm haven for the spirit, to help the living remember the dead.

Akan Memorial Terra-cottas

Akan funerary pottery exists in two forms: portraits or full-length figures for an elite social class, usually royalty, and vessels for more common people. The spiritual tradition and its form in art are known to have existed for several hundred years. Ancient connections in the art of terra-cotta may exist between the Akan culture of Ghana and traditions in Mali and Nigeria—the Nok, Ife, and Benin.

The Akan Culture

In the 1700s, when this Twifo-Hemang portrait was made, the Akan culture of Ghana had just been established as a confederation of societies, including the Fante, Aowin, Anyi, Akie, Abron, Twifo-Hemang, and Asante, the largest.

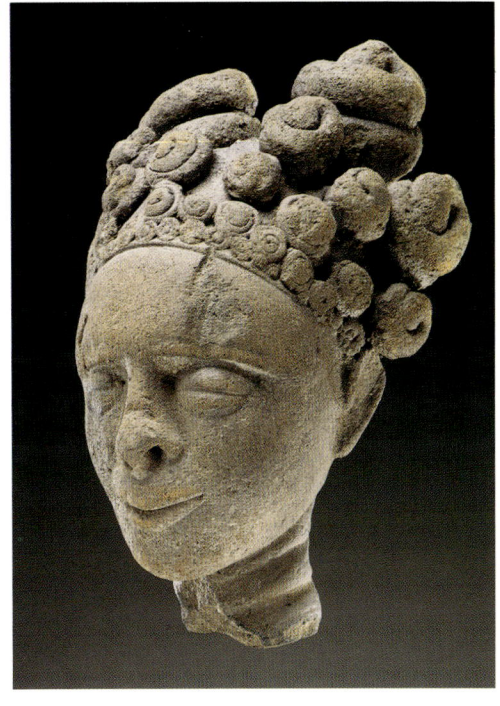

Memorial Portrait Head
Akan Culture, Ghana, circa 1700s
Terra-cotta with traces of pigment; 11 inches high
Virginia Museum of Fine Arts Purchase, The Arthur and Margaret Glasgow Fund, 88.42

Gold Necklace

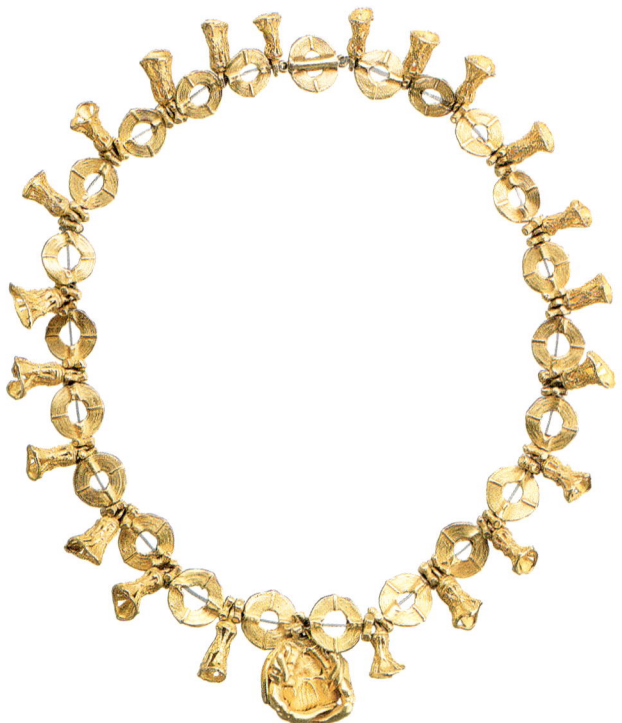

A lively assemblage of shimmering gold disks and bells surrounds a freshwater crab, cast from life, to form a necklace fit for royalty. Through it, we glimpse the golden heritage of Ghana's Akan culture, suggested by a proverb: "the crab knows where the gold dust is found." Both embellishments—the adage and the ornament that evokes it—descend from the Akanni's kingdom of gold dust and nuggets, transformed into the Akan confederation in the 1700s and once known as the Gold Coast.

Like golden dust, proverbs and precious objects grace the Akan culture, where words and images illuminate one another by adding depth, resonance, and meaning. The pendant crab, its claws curled and folded, rests at the center of the necklace, which consists of delicately grooved disks alternating with tiny bells and small gold crosses. The crab, an Akan symbol for the queen mother, may have

been selected as the focal point, because the piece was meant to adorn a woman of royalty.

More than decoration, Akan jewelry carries spiritual overtones. Its images convey ideas, as symbols of royal power. Chameleons, scorpions, birds, frogs, and mudfish animate finger-rings; stars and half-moons brighten crowns; and bells call to spirits from the necklaces they enliven. These necklaces display assortments of beads, nuggets, cones, shells, and geometric shapes cast in gold and strung in dramatic and deliberately asymmetrical arrangements. Carefully composed symmetry makes this piece unusual. Although it may reflect European or Islamic influences, its freshness is distinctively Akan. Akan goldsmiths, while adapting foreign materials and techniques over the centuries, have preserved the integrity and the beauty of their jewelry.

Where the Crab Finds Gold Dust

Ghana has long been enriched by its gold deposits, controlled by Akan kings as measures of wealth and god-given power. The Akan culture comprises several related groups who speak dialects of the Twi language and share a long history of foreign trade. A three-hundred-mile stretch of West African coast was known as the Gold Coast until Ghana's independence in 1957.

Akan Jewelry and Ornament

Akan goldsmiths fashion their greatest natural resource into crowns, necklaces, bracelets, armbands, and rings, as well as gold-ornamented caps and sandals. A round, gold pectoral called a Soul-Washer's Disk (in the Virginia Museum's galleries) is made to be worn primarily, but not exclusively, by the okra, *an official who purifies the chief's soul. Produced by a culture that values the beauty of nuance and interpretation in its visual and verbal arts, the disk may, however, serve multiple purposes and carry many meanings (see the* Royal Linguist's Staff, *opposite).*

Akan Goldsmithing and European Trade

Portuguese trade with West African cultures began in the late 1400s, and travelers noted the "countless bells and large beads of gold" that adorned the golden chains and regalia of Akan chiefs. European drawings by Jean Barbot, made during the late 1600s and published in 1732, record the spiraling, filigreed, conical, disk-shaped, and beaded forms of Akan gold necklaces seen today.

Gold Necklace
Akan Culture, Asante Kingdom, Ghana, 1800s
Gold; 15¾ inches long
Virginia Museum of Fine Arts Purchase, The Adolph D. and Wilkins C. Williams Fund, 88.73

Royal Linguist's Staff

Perched atop a carved staff, a hen turns her head in deference to a rooster, and golden words take gilded form: "the hen knows when it is dawn, but leaves it for the cock to announce." With this Akan proverb illustrated as its finial, the staff is carefully sculptured in diamond shapes and spirals, linked at the center by the "knot of wisdom," and covered top to bottom with paper-thin sheets of gold.

An *okyeame*—a top-ranking advisor to an Asante king of the Akan culture in Ghana—once held this object. It is an *okyeama poma,* also known as a "linguist's staff," perhaps because advisors served as bilingual messengers between the Akan and Europeans, centuries ago. Shimmering in gold and symbolizing far more than its simple name and form suggest, this staff is a fitting attribute for an ambassador skilled in the subtle statements required of political position. A master orator and diplomat, the *okyeame* counsels the chief, interpreting his communications and embellishing them with meaningful maxims. Interpretations of this proverb are many: as hen is to rooster, so advisor is to chief, wife to husband, youth to elders, individuals to community. Wisdom is accorded each party as social hierarchy is reinforced.

The roots of the word of *okyeame* have been translated as someone who "walks gracefully" *(kyea)* and someone "who completes" *(kyem).* The title aptly describes the counselor who does indeed walk gracefully before the king. The *okyeame* carries a gilded staff, carved with an image to convey a particular role, such as "sweetening the chief's words," it is said, or acting as his advisor. Although its use may be traced to the 1600s, the "linguist's staff" began to grow into an ornate art toward the end of the 1800s. At that time, a variety of proverbs found form in the art of golden finials.

Akan Words and Images

Words and images arc across the Akan culture, illuminating an aesthetic at least three hundred years old. Proverbs—both spoken and sculptured—preserve tradition and provide models for behavior in a society that values eloquent speech, well-crafted oration, sculpture, textiles, and jewelry (see the Akan Gold Necklace, *opposite, and* Memorial Portrait Head, *p. 37).*

Proverbs and Finials

Proverbs transformed into figures on Akan staff finials usually express one of four subtle themes: the ruling family's continuity ("the food is for the man who owns it and not for the man who is hungry," pictured by two men seated at a table); a chief's preeminence ("only an elephant can uproot a palm tree"); a chief's responsibility to his advisors and state ("one head does not go into council," expressed by many figures on a finial); and proper social behavior ("when you climb a good tree you get a push").

Linguists' Staffs Today

It is said that the first okyeame *was an old woman, Nana Amoah, who served as intermediary between the king and his community around 1600. Upon her death, Nana Amoah's son inherited her important position and her walking sticks. Gilded staffs exist today in Ghana. Depending upon his status, a chief may rely on one advisor or many—in appointed or inherited positions— and he may own several staffs for various needs. A variety of other occupations and associations have also adopted staffs (painted not gilded): merchants, musicians, carpenters, fishermen, and priests.*

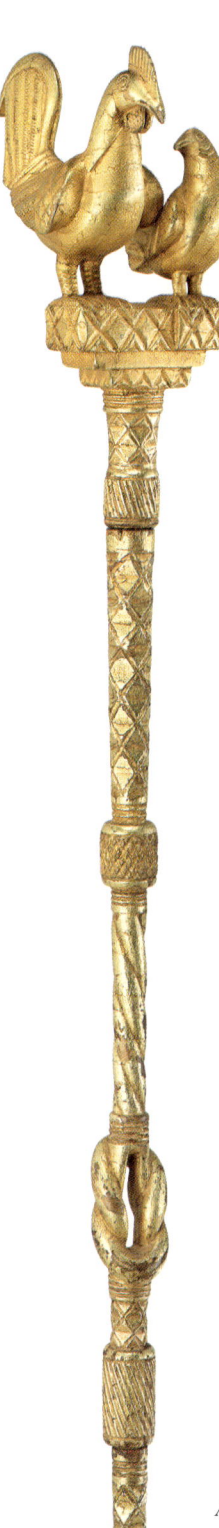

Royal Linguist's Staff
Akan Culture, Asante Kingdom, Ghana, 1900s
Wood, gold leaf; 65½ inches high
Virginia Museum of Fine Arts Purchase, The Kathleen
  Boone Samuels Memorial Fund, 86.200a/c

Eshu Staff

"Good luck and bad luck march together" *(tibi tire)*. Eshu, the messenger of the gods, conveys the wisdom of this Yoruba saying to remind us of life's unpredictability. Carved of wood and dyed deep black, Eshu raises his flute to his lips to announce his role as mediator between the human and the divine. For the Yoruba of present-day Nigeria and the Republic of Benin, Eshu stands at the threshold between the invisible realm of the spirit *(orun)* and the tangible world of the living *(aye)*. A cowrie-shell mantle, signifying wealth and power, covers his shoulders, while blue glass beads drape from his neck and cloth pouches dangle from his arms. A headdress, incised with cowrie patterns and carved with medicine gourds, arcs dramatically behind his head.

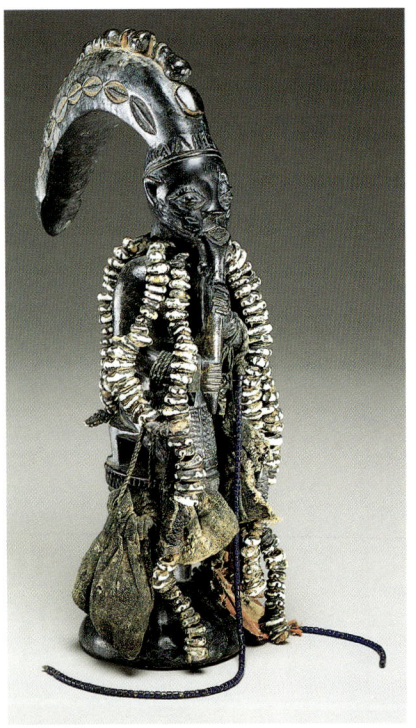

Eshu's contrasting colors and textures—cowrie white set against indigo black, lustrous wood enhanced by shell and fabric—hint of dualities harbored by people and gods alike: light and dark sides, positive and negative forces, strong and weak character, wise and foolish behavior. Eshu helps to balance these creative and destructive forces for a constructive life. He is the guardian of ritual, invoked to encourage gods to grant prayers for reconciliation. Eshu can facilitate the good, but he can also provoke the bad. He can help or he can hinder. Songs tell of his cunning, to turn right into wrong and wrong into right. Wherever quarreling, transition, or change occur, Eshu is there. If unacknowledged, Eshu the transformer becomes Eshu the trickster, and life, according to Yoruba lore, becomes "the bailing of waters with a sieve."

Like the forces that Eshu represents, his sculpture reveals surprises. Walk around Eshu to see a second face projecting from the tip of his curving headdress. His two faces symbolize his passage between the spiritual and the earthbound, and his nature to resolve or to make trouble. Two-faced, the messenger of dualities wears a phallus-like coiffure. It carries energy and vitality; it provokes a worshiper's response; it frees Eshu from the Yoruba code of duty to bear one's own burdens upon one's head. Eshu's headdress actually serves as a hook, to be worn over a male devotee's right shoulder as he dances to elicit the god. Eshu guides and corrects action; he teaches self-knowledge, even if by negative example, to test character. A careful look reveals the soles of Eshu's feet: Eshu himself kneels upon a stand, in reverence for the forces of life *(ase)* that he represents.

The Yoruba Pantheon

Yoruba gods and goddesses divide into soothing, cool, and temperate deities (orisa funfun) and aggressive, hot, and demanding spirits (orisa gbigbona). Eshu, the "hot" god of examination and effective action, is the counterpart of Ifa, the "cool" god of knowledge and fate. Theirs is a delicate balance: Eshu can create chaos to disrupt Ifa's order; Eshu may reveal negative aspects that, if heeded, may lead to Ifa's positive ones. If respected, Eshu intercedes for human beings; if angered, he wreaks havoc.

Eshu in Sculpture

Eshu takes the form of dance hooks or staffs such as this one, full-length statuettes, and altar figures. Images of Eshu, the god of the crossroads, are danced or kept in shrines in the marketplace and over doorways in the home, to protect against trouble.

Yoruba Sculpture

People are the essence of art for the Yoruba, a culture that evolved from ancient urban city-states. Sculpture exists to praise society and gods with beautiful forms that express moral values based on composure, obligation, and understanding.

Eshu Staff

Yoruba Culture, Nigeria/Republic of Benin,
  1800s–1900s
Wood, cowrie shells, glass beads, string, cloth, seeds;
  15³⁄₈ inches high
Virginia Museum of Fine Arts Purchase, The Arthur
  and Margaret Glasgow Fund, 88.43

Buffalo Mask

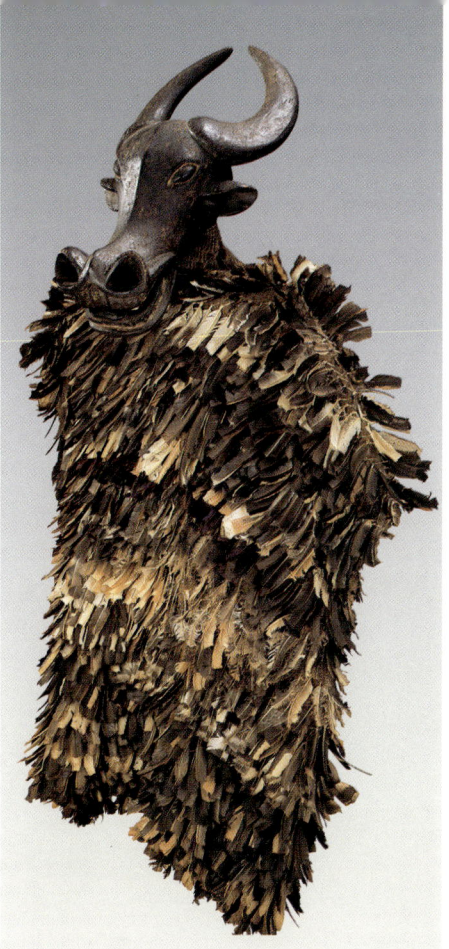

A messenger in the Cameroon Grasslands, the Buffalo Mask announces the presence of the governing council *(Kwifoyn)* for the king *(Fon)*. Its majestic head is made of carved wood, a highly valued art practiced by Cameroon sculptors and kings alike. Smooth surfaces sweep from curving horns to sloping muzzle; upturned nostrils flare, as if to snort, above squared teeth and tongue. With watchful eyes and ready ears, the buffalo stands primed to assess the viewer who stands before it.

Called a "crest" mask, the buffalo's face actually rests on top of the disguised wearer's head (impressions of human features are visible in the fabric just below the wooden carving). Feathers form the broad body; burlap fibers secure the quills, while plumes rise and fall, lifted by the air. This hybrid being—part animal, part bird—expresses the "dance" of the Grasslands, between culture and nature, human beings and animals, dependence and danger. Animals in the African Grasslands—by helping to sustain and to interpret human life—hold a sacredness, and are believed to possess a soul and have magical powers. These powers enter the mask when it is donned, transforming the wearer into an agent of higher purpose. Photographs of buffalo masks in use reveal two of their functions: as "runners," feather-cloaked messengers convey the *Kwifoyn's* decrees in the marketplace; and as "leaders," cloth-covered figures direct other masked performers to and from community celebrations of the passages of life.

Movement is the essence of most African masks, part of a spectacle of percussion and song. Because of its connection to government, however, the Buffalo Mask is more often considered "regulatory," a mask of annunciation rather than action. It evokes the power of the African "cape" buffalo, an enormous and unpredictable creature worthy of respect and wariness. The buffalo embodies paradoxes, both real and imaginary: mysteriously active at both dusk and dawn, docile by nature but ferocious when wounded, visible and yet invisible. Buffalo emerge unexpectedly from mud ponds and brushwood, where they hide despite their size, and they confuse their adversaries by changing directions of attack.

Admired for cunning and strength, the African buffalo corresponds to the ideal ruler: intelligent and peaceful, although aggressive when threatened. Aware of life's ambiguities, a king must be mindful of universal forces, good and evil, positive and negative. He must act decisively, despite divided loyalties, often meeting with his council "invisibly" in secret, to enforce social laws and values, to control disruptions, to dispense justice, and to stem malevolence. The Buffalo Mask serves the *Kwifoyn* and the *Fon* until his reign has ended. Then, the new king sanctions the carving, owning, or wearing of a new royal mask, to continue the cycle of life.

A Vanishing Presence

The central highlands of present-day Cameroon support numerous cultures. Half a million people in the western savanna alone speak 24 different languages; styles of buffalo masks vary. Often made by itinerant artists in similar styles, masks are hard to trace to their sources. It is said that with this century's increase in firearms—decimating herds of buffalo and elephants—traditional praise songs, mask dances, and celebrations are vanishing.

Buffalo and the Cameroon Council of Bamum

In Bamum, where this mask may have originated, the king's councilmen sit on bleached buffalo skulls and wear neck rings of miniature buffalo heads while in session. Other sculptured symbols of the royal hierarchy include the leopard, the elephant, and the serpent.

Buffalo Mask
Cameroon, possibly Bamum, 1800s–1900s
Wood, feathers, burlap, string; 72 inches high
Virginia Museum of Fine Arts Purchase, The Arthur
  and Margaret Glasgow Fund, 87.464a/b

Trio of Masks

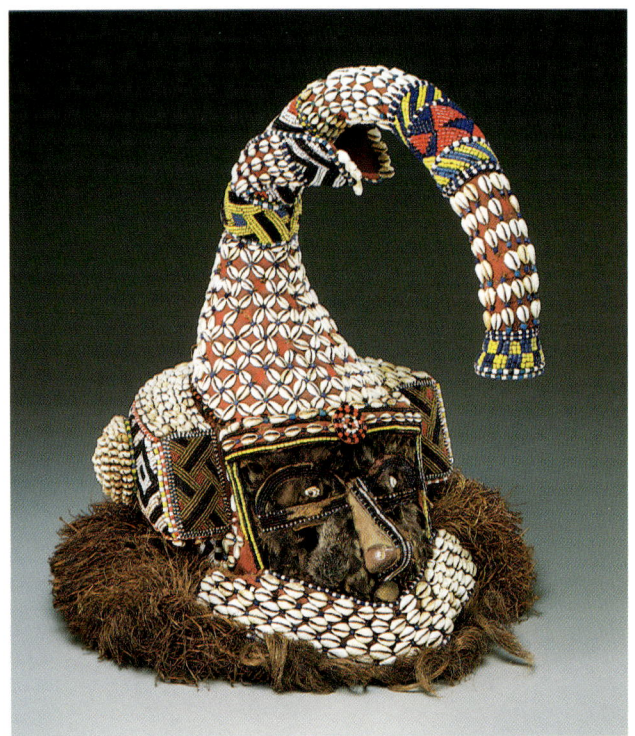

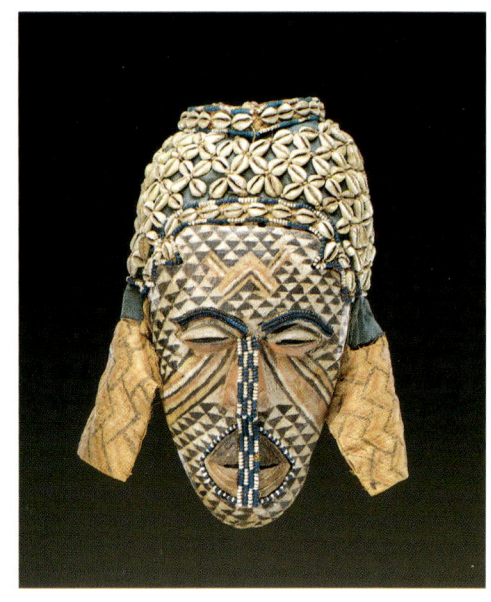

Three masks tell the story of the Kuba culture's origins, one of many African myths that explain the beginnings of royal houses, which are often said to descend from divine beings. Colorful glass beads and white cowrie shells decorate ancient faces that speak of beauty and desire, creation and destruction, silences and curses, blindness and insight.

From the Democratic Republic of Congo (formerly Zaire), the *Mukenga Mask* (left) represents a king of the Kuba culture. The royal visage is a regional variation of Woot, the legendary founder of the Kuba kingdoms. The elaborate elephant-trunk headdress—its fields of petal-patterned shells interspersed with beaded lozenges and chevrons of blue, red, yellow, and black—refers to the

king's commanding power. The animal fur covering his face and the palm fringe *(raffia)* encircling his neck signify his strength (see the Cameroon Grasslands *Buffalo Mask*, p. 41). His cowrie-shell collar designates his wealth and power (see the Yoruba *Eshu Staff*, p. 40).

Woot's love for his sister, Mweel—as some "rememberers" say—disrupted the harmony of his culture. Exiled by his community, Woot cursed his kingdoms with famine and darkness, until Mweel persuaded him to forgive his people and to restore the sunshine. Still, he led a band of followers away, forging new terrain on Earth and founding tribes with twisted tongues, forever speaking different languages. Here, Woot's beloved sister, champion of her culture and mother of

his child, takes her place in the *Ngady amwaash Mask* (center). Mweel wears a crown of cowrie shells, crisscrossed like the king's. A soft blue aura inhabits her mask: blue beads form her eyebrows, arching over painted almond-shaped lids, while clusters of blue beads alternate with white as they descend along her nose to cover, and to outline, her mouth. Decorating her skin, black and white triangles add quiet drama as they give way to black, white, yellow, and red stripes under her eyes, said to be the traces of tears.

The third mask, *Bwoom* (right), introduces the king's brother and, with him, other tales. A rival for Mweel's attention and a representative of commoners, Bwoom is fashioned with forceful features

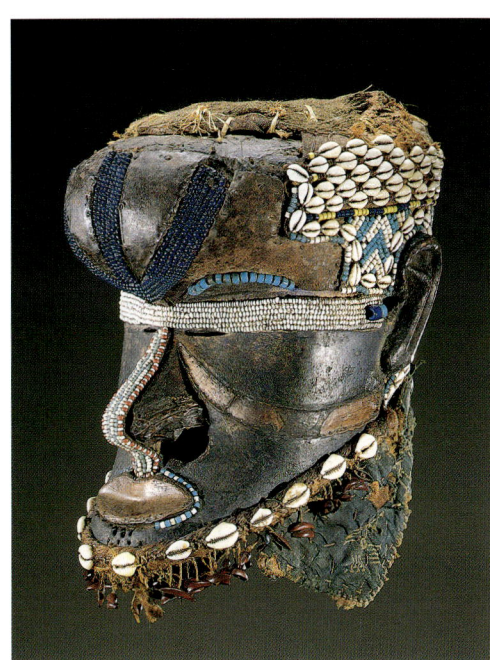

The Kuba Culture

The Kuba culture boasts of ancient kingdoms rich in ivory trade, artistic traditions, myths, legendary histories, and royal lineage. Among the nineteen or so groups that form the Kuba confederation are the Bushoong, Ngeende, Ngongo, and Pyaang. Cultural specialties include metalwork and wood carving, traditionally the province of men; and miniature funerary sculpture, the province of women. Geometric designs embellish objects of the most utilitarian nature, and patterns reappear in beaded, woven, and carved forms (see the Woman's Wrap Skirt *in the Virginia Museum's galleries).*

Identifying the Masks

Kuba masks serve different roles and legends, depending on the occasion; their use may date to 1600, when the lineage of Kuba kings is said to have begun. Ten types of Kuba masks have been identified; the three discussed here relate to cultural origins. The Mukenga Mask *may stand for Woot, or his son, or a wise and experienced elder. Masks of this type are often buried with deceased leaders. The first dynasty's Queen Ngokady is said to have introduced the* Ngady amwaash Mask, *or Mweel, to celebrate the role of women in Kuba culture. Mweel's mask is, however, danced by men. Bwoom is sometimes danced as a nature spirit—his name interpreted as "divination"—or as a village leader in boys' initiations. By 1800, Bwoom had joined the court dance, to compete unsuccessfully for the king's wife. At court, Bwoom's is the more active dance, and masks of this type are preserved as symbols of family continuity.*

Mask Dancers

Only those of royal lineage may wear the Mukenga Mask; *only special society members participate in rites-of-passage ceremonies in which the masks are worn, for initiations or for funerals.*

Trio of Masks

Kuba Culture, Democratic Republic of Congo (formerly Zaire), 1800s–1900s

Mukenga Mask

Wood, animal fur, raffia cloth, cowrie shells, glass beads, string; 19 1/2 inches high
Virginia Museum of Fine Arts Purchase, The Arthur and Margaret Glasgow Fund, 87.82

Ngady amwaash Mask

Wood, paint, glass beads, cowrie shells, string, raffia cloth; 12 1/2 inches high
Virginia Museum of Fine Arts Purchase, The Arthur and Margaret Glasgow Fund, 87.83

Bwoom Mask

Wood, copper, cloth, glass beads, cowrie shells, seeds, string, traces of paint; 19 1/4 inches high
Virginia Museum of Fine Arts Purchase, The Adolph D. and Wilkins C. Williams Fund, 77.13

carved of wood—forehead, nose, chin, and ears. Inlays of metal define his lips, nostrils, and cheekbones. Cowries encircle his head and jaw; blue and white beads form chevrons, like hair, around his head. Beads trace the contour of his nose; a white-beaded band binds his eyes, while a deep blue-beaded trident marks his brow.

These three masks summon ancestral protagonists in the ongoing drama of life. Geometrically patterned tunics and raffia gloves and shoes would have disguised the dancer's entire body. The dancer's eyeholes are often pierced beneath the mask's eyes or within the nostrils. This trio is often, but not always, danced together; careful choreography helps onlookers to recognize each one's identity and role.

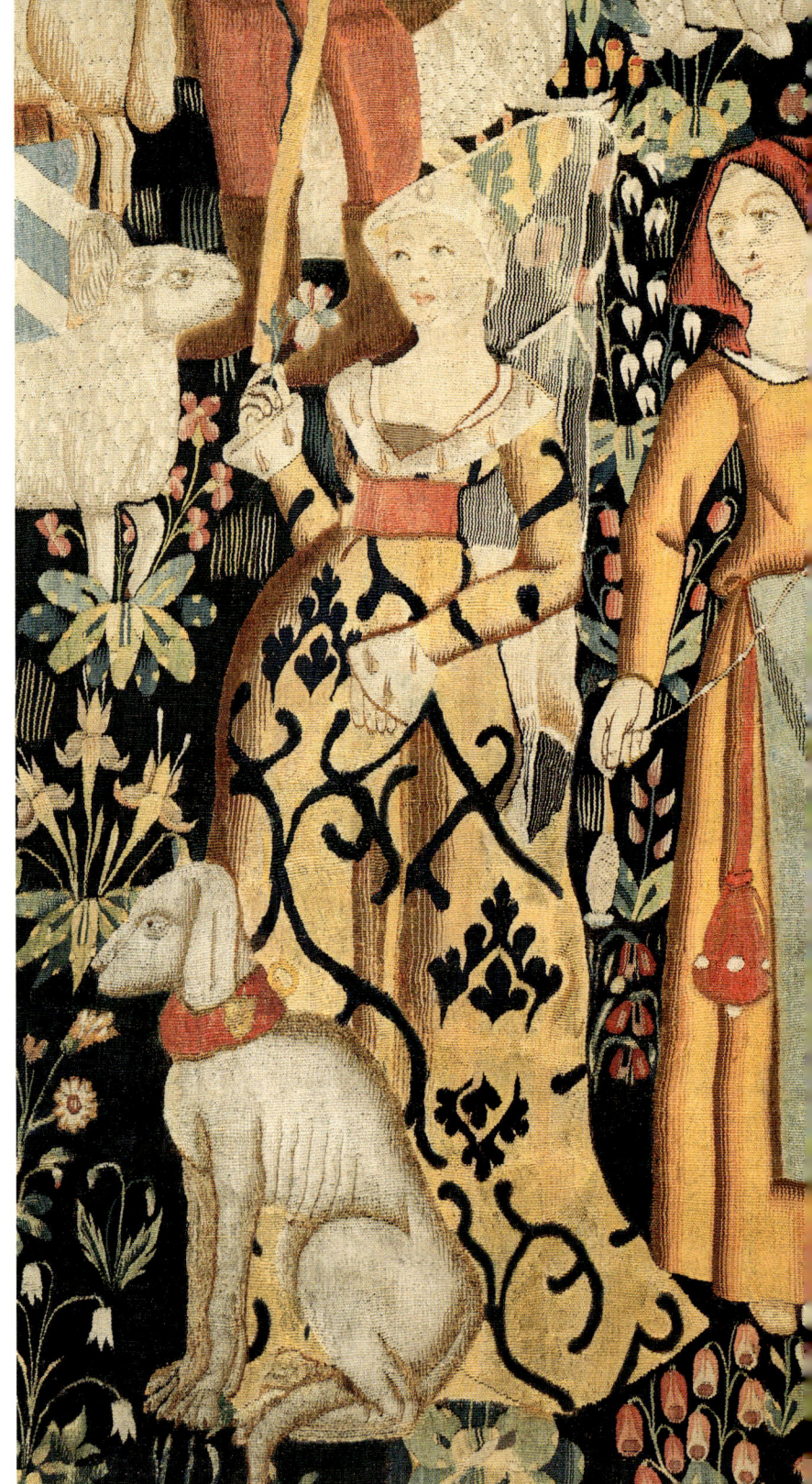

CHAPTER 5

Byzantine and Western Medieval Sculpture and Decorative Arts

Late Roman and Byzantine

English

French

German

Mount with Odysseus

One thousand years after Homer is said to have recited the *Odyssey,* an artisan from the Late Roman Empire (A.D. 200–400) cast Odysseus's encounter with the Sirens in bronze. These half-woman, half-bird demons of the sea wrecked sailors' ships, luring them to watery graves with their song. Warned of the peril by the enchantress Circe, Odysseus heeds her advice. He plugs his "oarsmen's ears / with beeswax kneaded soft" and, so that he could hear the "harpies' thrilling voices," orders his men to tie him to the mast. Here, a single helmsman holds the main sheet and rudder, ready to sail past the temptresses' song.

Both men are bearded and have a mantle draped over one shoulder; the hero wears a cap and boots. A broken finial tops the mast, and a sail unfurls. A shield decorates the ship's prow, and lattice-work railing surrounds the deck, as waves lap against the hull. Below, a hollow base suggests that the bronze, now aged with a green patina, was originally mounted to another piece. It may have ornamented a chariot, for use in victory celebrations and funerary rites, or a ceremonial boat, used in processions.

Only eight-and-a-half inches tall, this *Mount with Odysseus,* and many other bronzes of its type, connected the world of classical antiquity with the medieval worlds of western Europe and eastern Byzantium (see the *Athena-Minerva Weight* in the Virginia Museum's galleries). Late Roman and Byzantine artists depicted Christian saints in holy icons and mosaics, as well as mythological Greek and Roman figures in secular mosaics, textiles, ivory carvings, and bronze sculpture created for the home.

Though the Sirens' episode is a rare subject for a bronze mount, the story does appear on Late Roman sarcophagus lids and mosaics in Late Roman baths; early Christian writers at the time likened Odysseus's voyage homeward, through a world filled with Siren-like temptations, to a Christian's path to heaven. While this mount may only hint at the complex interweaving of the Classical and Christian worlds, it clearly represents subjects, themes, and materials that lasted for some 1200 years in Late Roman and Byzantine art.

Late Roman and Byzantine Empires

The Roman Empire extended east from Italy across Greece and Asia Minor to Syria and Mesopotamia, and west across Northern Africa, Spain, and France to Germany and Britain. Religious practices evolving from worship in classical temples to prayer in Christian churches led the Roman emperor Constantine to officially recognize Christianity in A.D. 313. The great age of Byzantium dawned after he moved the capital of the Empire from Rome to Constantinople (now Istanbul) in 325 and political power shifted to the East. At various times during its long history (until circa A.D. 1450), the Byzantine Empire reached as far as the Roman Empire. Byzantine artifacts have been found from Britain to Syria.

Late Roman and Byzantine Art in the Galleries

The Virginia Museum's holdings date from A.D. 250 to 1450. The collection includes fine examples of gold-and-gemstone jewelry (see the Openwork Armbands, *p. 46), as well as pottery, bone and ivory carvings, textiles, silver patens, and bronze, wood, and stone sculpture.*

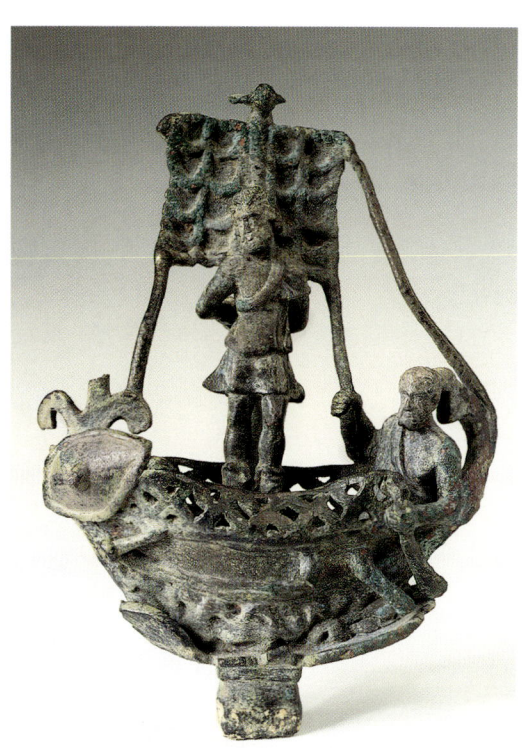

Mount with Odysseus
Late Roman, A.D. 200–400
Bronze; 8½ by 6¾ by 3½ inches
Virginia Museum of Fine Arts Purchase, The Adolph D.
  and Wilkins C. Williams Fund, 67.20

Openwork Armbands

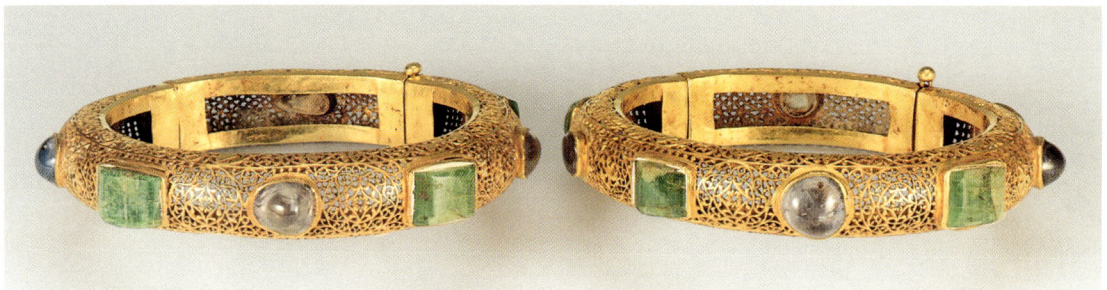

Byzantium, a world of "hammered gold and gold enameling" described by the Irish poet W. B. Yeats, is best remembered for its architecture, icons, mosaics, and jewelry. Here, two openwork armbands, believed to have come from Syria, are among the finest surviving examples of the *opus interrasile* technique, a filigree style fashionable during the Late Roman and Early Byzantine periods. Sheets of gold have been carefully drilled and chiseled to create a lacy design of ivy scrolls and geometric patterns, supported inside by solid strips of gold. Four pale to deep blue sapphires and four emeralds rest in bezels around the circumference of each piece. Made in two sections held together by a hinge and pin, each armlet would have been worn just above the elbow.

Men, women, and children of the Late Roman and Early Byzantine Empires shared a love of jewelry: armlets and bracelets, necklaces, headbands, and belts. Mosaic portraits depict the Byzantine Empress Theodora, Emperor Justinian, and members of their court, dressed in gowns of gold embroidery and gemstone borders, jeweled crowns, necklaces, and pendant earrings. Here, the fine quality of the gems and the gold, finely wrought and weighty, suggests that these armlets belonged to a member of the ruling class and that their cost was very dear.

The Price of Jewels

Ancient and medieval records tell us of the relative value of Late Roman and Byzantine jewelry. Soldiers received about four soldi *a year, and a year's worth of bread cost one* soldus *(a basic monetary unit). Around A.D. 500, a pair of earrings cost eight* soldi, *a necklace twenty.*

The Gift of Jewelry

Ancient jewelry has been found throughout the Roman and Byzantine Empires. The Imperial court bestowed gifts of jewelry upon generals and diplomats (see the Presentation Ring *in the Virginia Museum's galleries); jewelry was offered in friendship with blessings and good wishes (see the* Signet Rings *and* Amulets *in the galleries) and was commissioned in celebration of weddings (see the* Marriage Ring *in the galleries). It was not uncommon for the elite to commission luxury objects by local artists. The middle class did so as well, though theirs were sometimes of less expensive gilded bronze and glass, instead of gold and gems.*

Conservators' Analysis of the Armbands

Analyzing the composition of gold and the technique of perforation, conservators have concluded that these Byzantine armbands were cut from the same sheet of metal, pierced entirely from the front, and supported by bands of gold soldered to the inside.

Pair of Openwork Armbands

Late Roman, A.D. late 200s–early 300s
Gold, emeralds, sapphires; 4½ (diameter) inches
Virginia Museum of Fine Arts Purchase, The Adolph D. and Wilkins C. Williams Fund, 67.52.31.1/2

Window with
Two Roundels and Ornament

From Canterbury, England, medieval stained glass admits light to reveal its jewel-like colors, as it once did in the Gothic cathedral of Christ Church, the site of Thomas à Becket's shrine. Ornamental motifs surround two roundels of Christian scenes, made around A.D. 1200 and set within fields of royal blue. The upper medallion features the *Last Judgment:* Christ is seated above a yellow-and-white arch that separates the blessed from those awaiting judgment. The Virgin Mary and John the Evangelist, both wearing green mantles draped over blue robes, sit to his right and left. Saints and Apostles, in white robes with purple mantles, surround them. Each of the blessed radiates a red nimbus or halo; below them, figures dressed in yellow, white, purple, and green robes seek salvation. Most of the glass is original, although the figure of Christ has been replaced with new glass and cames, grooved lead rods.

The glass and leading of the lower medallion are almost entirely original, though the heads of the figures have since been restored. Medieval glass resonates in deep hues of yellow, green, red, and purple. A young, beardless man with a red halo instructs from a book, while listeners gesture in response. The subject is probably *St. Stephen Disputing with the Sanhedrin* (New Testament, Acts 6–8). The disciple Stephen angered the council in Jerusalem with his sermon about Jesus and the House of David. He was later stoned to death and became the first Christian martyr (see the German sculpture of St. Stephen in the Virginia Museum's galleries).

Roundels with figures represent one of five types of stained glass to be found in the early Gothic cathedrals of England, including windows with the Tree of Jesse (the ancestors of Christ); windows with large holy figures; "rose" windows of kaleidoscopic scenes; and windows with purely decorative colors and patterns. Some of the best examples are preserved in Canterbury Cathedral; these roundels have been called some of the finest glass now outside of the Cathedral itself.

Medieval Stained Glass
Monasteries and later professional guilds perfected the art of medieval stained glass, which depicted the history and the doctrines of Christianity. Scenes from the "New" Testament paired with scenes from the "Old" Testament strengthened the Christian message, filling chapels with what Abbot Suger, father of the Gothic cathedral, called "the wonderful and . . . most luminous windows" (see the Virgin and Child, *p. 48). Of a fragile nature, much of the medieval stained glass in European churches and synagogues has perished—destroyed during periods of political turmoil.*

Making Stained-Glass
Stained-glass techniques have hardly changed since the Middle Ages. The stages recorded by the monk Theophilus in his craftsman's manual around 1140 are practiced today: an artisan cuts the colored glass from a full-sized pattern, then stains or paints details on its surface, fires the glass, joins the pieces with lead strips, and weatherproofs the glass and leading before fixing it within its window-frame (see Tiffany, *p. 100,* Lalique, *p. 101,* Wright, *pp. 102–103).*

The History of the Museum's Panel
These roundels were removed from Canterbury Cathedral before 1852, when George Austin restored the stained glass in various chapels. Around 1900 a member of the Caldwell family—by trade Canterbury Cathedral glaziers from the 1890s through

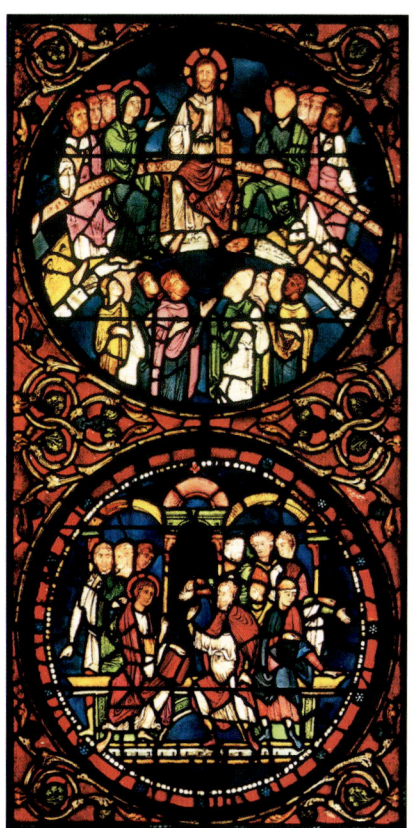

the mid 1900s—restored the medallions, originally made for two different settings, into one piece with a background support. Collector John Hunt, of Ireland, acquired the original glass, which was exhibited at the Louvre in 1968 (L'Europe Gothique) before the Virginia Museum purchased it in 1969. Replicas of these roundels in the Museum are now located in the Cathedral's Chapel of St. Gregory.

Window with
Two Roundels and Ornament

English (Christ Church Cathedral, Canterbury); upper, before 1207; lower, circa 1180
Stained glass with leading; roundels: 31½ (diameter) inches
Virginia Museum of Fine Arts Purchase, The Adolph D and Wilkins C. Williams Fund, 69.10

Virgin and Child

Mary, venerated as the Virgin Mother of God, affectionately cradles the Christ Child in the crook of her arm. The two express loving devotion, as the child reaches out to his mother, and she attentively turns toward him. The warm color and smooth surface of the marble enhance their tender exchange. This *Virgin and Child*—a favored subject in French and Italian Gothic sculpture, often carved in wood, alabaster, ivory, or marble—may have stood on or near an altar as an object of personal prayer. Many statues of the mid 1300s from the Ile de France, the region surrounding Paris, resemble this one. The Christ Child sometimes holds a bird, as he does here, and Mary a flower-stalk or scepter entwined with flowers—a symbol of the Tree of Jesse, the ancestors of Christ (see the English *Window with Two Roundels,* p. 47). The object in this Virgin's lowered hand could have held a flower.

While a veil or crown usually covers the Virgin's head in statues of this type, here Mary's curls are unadorned. Draped gently over her shoulders, her mantle wraps around her body and falls into graceful folds. Her tunic, girded with a sash (see Andrea di Bartolo, p. 53), breaks slightly at her knee and foot as it falls in soft folds to the floor.

The Christ Child's small, cupped hand conceals a hollow space in the center of the Virgin's chest. The opening may have held a jeweled ornament. Rosette-shaped brooches clasp Mary's mantle and attract the Child's attention in other medieval statues from Parisian workshops. One such statue was made for the church of St. Denis, where the Gothic style is said to have originated.

The bird in the infant's left hand may be the dove of the Holy Spirit or perhaps the European goldfinch, which is said to have plucked a thorn from the crown that Christ later wore as he carried the cross.

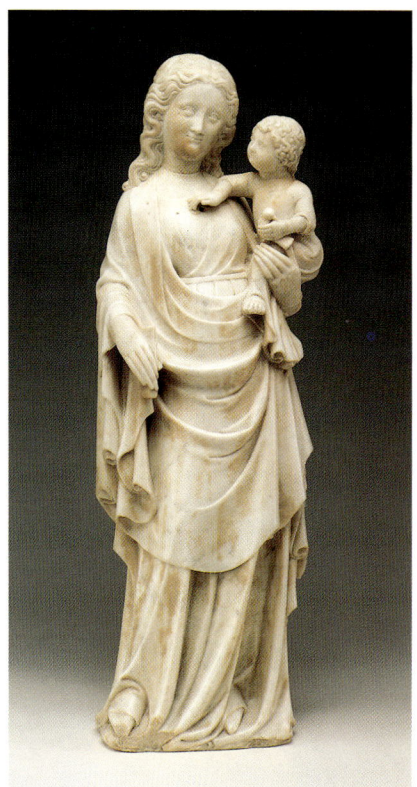

According to the legend, a drop of the Savior's blood spilled forth and forever marked the bird's head with red plumage. The goldfinch has been depicted in the hands of the Christ Child in French and Italian art from the 1300s, as a symbol of the Incarnation and the Passion.

This sculpture's elegant form characterizes the Court Style of medieval Europe, originating with the patronage of princes. Adapted by sculptors and manuscript painters in the courts of France, Italy, and Germany, the style came to be known as International Gothic.

Gothic Cathedrals

The historical province of the Ile-de-France is considered the birthplace of the Gothic style. There, around 1140, one of the largest economic enterprises of medieval Europe began with Abbot Suger's Church of St. Denis (see the sculpture of St. Denis in the Virginia Museum's galleries). Architects, masons, sculptors, metalworkers, and stained-glass makers created cathedrals that express devout spirituality: pinnacles and spires of soaring heights, holy figures sculptured in marble to enliven column capitals and portals, immense ribbed vaults spanning vast interiors filled with radiant light and adorned with carvings (see the English Window with Two Roundels, *p. 47; and the German* Figures from an Altarpiece, *p. 50). The Gothic cathedral, built with regional variations, appeared first in northern France, then in England, Germany, Spain, and Italy between the 1200s and the 1500s. By the mid 1300s, prominent sculptural styles and local variations had fully evolved, including the suave Court Style, represented by this* Virgin and Child, *that spread from the Ile-de-France to Burgundy to Tuscany.*

Virgin and Child

French (probably Ile-de-France), circa 1350
Marble with traces of gesso; 28 by 8½ by 4¾ inches
Virginia Museum of Fine Arts Purchase, The Adolph D. and Wilkins C. Williams Fund, 68.22.2

The Marriage of Rigault d'Oureille and Catherine de Rance

This tapestry has been called "enchanting in its simplicity," though its simplicity belies a complex interweaving of cultures, artists, subjects, and patrons. Judging from the coats of arms that appear in the middle ground and a castle in the background, the subject is believed to be the marriage of Rigault d'Oureille, a diplomat in the courts of two French kings, to Catherine de Rance in 1476. The castle (upper left) has even been identified as Rigault's Chateau Villenueve, near Issoire, which still exists today. In due time, scholars may clarify our knowledge of the tapestry's origins. Meanwhile, this woven work reveals a colorful world of enchanting medieval motifs, cast in green, blue, reddish-orange, and gold, to delight the eye and the imagination.

The art and industry of large-scale tapestries began in France and Flanders in the 1300s. Traces of an international Court Style (see the *Virgin and Child,* opposite) are preserved here in the theme. A "marriage" takes place in a pastoral setting, a garden of love that served for centuries as the perfect place for courtly romance in European prints, manuscript illuminations, and paintings (see Watteau, p. 62). The brocades and headresses worn by the aristocratic couple—a woman in an elegant hennin and a man in a chapeau—set them apart from less finely clothed musicians playing bagpipes, flutes, and horns (see Molenaer, p. 59), shepherds tending flocks of sheep, and women spinning and harvesting.

The artisan has woven a floral carpet, where grazing lambs emerge behind their caretakers, and a hare peeks out from foliage. One boy, boosted by another, bends a branch of an orchard tree so that a woman may pluck a pear (see Cassatt, p. 90). A terraced landscape of tree stumps—whose trunks and limbs have been lopped off to strengthen roots and prevent erosion—rises to distant turrets, battlements, and bannered rooftops. When seen from afar, the tapestry offers a colorful Franco-Flemish panorama of cityscape and countryside, but the scene is just as intriguing when threads of warp and weft are examined up close.

Franco-Flemish Tapestries

This tapestry dates from the late 1400s when the great tapestry centers were shifting east from Paris and Arras to Tournai, Bruges, and Brussels. French and Flemish tapestries, largely made of wool with silk highlights, were exported to England, Italy, and countries in between. Themes preferred by patrons ranged from pastorals and hunting scenes to histories (the Trojan War or the Life of Alexander the Great), religious scenes, and depictions of battles. These pictorial wall hangings decorated great halls and rooms in large stone homes, colorfully insulating interiors from the cold. From 1500 through the early 1600s, the torch of tapestry-weaving passed from France to Flanders. But with the establishment of the Gobelins manufactory under Louis XIV, the center of the tapestry industry returned to France in the late 1600s. (see the Flemish and Gobelins Factory tapestries in the Virginia Museum galleries.)

The Marriage of Rigault d'Oureille and Catherine de Rance
French, 1476
Wool; 96 by 136 inches
Virginia Museum of Fine Arts Purchase, The Adolph D. and Wilkins C. Williams Fund, 54.11.1

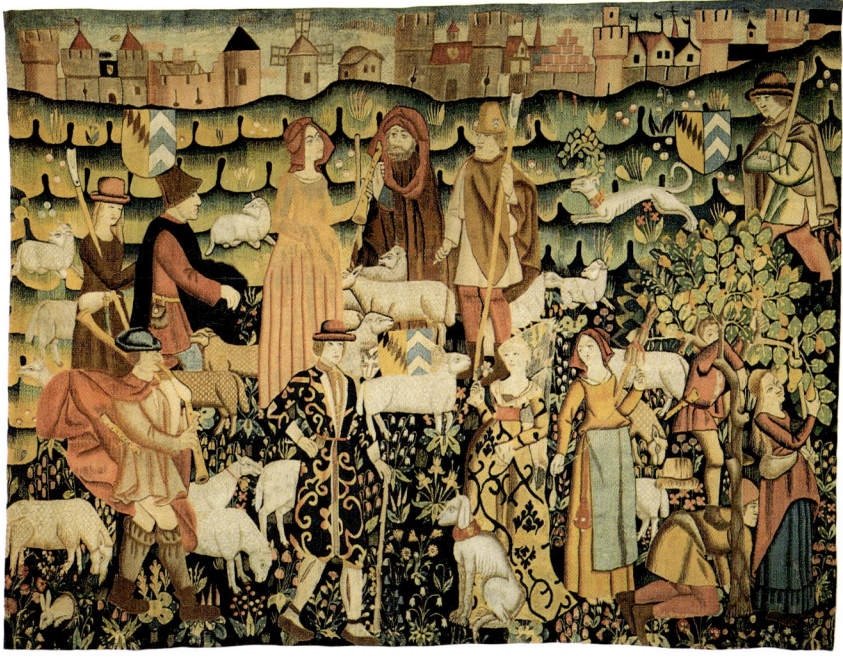

Figures from an Altarpiece:
St. John the Baptist, the Virgin and Child, and St. Gregory

Since the early 1300s, sculptors in medieval Germany carved religious figures of wood, as if freeing their forms from tree trunks. After painting and gilding the sculpture, they placed it in boxlike wooden altars, flanked by carved or painted side panels. It has been said that these "winged" altarpieces are among "the greatest glories of the German churches."

Wooden altarpiece figures—whose naturalistic faces and gestures caught light and shadow—were meant to stir emotional feelings of piety and mysticism. In their original setting, *St. John the Baptist,* the *Virgin and Child,* and *St. Gregory* would have stood side by side, probably at the same height, within their painted altar surrounded by stained glass windows and wooden choir stalls. Their pale faces, flushed cheeks, and golden drapery would have seemed at once eerily lifelike and deeply mysterious.

The thin figure of *St. John the Baptist,* the last of the Old Testament prophets and first of the New Testament saints, is bearded, barefoot, and draped with a mantle. His robe is carved to look like camel's hair, befitting his ascetic life in the desert (*Matthew* 3:4); he carries a lamb, for John called Jesus "the Lamb of God" (*John* 1:29). The Virgin Mary, Queen of Heaven, holds the Christ Child and wears a crown. Her full drapery falls to a crescent moon carved at her feet.

The moon, an ancient symbol of chastity, may refer to Mary's Immaculate Conception, born of St. Anne without original sin to become the mother of God, according to Christian doctrine. Next to Mary, the beardless St. Gregory wears a papal tiara; he blesses with one hand and carries a book by its soft "leather" binding in the other. Known as "Gregory the Great"—one of the four Latin (Western) Church Fathers—he became Pope in 590.

This holy trio is made of lindenwood, from the linden or limewood tree, native to southern Germany. Scholars have determined that three generations of limewood sculptors (1475–1525) perfected the art of carving the soft wood into altarpiece figures. Albrecht Dürer's 1494 watercolor depicts three lovely limewood trees; less than ten years later, this sculptor transformed limewood into three graceful figures. Their swaying curves convey human spirituality through expression and gesture, while remaining true to the essential nature of the wood.

Folklore and Limewood
Medieval folklore tells of the holy, healing properties of limewood trees (grunen linden): Linde *referred to holy groves, the site of medieval pilgrimages; people hung votive offerings on the branches of the tree to ward off illness, applied its leaves, bark, and blossoms to their bodies, and ingested the seeds.*

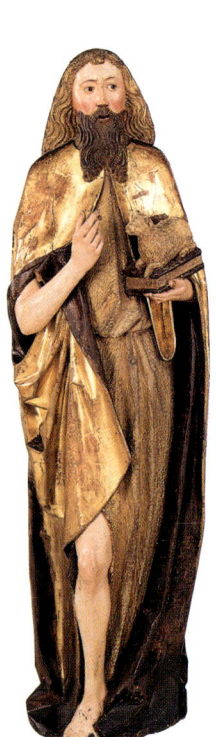
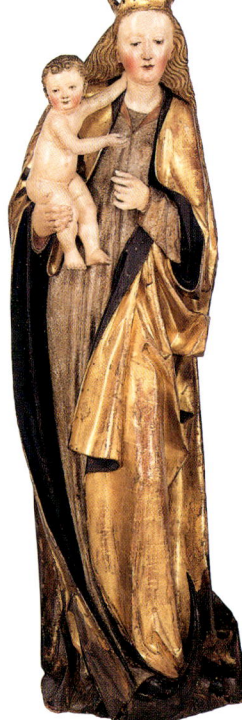
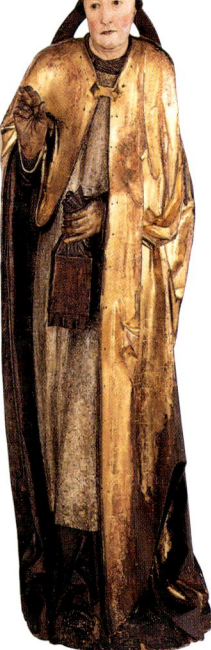

Figures from an Altarpiece:
St. John the Baptist, the Virgin and Child,
and St. Gregory
German, circa 1502
Lindenwood with polychromy and gilding; each
  approximately 89½ by 88½ by 15¾ inches
Virginia Museum of Fine Arts Purchase, The Adolph D.
  and Wilkins C. Williams Fund, 68.9.2a/c

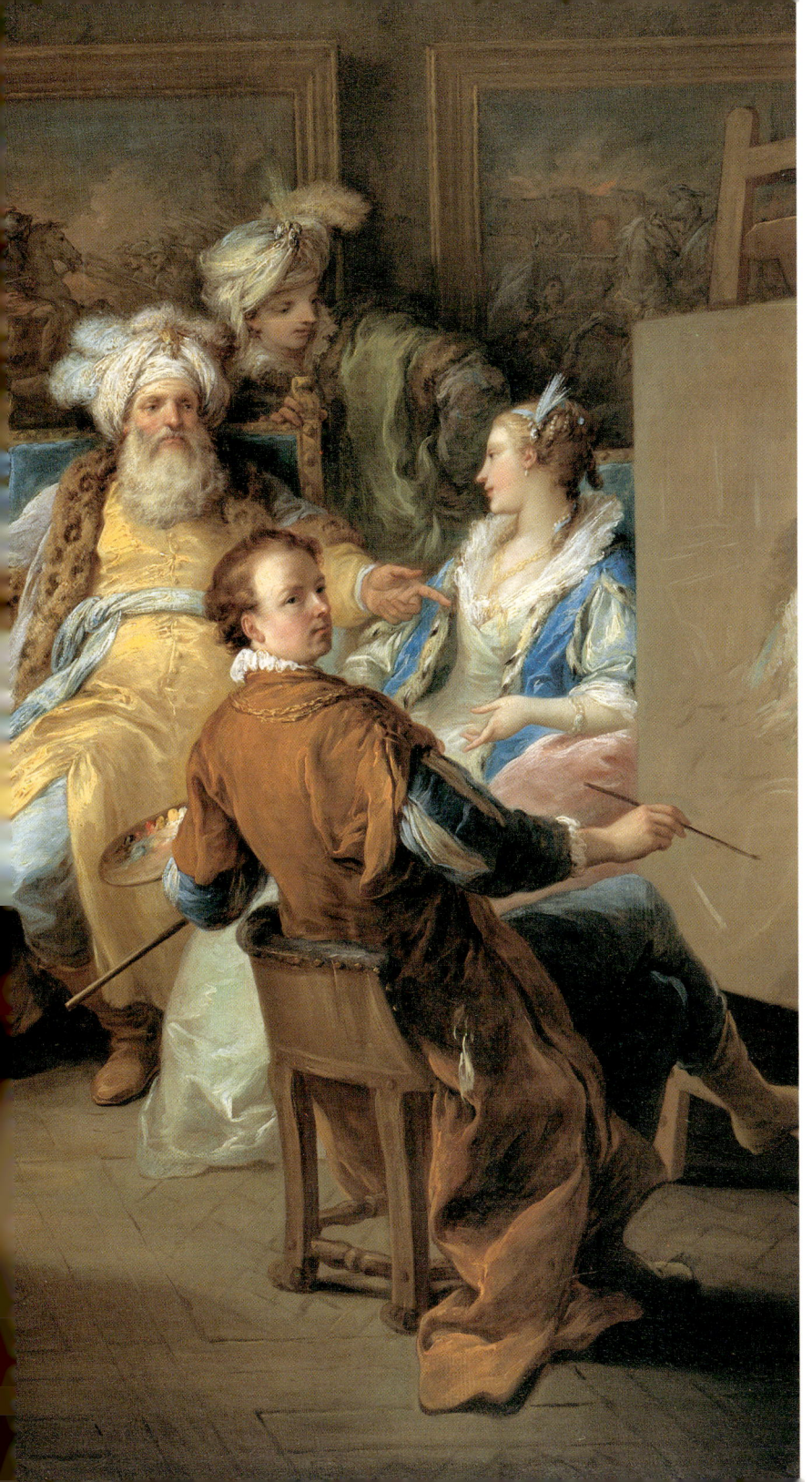

Altichiero Altichieri
Crucifixion with Saints and Donors

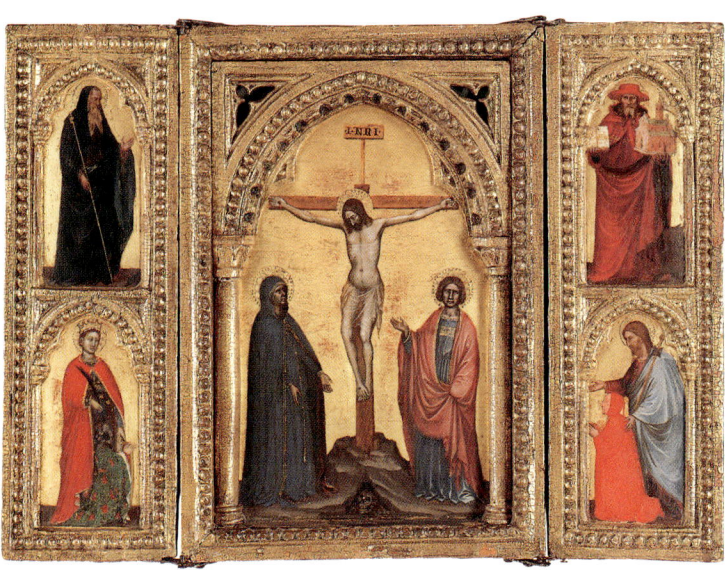

This *Crucifixion,* a central image of Christian faith, inspires contemplation. During the late 1300s, at the dawn of the Italian Renaissance, such small devotional pictures were common in Verona, Padua, and Venice. Altichiero Altichieri, the most prominent fresco painter of the Veneto region made this image, now a rare example of his work on panel. Its richness—a deep palette of dense color transformed into expressive faces and folds of cloth—speaks of his style.

Draped in her blue mantle, a symbol of Heaven, the Virgin Mary mourns the crucified Christ while St. John the Evangelist directs the viewer to meditate upon the image. Their distressed faces poignantly register their grief, yet their presence beneath the cross offers hope for salvation. Christ died to redeem the sins of Adam, and it is said that the Crucifixion took place on the site where Adam lay buried. Adam's skull lies here at the foot of the cross.

The saints enframed by arches on the side panels lived during the early, formative centuries of the Christian era. St. Anthony Abbot, a desert hermit and the founder of monasticism, appears in his monk's black cowl (upper left). The bell around his wrist wards off evil temptations; the tiny pig at his feet refers to the swine raised by his monastery during the the Middle Ages. Beneath St. Anthony stands St. Catherine, Queen of Alexandria. She wears a golden crown and royal brocades; she holds a martyr's palm and wheel, symbols of her persecution. Known for her legendary erudition, she once converted fifty philosophers sent by the Roman Emperor Maxentius to debate Christian precepts. Opposite St. Anthony, stands St. Jerome in his red Cardinal's hat and robe (upper right). Like Anthony he founded a monastery; like Catherine he was a scholar. The lion at his feet, now abraded, refers to his years as a desert hermit. His open book

reminds us that he translated the Bible from Greek into Latin; his miniature church symbolizes his position as one of the four Fathers of the Latin Church, guardians of the Christian faith. Beneath him is a panel showing St. James the Greater. Like John the Evangelist, James wears robes of blue and rose, for he is John's brother, and also like him, an Apostle. Known as the patron saint of pilgrims, James rests his pilgrim's staff against his shoulder, while he directs the prayer of a kneeling man in a hooded red robe.

As James guides his ward's attention toward the central Crucifixion scene, he also guides the viewer's. A closer look reveals a woman praying at Catherine's feet. She wears a green gown with red flames; her head has been worn away through time. This couple, from a prominent family of Verona or Padua, commissioned this triptych depicting their patron saints, to express their religious devotion (see Moroni, p. 54).

The Kneeling Donors

At one time, overpainting completely covered the female donor within Catherine's robes. The male donor had been reworked. The clumsiness of these two areas aroused scholars' suspicions; cleaned in 1981, the painting now reveals the first set of donors as Altichiero had originally painted them.

Crucifixion with Saints and Donors, 1380–85
Altichiero Altichieri (Italian, circa 1330–1385)
Tempera on wood; central panel: 12¾ by 8¾ inches; each wing: 12¼ by 3¾ inches
Virginia Museum of Fine Arts Purchase, The Arthur and Margaret Glasgow Fund, 59.5

Andrea di Bartolo
Assumption of the Virgin

A Christian miracle—the *Assumption of the Virgin*—unfolds in flowerlike color and shimmering gold in this Italian painting from the late 1300s. Choirs of angels accompany the Virgin Mary, mother of Jesus, as she is drawn body and soul into Heaven after her death. At the top, coral-colored cherubs spread their wings to welcome her; below, music-making angels—dressed in deep greens, light lavenders, pale blues, and soft roses—play flutes and harps to surround her with sweet song. Beneath them, St. Thomas the Apostle (traditionally known as "Doubting Thomas," because of his skepticism) reaches up to catch the red sash (traditionally called a "girdle") that has fallen from Mary's robe. She has dropped the sash for Thomas as proof of the miracle he witnesses.

The "Queen of Heaven," Mary is enthroned at the center of the painting. She is draped in a light-blue mantle richly ornamented in gold detail, and she is larger than her heavenly hosts. Her presence, radiance, and magnitude indicate her importance in the Christian faith as the Mother of God. She was also believed to be the protector of the city of Siena, where Andrea di Bartolo was born.

This "ancient city of the Virgin," as Siena was known at that time, had experienced a golden age of painting during the 1300s. Sienese religious painting was appreciated then, as it is now, for its elegant line, ornate gold patterns, and delicate color. Andrea, son of artist Bartolo di Fredi, signed his picture at the bottom with words that acknowledge this heritage: *Andrea di Bartolo, of Master Fredi, Sienese painter.* The words that follow Andrea's also recognize a family and a civic bond. They tell us that a woman from Urbino paid Andrea for the picture and dedicated it to her deceased husband and son, who are depicted on either side of the inscription.

Andrea's picture still serves in many ways to connect the living and the dead. Painted to express the faith of the family and to inspire devotion, Andrea's vision of Mary's assumption into Heaven offers the promise of eternal life—for the Apostle Thomas; for the widow, her husband, and her son; for Andrea and his father; for the viewer who believes.

Art in Early Italian Churches

The family and the community played a vital role in the creation of Italian Medieval and Renaissance art. Prominent families often donated paintings and sculpture, in memory of deceased relatives, as decoration for chapels in Italian churches. Andrea's painting once held an honorary place above an altar in such a chapel.

The Art of the Altarpiece

Altarpieces usually consisted of a central holy figure surrounded by saints, church fathers, prophets, and apostles, whose images and stories were painted on smaller surrounding panels attached to the sides, top, and bottom. Ornate gold frames encased the panels, much like the one that now frames Andrea's picture (although this one is a late nineteenth-century frame, made to suggest what Andrea's lost original may have looked like).

Andrea's Signature

This painting is only one of four pictures that Andrea signed, at a time when artists' signatures rarely appeared on their works.

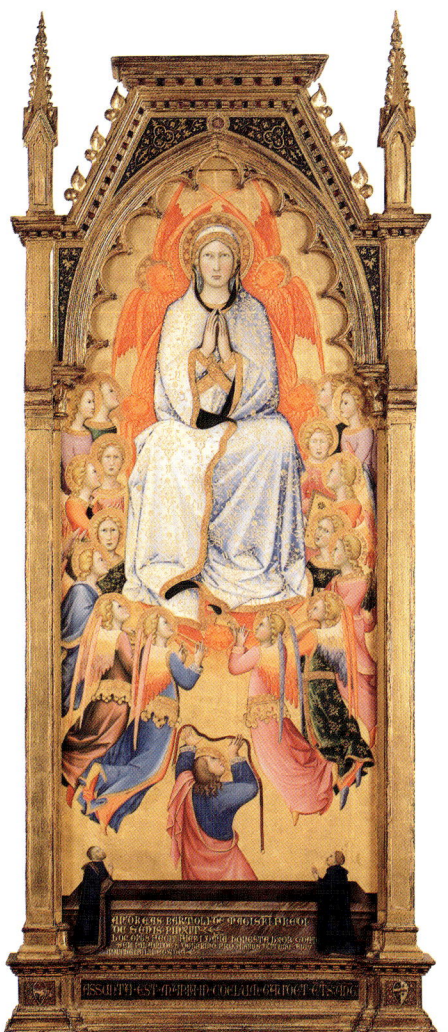

Andrea's Inscription
"This work was commissioned by [Dominica,] true wife of the late Ser Palamides of Urbino, for the souls of her husband and of their son Matthew."

Assumption of the Virgin, circa 1390s
Andrea di Bartolo (Italian, active 1389–1429)
Tempera on wood; 80 by 33½ inches
Virginia Museum of Fine Arts Purchase, The Adolph D. and Wilkins C. Williams Fund, 54.11.3

Giovanni Battista Moroni
Two Donors before the Madonna and Child and St. Michael

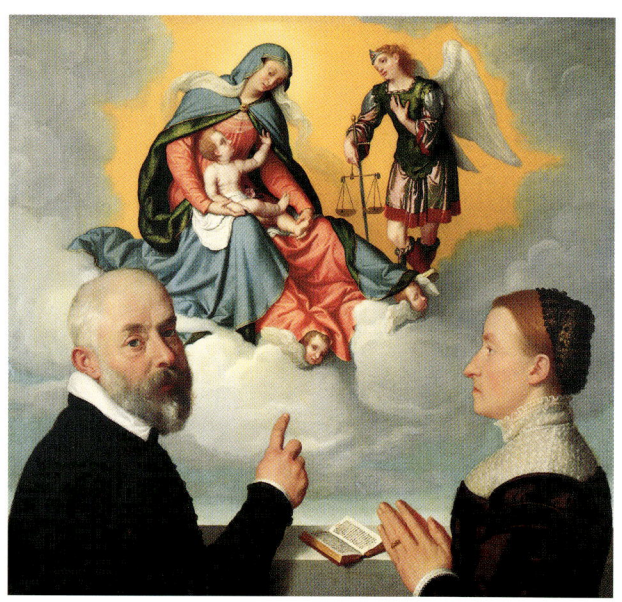

Clouds part and the heavens open to reveal a golden vision of the Madonna and Child. A devout couple beholds the celestial scene. They fold their hands piously and direct us to the Holy Mother and Son. Across an open prayer book resting on a parapet, physical and spiritual worlds begin to merge miraculously. A generous blue mantle enfolds Mary as she tenderly cradles her child's hand and foot; cherubs (*cherubim,* one of the highest orders of angels) peek from clouds beneath her feet. In adoration, the Archangel Michael covers his heart with his hand as he rests against the hilt of his sword. This winged warrior slays Evil. He wears a cuirass, boots, and a radiant tunic reflecting light, like armor. He also weighs souls. By a slender thread, he balances the scales that serve to judge humanity. The couple has commissioned this painting as an expression of faith and good works; they hope that their intercessors, St. Michael and Mary, will lead them to their Heavenly Father.

Born near Bergamo, in northern Italy, Giovanni Battista Moroni painted altarpieces and portraits throughout the region. Titian, the Venetian titan of painting, advised Bergamese patrons to seek Moroni for their portraits. Moroni often set his sitters against backgrounds of religious imagery, blurring the boundaries between the natural and celestial realms. At the time, the Catholic Church advised that religious art be simple and direct, to make its meaning clear and accessible. In Moroni's devotional portraits, visionary figures seem as palpable as the sitters themselves. His paintings often decorated chapels in churches and in homes.

Here, his patrons dress in the somber fashions of the day—the blacks, browns, and whites of the Spanish style that traveled east to northern Italy and then north to Holland by the 1600s. Delicate detail—a lace bodice and snood, an embroidered collar and cuff—is pure and parsimonious. As they witness the glorious color of their holy vision, the couple invites the viewer to share their experience. "Imagine the actual place where you would find that which you want to contemplate," counseled St. Ignatius of Loyola, Spanish founder of the Jesuit school. He preached in Bergamo in 1551 and had just died the year before Moroni may have started this picture. Here, painter and patrons imagine Heaven, an actual place in which to contemplate this holy trio.

Painting and Religious Reformations
In response to the Protestant Reformation in Northern Europe, initiated by Martin Luther in 1517, the Roman Catholic Church sought reformations of its own, in what has come to be known as the Counter-Reformation. In order to counter factionalism and to keep its members, the Catholic Church established the Council of Trent (1545–64). Religious art in Italy was affected by the Council's prescriptions; Moroni's imagery reflects the reforms. His painting presages the Baroque age of dramatic religious paintings, which were intended to spark viewers' emotions and inspire spiritual transformation. Foreground figures painted by Baroque artists after Moroni increase in size and physical presence, as though about to spill into the viewer's space (see Luca Giordano's St. Paul the Hermit *in the Virginia Museum's galleries). The more real and immediate a religious painting seemed, the more convincing it might be for the viewer.*

Moroni's Sitters
Moroni worked for city officials and local patrons. Though at one time believed to be the governor of Brescia and his wife, this couple has not been identified. St. Michael, however, was most likely their patron saint. In Moroni's portrait, the two invoke the archangel and display prayer book, wedding ring, and austere dress in a painted testament to religious devotion.

Two Donors in Adoration before the Madonna and Child and St. Michael, *1557–60*
Giovanni Battista Moroni (Italian, 1520–1578)
Oil on canvas; 35¾ by 38½ inches
Virginia Museum of Fine Arts Purchase, The Adolph D. and Wilkins C. Williams Fund, 62.20

Salvator Rosa
The Death of Regulus

As a landscape painter, Salvator Rosa depicted thorny trees bending against darkening skies; as a poet, he wrote scornful satires that take root in classical morality. Rosa espoused the philosophy of the ancient Stoics; he founded and acted in a theatrical company; and he moved within the learned, academic circles of Rome and Florence in the mid 1600s. Of all of his accomplishments, he wanted most to paint the great stories of heroes and heroines—recorded in biblical books, ancient histories, and myths. *The Death of Regulus* ranks among Rosa's best efforts in history painting.

Nature itself seems to brood in response to the event. Rosa casts the wind-blown scene in clouds and shadow, as if to echo the harshness and the horror of the event. The place is Carthage, the ancient Phoenician colony in northern Africa; the time, 255 B.C., during the Punic Wars with Rome over territories such as Sicily. Marcus Atilius Regulus, the Roman consul captured by the enemy, has just returned from a paroled mission to negotiate peace with Rome in Carthage's favor. Instead, he urged the Romans to continue to fight, and, knowing he would face certain death, he honored his word to return to the Carthaginians.

His legend became a model of civic virtue and duty in Italian art and literature between the 1400s and the 1700s, when Stoicism enjoyed a revival in Europe. Here, soldiers enclose the captive Regulus in a spike-studded barrel. An active chorus of witnesses gathers, as though on a stage. Dramatic gestures convey emotions: onlookers raise their hands, point, supplicate, and decree. In contrast, Regulus stoically accepts his sentence. Passively he lies within the barrel that will seal his fate.

Rosa covers the canvas with expressive brushwork, some of which has become transparent over time to reveal the figures that the artist had overpainted (left). Reflections in clouds and armor, highlights within muscle or wood, and an executioner's blood-red kerchief provide the only relief to Rosa's typically dark tones. Rosa is known for the originality of his rugged landscapes and brisk pen-and-ink drawings; the classical subjects, gestures, and stage settings of his history paintings reflect the standards of this highly regarded art form in Europe at the time (see Poussin, pp. 60–61).

Stoics in a Barrel

Atilius Regulus of ancient Rome personified Stoicism by embracing an indifference to fortune, whether good or bad. His valorous death was legendary; he may actually have died of natural causes while in captivity. A century before Rosa painted Regulus's story, Giulio Romano (Raphael's close assistant) *introduced the barrel-torture for one of a series of frescoes dedicated to Stoic virtue in the Room of Atilius Regulus (about 1530) in Palazzo del Te, Mantua.*

Rosa's Legacy

Rosa's etchings of small figures and Roman ruins inspired art in the 1700s, including Giovanni Panini's idealized views. Rosa's fascination with the macabre also influenced Alessandro Magnasco's paintings (see Panini and Magnasco in the Virginia Museum's galleries). He made etchings of this picture, as well as of warriors, robbers, and moody landscapes, and he came to embody the Romantic concept of the Sublime.

The Death of Regulus, 1650–52
Salvator Rosa (Italian, 1615–1673)
Oil on canvas; 60 by 86½ inches
Virginia Museum of Fine Arts Purchase, The Adolph D. and Wilkins C. Williams Fund, 59.15

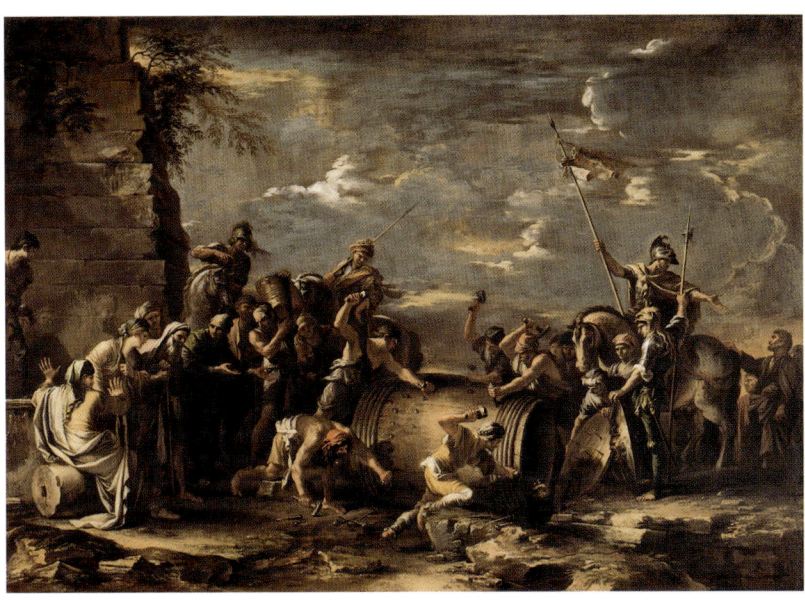

Alexander Keirincx
Landscape with Cephalus and Procris

Alexander Keirincx's enchanted forest evokes descriptions ranging from "lace-like" to "gnarled" or "fantastic." Dark moss-colored woodlands flecked with red and silver give way to soft green trees. Feathery leaves fade into a blue-green distance, where a thatched hut sits along a river bank. Travelers make their way across a wooden bridge through this Flemish countryside. Noticing their presence, a mountain goat looks up; a river tumbles over rocks into a calm pool where lily pads float and reeds reach to catch sunlight. Above the treetops, birds flit in the early morning air. The artist has created the scene in part from his imagination and from his observations in the early 1600s.

Into this charming setting, Keirincx places a scene from the myth of Cephalus and Procris. The ancient Roman poet Ovid tells the tale of this passionate but ill-fated pair, whose jealousy and mistrust led to tragedy. Here, the young couple meet in Ovid's "cool shadows" of "deep woods" to exchange gifts and vows. Procris offers her husband gifts from Diana, virgin goddess of the hunt: a golden-speared javelin and a swift hound, named Laelaps. Leafless branches and ivy-laced bark bend toward the lovers, as Keirincx frames their last happy moments together.

Delicately painted, the figures seem as ephemeral as the forest breeze that catches their golden curls, red cloak, and dress of gold, blue, and rose. Later, Procris will become suspicious of Cephalus's fidelity, as he had once been of hers, and she will spy on her husband while he hunts. She dies by her husband's hand, when he mistakes her for his prey and hurls his javelin, a gift of love and an instrument of death.

Working within an older tradition of Netherlandish landscape painting, Keirincx couches his story within a vast, expressive terrain. His fanciful vista, full of enchantment and omens, comes from a unique artistic vision influenced by other Flemish painters (see Jan Brueghel in the Virginia Museum's galleries). With jewel-like colors, Keirincx brings Ovid's "cool valleys" and "morning breezes" to life, in a painting as transporting as the poetry itself.

The Netherlands
The Netherlands once included Holland, as well as Belgium and parts of France (Flanders). In the mid 1600s, boundaries were more or less drawn by treaties and religious affiliations: the northern Protestant provinces (Holland) and the southern Catholic provinces (Flanders).

Aurora and Cephalus
Ovid (born 43 B.C.) writes in his Meta-morphoses, *a compendium of myths, that Aurora, the Roman goddess of dawn, loved the young hunter Cephalus. Jealous of his devotion to Procris, Aurora first caused Cephalus to doubt his wife's faithfulness, which led to tests, treachery, and death. An older, ancient Greek version of the story of Aurora and Cephalus (in Greek, Eos and Kephalos) appears on the back of the Red-figured Calyx-Crater (see p. 5).*

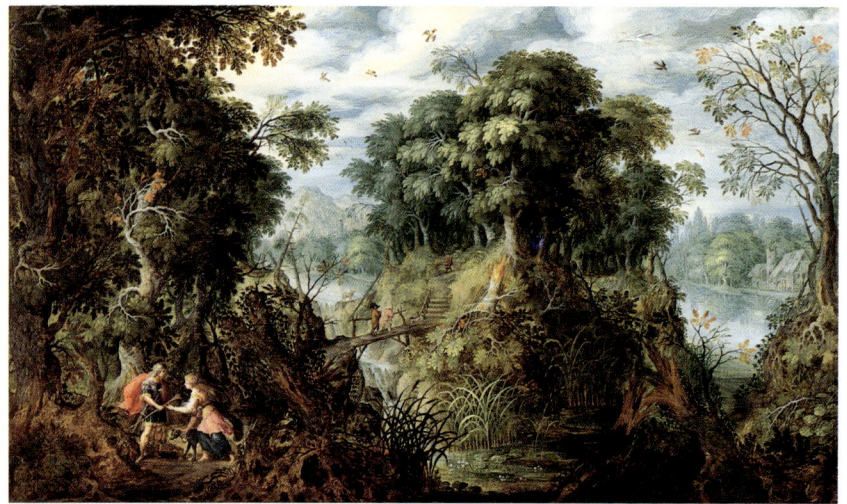

Landscape with Cephalus and Procris, circa 1620
Alexander Keirincx (Flemish, 1600–1652)
Oil on wood; 18¾ by 31¾ inches
Virginia Museum of Fine Arts Purchase, The Adolph D. and Wilkins C. Williams Fund, 84.77

Isaac Soreau
Still Life with Grapes, Flowers, and Berries in a Wanli Bowl

Green grapes, bright cherries, and variegated tulips introduce us to Isaac Soreau's delicate world. He paints dew drops and ripening raspberries, herbs and artichokes. He offers us an orderly array: sprigs of rosemary, a rose, a little lily of the valley, scattered nuts. A dragonfly clings to a tulip. A fly crawls along the table's edge; at the corner, a butterfly spreads its wings while another alights upon red grapes.

The simple beauty of Soreau's painting reflects the dawn of Netherlandish still lifes. By the mid 1600s, Dutch and Flemish painters had perfected the art. Pleasing to the eye, flower and fruit paintings tell us much about Northern European culture. Soreau's white and yellow tulips, striped with red or blue, capture the exotic wonders of the flower first imported from Asia Minor in Soreau's day. Tulips have been associated with Holland ever since.

Soreau's blue-and-white bowl represents porcelain that was exported from China to Europe at the time; in fact, the bowl bears the name of Wanli, the emperor of China from 1572 to 1619. Dutch artisans making fashionable Delftware adapted Chinese patterns, among them Soreau's long-legged white deer surrounded by blue foliage (left).

Soreau's fruit and flowers, while not necessarily symbolic, have ancient and medieval meanings. Fruit and flowers in general express fertility and abundance; the rose and lily of the valley are associated with Christian love and humility; butterflies and dragonflies with spirituality; the fly with material concerns. Classical and Christian traditions valued rosemary for its healing properties and held the grape and its wine to be sacred.

Born into a family of painters, Soreau emigrated with his father and brother

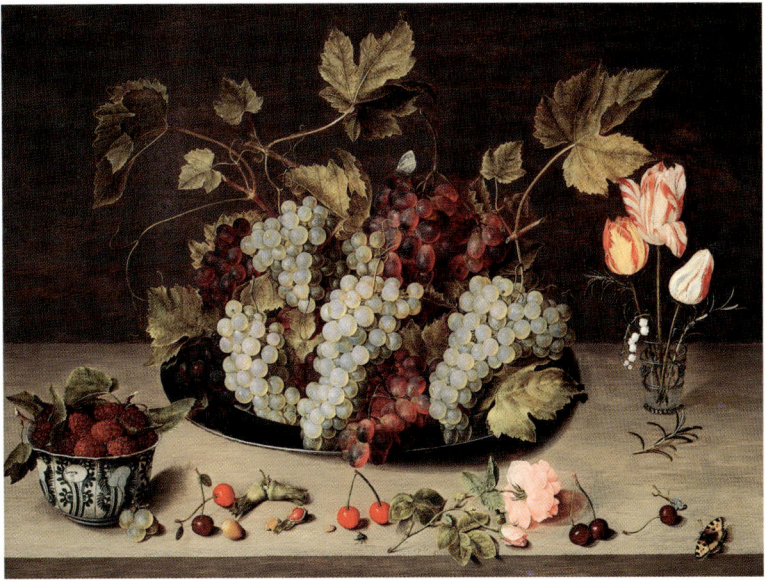

from Flanders to Germany. Although the full circumstances of his life have not yet come to light, his paintings are visions of clarity. Soreau imaginatively gathers blossoming flowers and maturing fruit from different seasons into his longer-lasting still lifes, modest but rich.

Soreau's Signature

Soreau signed only two of some thirty still lifes attributed to him; he dated one of the signed paintings 1638. His clear and lucid pictures share signature elements of composition—baskets of grapes; strawberries, blackberries, or raspberries in blue-and-white porcelain bowls; glass tumblers of tulips; cherries, artichokes, roses, lily of the valley— all carefully arranged on table tops. Other still lifes by Soreau may be seen in the Cincinnati Museum of Art; the Walters Art Gallery, Baltimore; the Ashmolean Museum, Oxford; and the Hamburg Art Museum.

Netherlandish Paintings

Landscapes and still lifes were the two most popular types of painting in the Netherlands—Flanders and Holland— during the 1600s. Both types evolved from medieval religious art of previous centuries. Landscapes first served as settings for biblical stories or classical mythologies before receiving prominence in their own right. Fruit and flowers appeared earlier as attributes of holy figures in religious paintings. Objects from nature were believed to embody divine elements, and thus were often given symbolic meaning (see Keirincx, opposite, and Molenaer, p. 59).

Still Life with Grapes, Flowers, and Berries in a Wanli Bowl, circa 1620
Isaac Soreau (Flemish, 1604–after 1638)
Oil on wood; 21⅜ by 29⅜ inches
Virginia Museum of Fine Arts Purchase, The Adolph D. and Wilkins C. Williams Fund, 84.78

Peter Paul Rubens
Pallas and Arachne

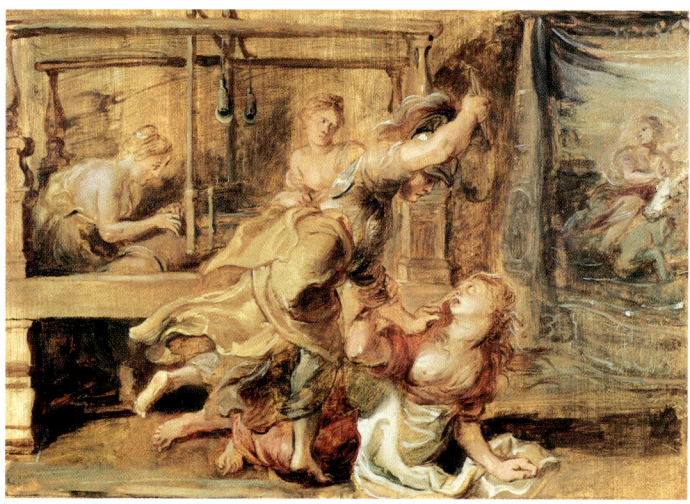

Peter Paul Rubens spins webs of color to paint the myth of how the spider, nature's weaver, came to be. The artist's "fury of the brush," as his technique was described in his day, matches the fury of the myth: a weaving contest between Pallas Athena—goddess of wisdom, war, and art and crafts—and her mortal challenger, Arachne. Arachne flouted her talents at the loom and failed to defer to Athena, her teacher. In their competition, Athena wove a tapestry of gods, with warnings to mortals who defy them. Arachne spun a flawless work showing how gods use mortals for their pleasure. Here, in her wrath, Athena strikes Arachne with the shuttle from a loom; in her agony and despair, Arachne will hang herself, only to be transformed by the goddess into a spider. Ovid tells us in his ancient Roman poem about the myth—"The spider has not forgotten the arts she used to practice."

Rubens' painting seems to vibrate with deft brushwork, as though echoing the hands that flew eagerly across the looms in contest. Although his image is a sketch for a larger, brighter painting, Rubens' fleet-footed color evokes the tapestries described by Ovid: "Like a rainbow…a thousand colors shining and blending, so the eye could never detect the boundary line." Browns, golds, reds, and blues spin across the painting, highlighted with white. Through Arachne's eyes and twisted body, Rubens captures her terror; as she writhes, her spidery feet foretell her fate.

Although a warning about hubris, Rubens' painting also testifies to the power of art. Layers of illusion play in his sketch. Rubens paints Arachne's "tapestry" in the background of his image: Zeus in the guise of a bull abducts Europa and carries her across the waves. Europa turns her head—echoing Arachne's actions—and calls to her companions. An anxious weaver in Athena and Arachne's realm looks up from the loom as if she hears the call.

A scholar and a diplomat, knighted in both England and Spain, Rubens painted prodigiously—classical mythologies, landscapes, religious works, and portraits. In 1636, Philip IV commissioned a series of more than one hundred pictures—many based on Ovid's *Metamorphoses*—for the royal hunting lodge outside of Madrid. During the next year, Rubens made small oil sketches like this one, to serve as designs for paintings to be worked on by his collaborators and assistants, and the master himself. By 1638, Rubens had delivered the finished paintings. Though only some of them still exist, about fifty oil sketches survive and have become popular with collectors, as displays of Rubens' technique and imagination. The sketches point the way to the rich and confident paintings—filled with robust human figures, energized brushstrokes, and intense, fluctuating color—for which Rubens is famous.

Rubens' Studio
From his house in Antwerp, Rubens' successful workshop produced paintings of translucent color, shimmering drapery, and voluptuous figures that inspired the phrase "Rubenesque." Rubens designed his art to be developed by his assistants on canvas, and then completed by him. The door to his studio measured only three feet wide but twenty feet high, to accommodate the grandiose paintings that Rubens shipped to destinations throughout Europe, including Spanish, French, and English courts.

Pallas and Arachne, 1636–37
Peter Paul Rubens (Flemish, 1577–1640)
Oil on wood; 20 by 24 inches
Virginia Museum of Fine Arts Purchase, The Adolph D. and Wilkins C. Williams Fund, 58.18

Jan Miense Molenaer
Allegory of Marital Fidelity

Here we have a sparkling Dutch vision of lavish lace, dotted doublets, and ostrich plumes. From the right, a gentleman in red velvet, hat in hand, offers a greeting; a woman in silvery blue and rose accompanies him. A musician plays his bass violin cello with his bow, while, at the center, a woman in satin and lace keeps time to sheet music. Behind her a man raises a pitcher to pour a perfect arc of water or wine into a goblet. To the left, a lutenist strums, while attendants rinse crystal in a golden basin, balance glasses on a serving tray, and check a tankard's diminishing contents. Jan Miense Molenaer, probably a student of Frans Hals, brushes this opulent world with brilliant color and exacting detail: pink ribbons flounce over shoes and garter stockings at the knee; blue bows adorn bodices; gold trim encircles hem, sleeve, and dog collar alike. Crowned by potted pink and blue carnations, an ivied wall encloses the terrace; outside, refinement gives way to a rustic brawl.

Dutch paintings, delicate counterpoints of surface charm and careful symbolism, can often puzzle as much as delight. Molenaer's image has been called a garden party, a musical company, a contrast in social classes, and a glimpse of life in Holland three hundred years ago. Titled *Allegory of Marital Fidelity,* it may demonstrate proper conduct for the couple on the right. A hand lifted to music emphasizes timing and measure. Water poured from one vessel to another symbolizes moderation, based on images of Temperance in medieval art. The little dog stands for fidelity and faith; stringed instruments for harmony and concord; ivy is associated with marriage, and carnations, with sacred love. Temptations should be heeded: the monkey often stands for unchecked sensuality and lust,

the cat for cruelty, or mischief at the very least. In Dutch art, men gazing hopefully and humorously into empty tankards represent the vice of gluttony, and peasants sometimes pose a threat to class boundaries; the murderous rustics here are said to represent the sin of anger.

Still, recent studies caution us to look more closely. Does the tankard-gazer look intemperate, or is he merely tending to his servant's task? Is extravagance growing in this garden? The musical party, gazing to the left outside the picture, disregards the knifing that occurs among the rowdies. Only the monkey and the cat seem to look directly at us. Seated on a block signed by the artist, the creatures catch our eye and urge us to think again. Are we meant to see trappings of wealth and idleness as well as those of poverty and ignorance? The richness of Molenaer's painting may lie, in part, in the questions it provokes.

"Man is a Bubble"

Three major subjects of Dutch painting converge in Molenaer's image: merry companies, banquet scenes, and outdoor festivities. However fun-loving they may be, Dutch paintings often warn of the dangers of overindulgence, the vanity of riches, and the brevity of life. "Man is a bubble," so the proverb goes; in Molenaer's painting, a fragile glass vessel floats like a bubble in the basin. As one scholar has observed, Dutch paintings of luxury, the celebration of the senses, and the love of merriment often express both fascination and fear.

Allegory of Marital Fidelity, 1633
Jan Miense Molenaer (Dutch, 1609/10–1668)
Oil on canvas; 39 by 55½ inches
Virginia Museum of Fine Arts Purchase, The Adolph D. and Wilkins C. Williams Collection, 49.11.19

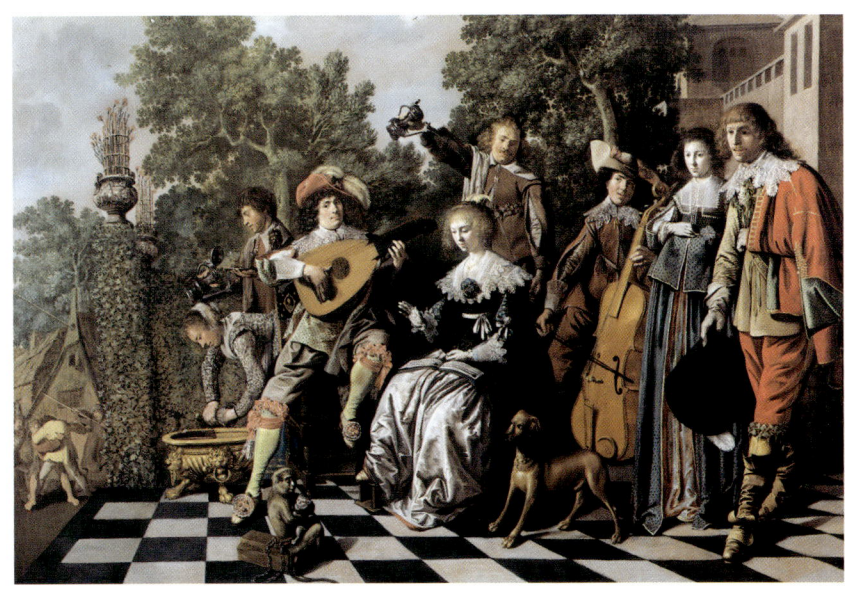

Nicolas Poussin
Achilles on Skyros

Nicolas Poussin, regarded as one of the greatest painters in the history of European art, once described the art of painting as "an imitation in lines and colors on any surface of all that is to be found under the sun." His work reflects his philosophy. Poussin depicts histories of ancient Greek and Roman gods and goddesses, fallen and triumphant heroes, Old Testament prophets and New Testament saints, as they meet their challenges and face their destinies. They enact their stories against carefully constructed backdrops that serve as suitable stages for each drama. Figures, drapery, trees, and columns exist together in a unified atmosphere of color, light, and air. Low-lying clouds touch the tops of rocky cliffs, leafy plants carpet the damp ground, and classical buildings emerge as the muted monuments of past civilizations. To Poussin, painting was silent poetry: indeed, we want to "read" his works as they unfold before us.

Here, the Greek hero Achilles reveals his true identity as a warrior (so skilled was Achilles that the ancient Greek poet Homer called him the "breaker of men"). While young women—King Lycomedes' daughters—admire conventional feminine adornments of pearl necklaces and earrings (center), Achilles admires his own image, bedecked in masculine trappings of helmet, sword, and shield (left). Until this moment, Achilles had been hiding, disguised in women's clothing and living in Lycomedes' kingdom on the island of Skyros. Achilles' mother, the goddess Thetis, had placed him there for his protection, knowing her son's future if he pursued his heroic calling to fight the Trojan War. When Achilles was

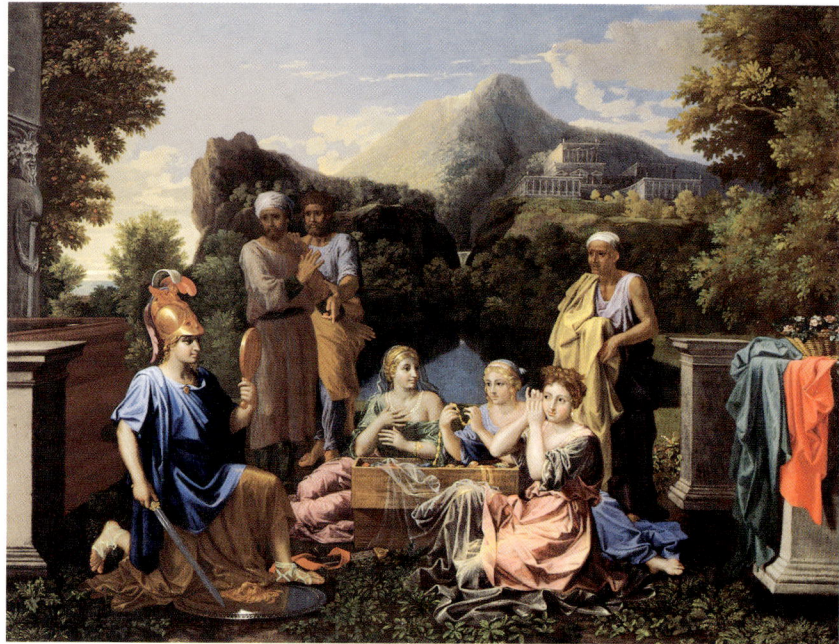

a child, Thetis had unwittingly determined his destiny, when she dipped him in the River Styx's waters of immortality but failed to submerge the heel by which she held him.

Poussin selects the fatal moment when Achilles' fellow warriors, Odysseus and Diomedes, trick him into divulging his secret. The visitors have just offered their island hosts a casket filled with gifts, and Achilles has naturally reached for weapons of war rather than jewels. His vanity flashes for a comic instant. But, he has just sealed his fate to join the battle, and die when Paris's arrow, guided by Apollo, strikes Achilles' vulnerable heel.

Mode and Measure in Poussin

Though Poussin's themes are passionately human—lost loves, virtuous deeds, tragic fates, life's transience, nature's cycles—his style is profoundly reserved and measured. Believing that the mode or style of painting should match its theme and subject, Poussin carefully selected the types of drapery and setting, the gestures of figures, and the overall composition to suit the tone of the myths, histories, and biblical stories that he depicted.

Turning Points in Poussin's Paintings

Though Poussin's figures can appear as impassive as the faces of Greek and Roman statues, the artist sometimes paints them with similar features reflecting an emotion—surprise, joy, wrath—appropriate to his subject. In each painting, Poussin captures one succinct moment to carry the story, embracing events leading up to it and foreshadowing consequences to follow.

Poussin's Clarity and Ambiguity

Surprising, amusing, bemusing, suspenseful, horrifying: so this picture has been described. Poussin's painting has a subtle, if unsettling, equilibrium, as he captures both the comic and the tragic aspects of Achilles' story, and the complexities of the Greek hero's character. Achilles' feminine attire amuses, while he reveals his warrior's deadly nature; his visitors betray their tensions as they trick him, while his carefree hostesses enjoy their presents, unaware. The figure on the right has been identified as a laughing male, as a grimacing female, and even as Achilles' mother, a sea-goddess. Poussin's subject had been painted in antiquity, and he would have read ancient descriptions of these lost pictures. Questions posed by the Greek writer Philostratus about one ancient painting of Achilles on Skyros—"What does the man behind them mean, the one who blows the trumpet? And what is the significance of the painting?"—could well have inspired Poussin to place elements of mystery in his "modern" version.

The Art of Europe in the 1600s

Poussin, a Frenchman, worked primarily in Rome—a center of European art in the 1600s. There, he ranked among the geniuses of the day who defined Baroque art: native Italians Annibale Carracci, Caravaggio, and Gianlorenzo Bernini; Claude Lorrain, Poussin's fellow countryman (in the Virginia Museum's collection); Anthony Van Dyck and Peter Paul Rubens (see p. 58) from northern Europe; the Spaniard Diego Velásquez.

Poussin's Place in European Painting

Poussin's art adds a strong link to the chain of European painting. His classical style was influenced by masters of the Italian High Renaissance—the order of Raphael, the drama of Titian. Poussin's pictures, in turn, led the way for the great French painters of the next three centuries: Jacques-Louis David, Jean-Auguste Ingres, Eugène Delacroix (see p. 71), Paul Cézanne.

Poussin-sized Painting

Poussin gave many gifts to the art of painting: succinct stories set in precisely measured spaces, a masterful ability to make mythological and historical moments visible, a clarity of form and color. His canvases of rational space and proportional figures became a standard in the art world and were known in the 1700s as "Poussin-sized."

Conservation and Cleaning

Recent cleaning of this painting has revealed details of Poussin's working methods, geometrical structures, and color that are typical of his later works: breathtaking blues contrasted with unusually soft and subtle shades of greens, golds, roses, and reddish-browns.

Academies of Art

The study of Antique and Renaissance art became part of a European artist's academic training during the 1600s and 1700s, particularly in Italy, France, and England. Poussin's art came to embody the academic tradition. Students copied ancient sculpture and studied ancient authors. Apelles' vow to draw every day, no matter how busy, inspired the proverb "no day without a line"—an ancient version of "practice makes perfect" that academy students would have understood. The Academy of Design was established in Florence in 1563; France's Royal Academy in Paris was founded in 1648 and the French Academy in Rome in 1666 (see Van Loo, p. 63, and Robert, p. 65). In 1768, the Academy of Arts in London received royal support (see Kauffman, p. 67).

Achilles on Skyros, 1656
Nicolas Poussin (French, 1594–1665)
Oil on canvas; 39½ by 52½ inches
Virginia Museum of Fine Arts Purchase, The Arthur and Margaret Glasgow Fund, 57.2

Jean-Antoine Watteau
The Gazer

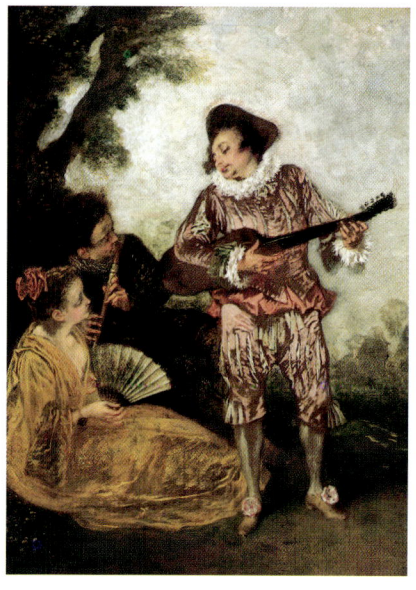

Jean-Antoine Watteau creates a world of fragile beauty. A woman tilts her head to listen to gentle music from a guitar and flute. She stirs the air with her fan; its pleats flicker with traces of color from Watteau's palette. As she leans slightly into the delicate breeze, she reveals her alluring décolleté, the low-cut neckline that was the fashion of the day. The guitarist, clearly distracted from his serenade, gazes intently at her. An engraving made from Watteau's painting about ten years later bears the Latin inscription "he thinks of something else" and the title "Le Lorgneur" (The Gazer or Ogler). We may never know what Watteau called his painting, or why he repainted the young woman. She originally sat lower in the picture, where the musician's glance would have met her eyes.

Watteau captures palpable beauty, tinged by ineffable mystery. He paints elusive pleasures—desired, attained, lost.

He washes languorous landscapes in golden light and catches the passage of precious time: a glance, a gesture, moments that cannot last forever. In Watteau's pictures, courtiers dressed in current fashions often mingle with costumed actors in choreographed scenes suspended between fantasy and reality. Here, colors from red ribbons, pink plumes, and white ruffs reflect within the stripes and sheen of the guitarist's clothing, a flounced costume suited for an actor.

Watteau's paintings of elegant, amorous excursions to parks or country settings came to be known as his *fêtes galantes*. These fragile paintings of fleeting moments have suffered the ravages of time. To achieve shimmering effects, the artist applied pearly coats of underpainting in white, blue, or rose. He brushed in the landscape and then, from his sketchbooks, selected suitable figures to paint in thick, rich pigments *(impasto)*. An impatient painter, he often used too much oil to spread his pigments quickly, creating thin layers of translucent color. His oil glazes have now cracked, darkened, or vanished; painted surfaces have wrinkled; and areas where the artist has changed his mind *(pentimenti)* sometimes show. As delicate and transient as Watteau's subjects, the very surfaces of his paintings have come to reflect the passing of time.

Preliminary Drawings

Watteau's preliminary drawings for the two musicians survive. X-rays of the painting reveal Watteau's original conception for the woman that also matches one of his drawings. Known as a painter of the "senses," Watteau purportedly felt that his final paintings never approached his achievements in drawing.

Watteau's Pastorals

Watteau painted the pastimes of French aristocracy; his pastoral picnics set the stage for flirtations, serenades, and minuets. The poignancy of Watteau's paintings tempers their prettiness and playfulness; sentimental scenes of romance become dreamy, intoxicating encounters under love's sway, tinted ever so slightly by hints of scandal. France's Royal Academy of Painting and Sculpture recognized Watteau's fêtes galantes as a new genre in 1717.

The Gazer: Variations on a Theme

Only about two hundred paintings by Watteau are known, and most were given titles after his death. The Gazer *has been called a lively example of Watteau's art and a rarity in American museums. Four versions of* The Gazer *exist: this image, painted on wood, was owned by Watteau's friend in 1727, purchased by the painter Charles-Antoine Coypel, and documented upon his death in 1753. An engraving was made in 1727, and two versions on canvas came to light in the mid 1900s.*

Watteau's Characters and Settings

Watteau painted scenes from the theater, filled with stock characters from the Italian acting troupe, the commedia dell' arte, active from the 1500s through the 1700s. He also painted small pastoral scenes for Rococo interiors, including the fashionable Parisian "hotels" for courtiers, ministers, and ambassadors.

The Gazer (Le Lorgneur), circa 1716
Jean-Antoine Watteau (French, 1684–1721)
Oil on panel; 12¾ by 9⁷⁄₁₆ inches
Virginia Museum of Fine Arts Purchase, The Adolph D. and Wilkins C. Williams Fund, 55.22

Carle Van Loo
A Pasha Having His Mistress's Portrait Painted

Carle Van Loo creates an exotic masquerade in his studio to delight his viewers. The artist—with brush, palette, and maulstick in hand—glances up from his easel and over his shoulder as if to acknowledge our company. Van Loo has placed himself in the midst of a Turkish fantasy, the European vogue during the mid 1700s, known in Paris as *turquerie*. *Turquerie*, like *chinoiserie*, consisted of imaginative artistic motifs that Westerners associated with "exotic" Eastern cultures. Here, the artist has been sketching a "Pasha's mistress." The self-important "Pasha"—an honorary title bestowed upon actual Turkish officials—directs our attention to the task at hand. With colorful flourishes of yellow, deep ocher, blue, and pink, Van Loo presents satin skirts and fanned collars, turbans topped by downy feathers, brushed leather boots and velvet jackets, fur-trimmed bodices and brims of hats.

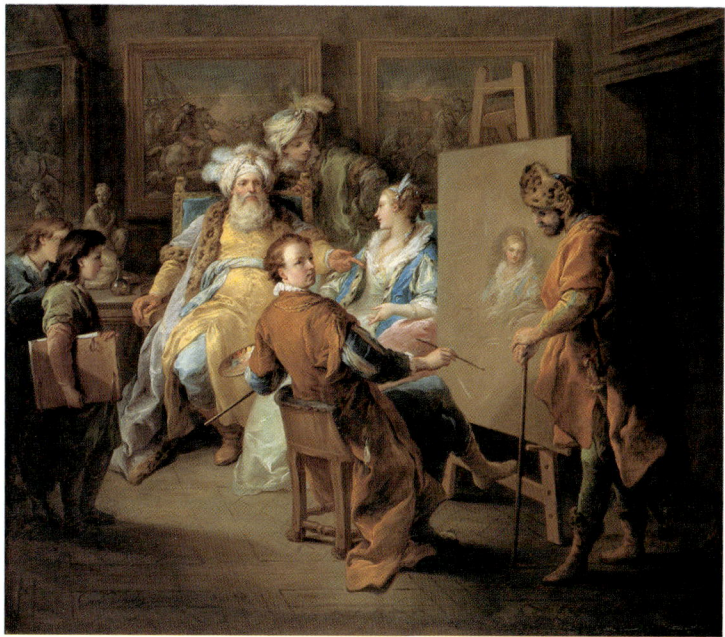

Casting himself as the consummate master, Van Loo alludes to famous artists of earlier eras. He knew the story, first told by Pliny the Elder, of the ancient Greek painter Apelles, who made a portrait of Alexander the Great's favorite mistress, Campaspe. As he painted her, Apelles fell in love, and so, the heroic Alexander "gave" Campaspe to him. Although several French and Italian artists painted this subject during the 1700s, here, Van Loo twists the tale, transforming it into his masquerade and joke. He plays the role of the ideal artist, an elegant easel painter; his model, who plays the Pasha's consort, is believed to be the artist's wife.

Carle Van Loo personifies the complex world of eighteenth-century European art: academies, fashions in taste, social roles for men and women. Born into a family of Flemish painters in Nice, he studied at the French Academy in Rome and held the titles of premier painter to France's Louis XV and director of the Royal Academy of Art in Paris. He also taught Jean-Honoré Fragonard. Van Loo's suave style displays the finesse of Rococo painting (see Watteau, opposite, and Fragonard, p. 64). Yet, the background details in his picture indicate the painter's mastery of the academies' exalted "grand manner": a knowledge of classical sculpture and the facility for history painting. So versatile, Van Loo became known in his day as Europe's premier painter, not merely the French king's.

Van Loo's Background

Van Loo nods to Apelles' painting of Campaspe as Aphrodite by including a cast of a Greek sculpture of the goddess in the background of this painting. The historical battle scenes may be copies of the Life of Alexander *on which Van Loo worked.*

The Salons

The Royal Academy in Paris began to sponsor public exhibitions of its members' art in 1667. Van Loo submitted this painting and its companion piece, The Pasha Giving a Concert for his Mistress, *now in the Wallace Collection, London, to the Salon of 1737.*

A Pasha Having His Mistress's Portrait Painted, 1737
Carle Van Loo (French, 1705–1765)
Oil on canvas; 26 by 30 inches
Virginia Museum of Fine Arts Purchase, The Adolph D. and Wilkins C. Williams Fund, 59.20

Jean-Honoré Fragonard
Landscape with Washerwomen

Jean-Honoré Fragonard's vision of Nature refreshes the viewer. Hills sparkle in clean country air. The weather is changing. Gathering gray-and-white clouds leave an imprint below, as they roll across the sky. Yellow light peeks through cloud cover, dances over treetops, and warms a winding path. It falls upon a hillside farmhouse, overgrown with vines. In pockets of sunshine and shadow, laundresses wash linens beside a spring-fed pond. A kerchiefed woman watches from the doorway; a tiny inscription on the lintel reads *Fragonard*.

"Beautiful dreams": so a biographer in 1821 described Fragonard's landscapes, praising "the magic of the skies…after a thunderstorm…when a cloudy sky lets a few shafts of sunlight shine forth." Here, earth and sky—a leaf-lined horizon and towering clouds—echo each other.

Fragonard's French landscapes have been called "Dutch" in spirit. His immense skies and fresh atmosphere were inspired by Dutch painters working 100 years earlier. Yet, Fragonard's touch is personal. With rapid brushwork, he seizes the moment, sketching scenes before they vanish from view and coaxing forms to emerge from shadow and light. Liveliness and gaiety infuse his pictures. His careful compositions seem transitory; a hint of urgency, exquisite and understated, haunts his scenes.

Fragonard spoke of beauty as "Nature in perfect health"; it has been said that he "seemed to invent Nature rather than to depict it." His landscapes—like his portraits and scenes from daily life—inhabit a lofty world, more ardent and much lighter than our own.

Fragonard's Fantasies

Though a master of landscape, Fragonard is famous for his effervescent fantasies— dashing portraits and romantic pictures of pink-cheeked women wooed by love-struck suitors. The artist's paintings led to his reputation as "red-cheeked…sparkling-eyed… carefree," which may have masked a purportedly modest and anxious temperament.

Fragonard and the Academies

In an era of strict hierarchies of painting— histories, portraits, landscapes, genre scenes, and still lifes, in that order, Fragonard painted all of these types except still life. He studied with François Boucher and Carle Van Loo (see p. 63). Although he won the French Academy's Rome Prize, he never fully adapted to academic competitions and official commissions. Still he sold his work, especially sketches, despite critics' assertions that his art was unfinished.

Fragonard and Hubert Robert

Lifelong friends born one year apart, Fragonard and Hubert Robert painted at the French Academy in Rome and traveled to Naples together. For a time, each lived in artists' quarters at the Louvre, the royal palace until 1792. When the National Assembly authorized the first public museum there in 1793, Fragonard and Robert participated in its formation. Of their drawings and paintings from Italy— cascading waterfalls, cypress-framed temples, laundresses on river banks—it has been said that "Hubert Robert loved ruins; Fragonard preferred trees…Robert was the painter of the past…Fragonard was the painter of the instant."

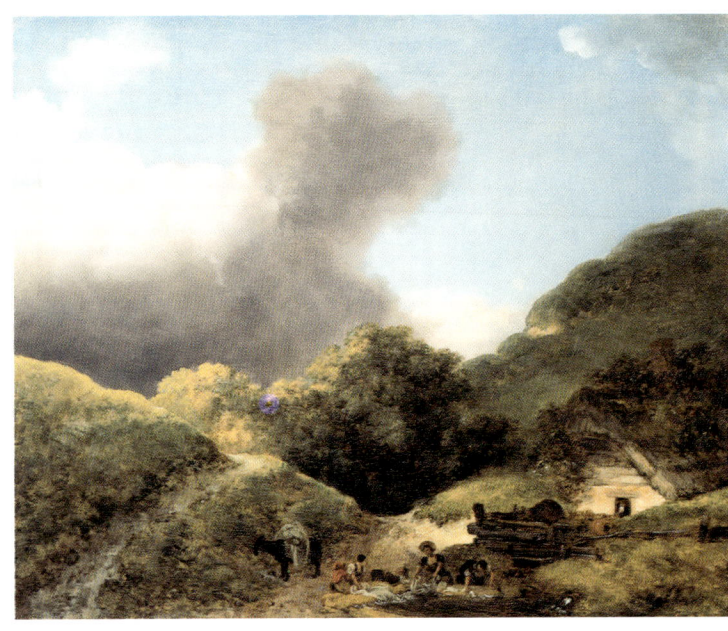

Landscape with Three Washerwomen, circa 1765
Jean-Honoré Fragonard (French, 1732–1806)
Oil on canvas; 15¼ by 18¼ inches
Virginia Museum of Fine Arts Purchase, The Adolph D. and Wilkins C. Williams Fund, 80.81

Hubert Robert
The Finding of the Laocoön

"Rome's very ruins tell of her former greatness." Inscribing this phrase on one of his drawings, Hubert Robert opens up his world of art to us. He loved to draw and paint ancient Roman sculpture and architecture: real or invented, slightly haunted, always graced by his imagination. He captures the visible layers of Rome's history—grandiose ruins to be pondered, just as they exist today. Here, the former greatness of Rome reveals itself in coffered barrel-vaults and stately Corinthian columns that reach enormous heights, dwarfing figures below. These ruins evoke, but do not copy, what Robert might have seen of ancient Rome in the mid 1700s. His dank and dark atmosphere suggests the mystery of antiquity, at once aged and ageless. A vast basilica looms before us. Ancient bronze statues of emperors and philosophers stand in shadowy corners as witnesses to the excavations, here invented by the artist. Scattered sculpture and stone slabs set the theatrical scene: one of the most famous antique statues, made before A.D. 100, has just been unearthed.

The *Laocoön,* a marble sculpture of writhing figures, inches its way forward, attached by a rope to a wooden winch that workmen struggle to turn. Light illuminates the crossing. It flickers across spectators in white blouses, red skirts, and blue cloaks and falls on the *Laocoön.* The sculpture actually came to light in 1506, discovered in a vineyard in Rome. Here, curious observers of Robert's own day step from city streets into the basilica to watch a wrinkle in time.

Travelers and artists flocked to Rome during the mid 1700s, attracted by antiquities such as the *Laocoön,* inspired by classical discoveries at Herculaneum and Pompeii and the idea of basking

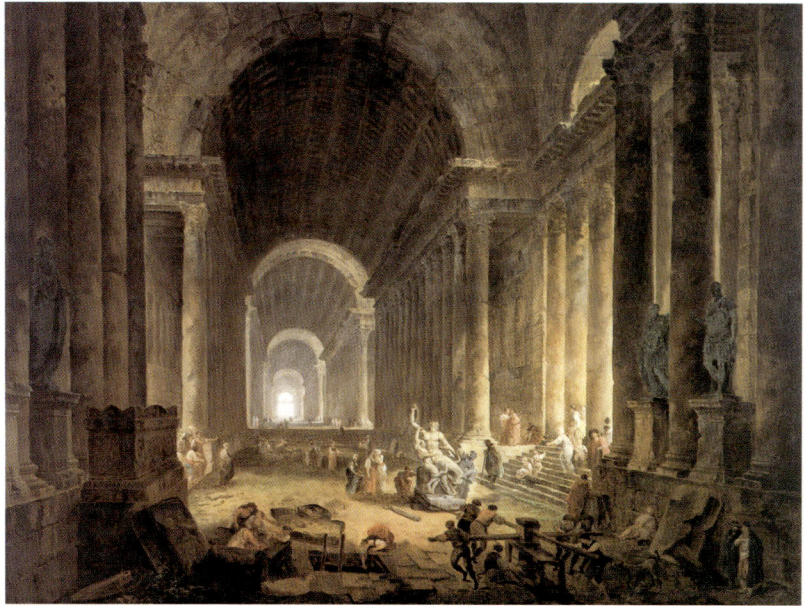

in the beauty of the Italian countryside. Robert sketched that countryside, as did his friend Fragonard, transforming the sketches into settings for ancient ruins—grottoes, temples, tombs, and toppled marbles. He returned to Paris with countless drawings of Italian buildings and landscapes, which provided sources for such paintings as *The Finding of the Laocoön.*

The Classical Revival

Visitors to Italy in the 1700s sought the "noble simplicity and silent grandeur" of classical art. So Johann Joachim Winckelmann, the father of archaeology and art history, described ancient art. He, like Robert, lived in Rome during the 1750s and 1760s. There, art students at the French Academy routinely copied casts of the Laocoön.

Robert's Popularity

Robert's views of Rome and Paris enjoyed great patronage (see Giovanni Paolo Panini, Rome's prominent "view painter," in the Virginia Museum's galleries). The philospher Denis Diderot admired Robert's paintings in the French Academy's salons; Catherine the Great (1729–1796) amassed one of the richest collections of Robert's work. After his return to France, Robert designed gardens for Versailles, served as curator of the Royal Museum at the Louvre, and submitted designs for the Louvre's grand galleries.

The Finding of the Laocoön, 1773
Hubert Robert (French, 1733–1808)
Oil on canvas; 47 by 64 inches
Virginia Museum of Fine Arts Purchase, The Arthur and Margaret Glasgow Fund, 62.31

Elisabeth-Louise Vigée-Lebrun
The Comte de Vaudreuil

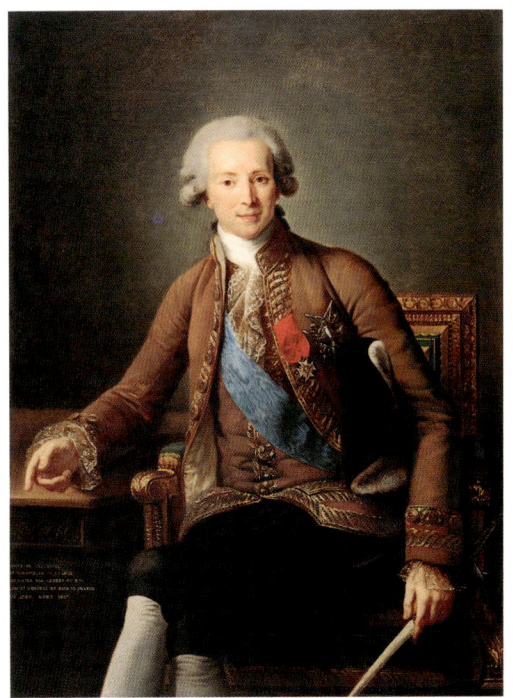

Elisabeth-Louise Vigée-Lebrun moved within a rarified atmosphere of royal and aristocratic patrons, social salons, art collectors and dealers. She painted the personalities of the eighteenth-century French court, as its center shifted from Versailles to Paris. Marie Antoinette called upon her for portraits, and the Comte de Vaudreuil was one of the artist's most avid patrons.

Here, Vigée-Lebrun depicts the Comte through smooth surfaces, attentive detail, and cheerful contrasts in color. In powdered wig and formal attire, he strikes a non-chalant pose, as though in the midst of speaking. In her *Memoirs*, Vigée-Lebrun praised the Comte's skills in conversation and storytelling; she acted upon her "Advice on the Painting of Portraits" by choosing a pose here, to "add to the likeness."

The Comte's gold-braided coat and vest, his lace jabot and cuffs, his black breeches and white hose attest to his position as one of the King's and Queen's court favorites. He displays orders of knighthood: a gold cross and silver badge. His striking blue sash and red rosette appear to be made of moire itself. He tucks his fur-lined tricornered hat beneath his arm and holds a sheathed sword. His portrait demonstrates the artist's counsel. Colors should be built from a dark base to mid-tones to golden highlights, shadows should be transparent, and backgrounds should be "subtle and uniform…neither too light nor too dark."

The artist and sitter traveled in the same social circles. A poet who knew them well called them "the Fairy and the Enchanter." Vigée-Lebrun's husband, Jean-Baptiste Pierre LeBrun, an art dealer and arbiter of taste, guided the Comte as he acquired an impressive collection of French art. Paintings by Vigée-Lebrun hung in the Comte's townhouse alongside pictures by Rubens and Poussin (see pp. 58, 60), Watteau, Van Loo, and Fragonard (pp. 62, 63, 64). The Comte owned Robert's *The Finding of the Laocoön* (p. 65), and Vigée-Lebrun painted Robert's portrait. Clients throughout Europe and Russia— countesses and counts, princes and princesses, actors and poets (including Lord Byron)—found Vigée-Lebrun to be engaging, and her portraits to be fresh, bright, and sparkling with finesse.

"Is she not astonishing"

So a critic quoted the reaction to Vigée-Lebrun's wit, grace, and talent, after the 1783 Salon, though he added: "what has contributed more than just a little to the spread of Madame Le Brun's fame is the fact that she is…young and pretty." An ideal courtier-artist, Vigée-Lebrun enjoyed a meteoric rise to fame as one of the foremost painters of her generation.

The Comte de Vaudreuil

Joseph Hyacinthe François de Paule de Rigaud came from a family of wealthy landholders in the Caribbean. He served in the Seven Years War. At court, his circle included his mistress, Marie Antoinette's favorite lady-in-waiting, and his companion, Louis XVI's younger brother. The Comte's critics called him insipid, modish, and spoiled; his supporters praised his charm and patriotic devotion to the art of his country. Vigée-Lebrun made five copies from her original portrait of the Comte.

Vigée-Lebrun, Kauffman, and the Academy

Like Angelica Kauffman (opposite), Vigée-Lebrun displayed artistic talent at a young age and was encouraged by an artist-father. At fifteen, she had a small list of clients for portraits. France's Royal Academy eventually awarded her one of its four positions allocated for women. Her Memoirs contain Jacques-Louis David's "compliment" of one of her portraits: "One would think that [it] was done by a man."

The Comte de Vaudreuil, 1784
Elisabeth-Louise Vigée-Lebrun (French, 1755–1842)
Oil on canvas; 52 by 39⅜ inches
Virginia Museum of Fine Arts, Gift of Mrs. A. D. Williams, 49.11.21

Angelica Kauffman
Cornelia Pointing to Her Children as Her Treasures

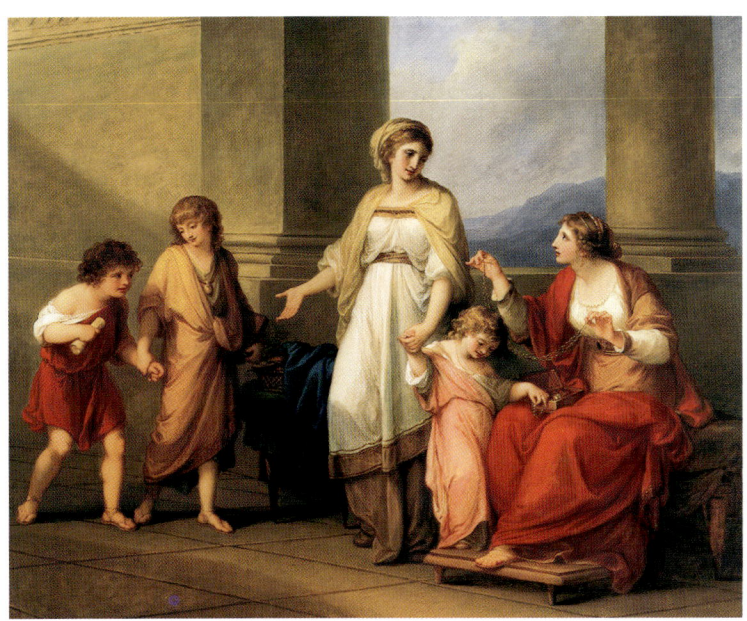

"These are my most precious jewels." This simple phrase earned admirable reputations for two women: one, the classic heroine of ancient Rome who uttered it, and the other, the Neoclassical painter who interpreted it while living in Rome, the Eternal City, almost two thousand years later. Pictured here, the noble Cornelia, around 200 B.C., presents her three children when asked by a Roman matron to display her most treasured objects. Cornelia became a classic example of family virtue, modesty, and devotion; in turn, her story provided "precious jewels" for Neoclassical artists such as Angelica Kauffman in the late 1700s A.D.

The painter's brush depicts fabrics washed in color, matte finishes as soft as velvet, and glistening eyes and earrings. Tunics and togas gracefully drape Kauffman's figures in red, gold, rose, and white. Slender golden sandals lace around toes. Ringlets graze napes of necks, eyelashes frame deep-set eyes, and aquiline noses form strong profiles. One poised hand leads to another, echoing spoken words and creating a gentle rhythm.

Clasping her daughter's hand, Cornelia gestures to her two sons. The little girl reaches for pearls from a jewelry box; the elder son guides his younger brother by the wrist. The young scholar in turn grasps a scroll, marked "ABC," an emblem of Cornelia's commitment to her childrens' education (see the Greek *Statue of a Young Boy,* p. 8). Like sculpture carved in classical relief, Kauffman's figures are set on a narrow stage against warm stone pillars that frame cool lavender-blue hills.

At sixteen, Kauffman made the pioneering choice to pursue history painting, considered the highest branch of the arts and the traditional province of men. By her mid-forties, two years after she created this picture, Kauffman had become the most successful living painter in Rome. The well-educated daughter of a Swiss mural painter, Kauffman studied in England and Italy, and she was a founding member of London's Royal Academy of the Arts with Benjamin West and Joshua Reynolds (in the Virginia Museum's galleries). The tributes at her funeral in Rome have been compared to Raphael's, whose classical style left footsteps for history painters to follow.

Art and Morality
Western art of the late 1700s encouraged moral improvement. It was the era of the Enlightenment, the American and French Revolutions, and the great discoveries of Greek and Roman antiquities. The English painter Joshua Reynolds advised that art, through ideal beauty and grand ideas, should better humanity. The French philosopher Denis Diderot argued that art should make virtue appealing and vice repugnant.

Cornelia, Mother of the Gracchi, Pointing to her Children as Her Treasures, circa 1785
Angelica Kauffman (Swiss, 1741–1807; active England 1776–1781)
Oil on canvas; 40 by 50 inches
Virginia Museum of Fine Arts Purchase, The Adolph D. and Wilkins C. Williams Fund, 75.22

John Wootton
A Bay Horse Got by the Leedes Arabian

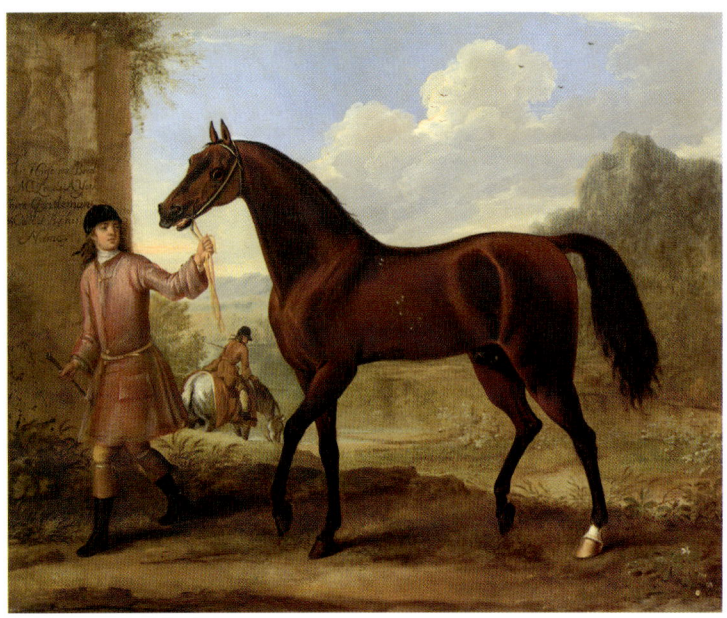

British Animal and Landscape Painting

Large-scale portraits of horses emerged in England during the late Tudor period (before 1603) and flourished during the late Stuart period (around 1700). Wootton's animal pictures and landscapes reflect the influence of Flemish painting, a tradition underlying English animal and sporting painting in general. Wootton's paintings also show the influence of Salvator Rosa's peopled landscapes (see p. 55); however, a century after Wootton painted, John Constable criticized Wootton's panoramas and took English landscape painting to new heights.

Patrons' Preferences

John Wootton painted portraits, horses and other sporting scenes, landscapes, and pictures of dogs. In his era, he was the highest paid painter of thoroughbreds. Nevertheless, the author and architect Sir Horace Walpole (1717–1797) remarked that the painter James Seymour was thought to be "superior to Wootton in drawing a horse" (see Seymour in the Virginia Museum's galleries; see also Benjamin Marshall, said to have been "the most professionally minded" painter of horses). Despite his criticisms, Walpole hung Wootton's portrait of Patapan, Walpole's pet dog, in the bedroom of his home, Strawberry Hill (see Reinagle, opposite).

A Bay Horse Got by the Leedes Arabian,
circa 1715
John Wootton (English, 1682/83–1764)
Oil on canvas; 39 by 49 inches
Virginia Museum of Fine Arts, The Paul Mellon
  Collection, 85.458

John Wootton introduces us to the world of thoroughbred horses at Newmarket, the mecca for racing enthusiasts in England during the 1700s. A groom leads a bay horse sired by the Leedes Arabian, a stallion brought to England from the Middle East. An inscription, painted on the wall (left), informs us: "This Horse was Bred / by Mr. Leeds a York / Shire Gentleman / & Called by his / Name." Wootton pictures the handsome horse in profile in the foreground plane to display champion features. The horse's eyes indicate a sensitive nature; his sheen attests to a well-cultivated coat; his golden hoof shows the mark of excellence. His groom dresses in a mauve riding jacket with flowing sleeves; this "Arabian" attire is meant to denote the stallion's lineage. In other portraits of Arabian horses, Wootton paints "exotic" palm trees and pyramids from Eastern lands.

Arabian stallions imported to England helped to establish the thoroughbred, enhancing the quality of horse-racing, and the quantity of horse-and-owner portrait commissions.

Some called Wootton the best painter of horses in England in his day, though not without controversy. He is said to have introduced light-filled skies and groups of figures to British landscape painting. Here, he sets his bay horse against a softly brushed ground, blue streams, and green trees beneath a lively sky. British nobility and literary circles praised the artist: the Prince of Wales favored Wootton's work; the poet Alexander Pope ("a little learning is a dang'rous thing") considered him to be the best landscapist in England. The simple clarity of Wootton's pictures makes them instantly recognizable (see the Virginia Museum's collection).

Philip Reinagle
Portrait of an Extraordinary Musical Dog

An engaging spaniel sits at a square piano and gazes at us earnestly, as only a canine can. Soft brown eyes express eagerness; silken ears frame a fetching face. A window, overlooking an English riverbank, brightens the music room of a countryhouse, as the pianist aspires to give song to an English anthem. Philip Reinagle presents this "Extraordinary Musical Dog," paws in place upon a keyboard, ready for a recital.

Perched upon a red piano stool and wearing a red collar to match, the spaniel has been playing "God Save the Queen," identified by a musicologist. If the viewer accepts the painter's invitation to sight-read the sheet music, the melody will surface.

The music is real, but is the "musician"? Records of a canine musical prodigy have been sought. Theories have been published: the spaniel is a portrait of someone's pet, or a parody of Romantic portraiture full of emotional intensity, or a lampoon of paintings and accounts of precocious child-musicians such as the young Mozart.

Such questions about Reinagle's spaniel-sitter, and the sponsor of the painting, only enhance the fun and wonder of it. Reinagle began his career as a portraitist before specializing in landscapes and sporting pictures. His twenty-four paintings of sporting dogs, including spaniels, served as standard references for later artists.

Here, Reinagle's picture captures the hearts of children, connoisseurs, dog fanciers, music buffs, and art lovers alike. Its charm induces pleasure and elicits smiles. During the great age of history painting in Europe, pet portraiture in England endeared even the irascible Samuel Johnson (1709–1784). The English essayist and lexicographer once remarked: "I would rather see the portrait of a dog I know than all the allegories you can show me."

British Sporting Art

British sporting art reached the height of popularity in the 1700s and early 1800s. It included pictures of horse-racing, fox-hunting, and fishing, as well as portraits of animals—wild but noble beasts, solid livestock, devoted pets. Whatever the subject, a love of English landscapes, country life, and leisure permeates British sporting art.

Of Sporting Scenes and Spaniels

Reinagle painted game birds, hunting scenes, and sporting dogs. Twenty-four portraits were engraved and published in an 1803 sporting periodical under the title "A Correct Delineation of the Various Dogs Used in Sports of the Field." Reinagle eventually was known as a restorer and copyist, particularly of Dutch landscapes and animal scenes from the 1600s.

Art and the Reinagles

Reinagle's father and three brothers were musicians in Edinburgh, London, and Philadelphia; his sister was a painter. Reinagle began his studies of art at London's Royal Academy in 1769; his membership finally culminated in his election to the rank of Academician in 1812. As a young man, Reinagle assisted the Scottish artist Allan Ramsay, who later became court painter to King George III of England (see Ramsey in the Virginia Museum's galleries). In the footsteps of their father, Reinagle's children, one of whom was named for Ramsey, exhibited landscape paintings at the Academy.

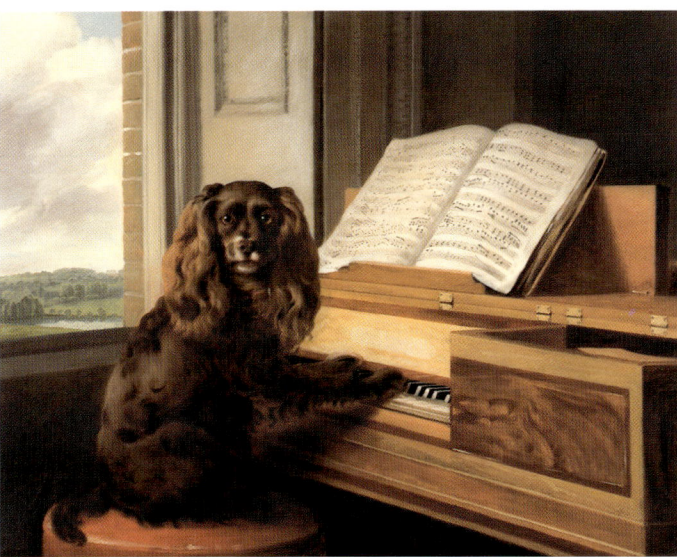

Portrait of an Extraordinary Musical Dog, exhibited 1805
Philip Reinagle (English, 1749–1833)
Oil on canvas; 28¼ by 36½ inches
Virginia Museum of Fine Arts, The Paul Mellon Collection, 85.465

Francisco Goya
General Nicolas Guye

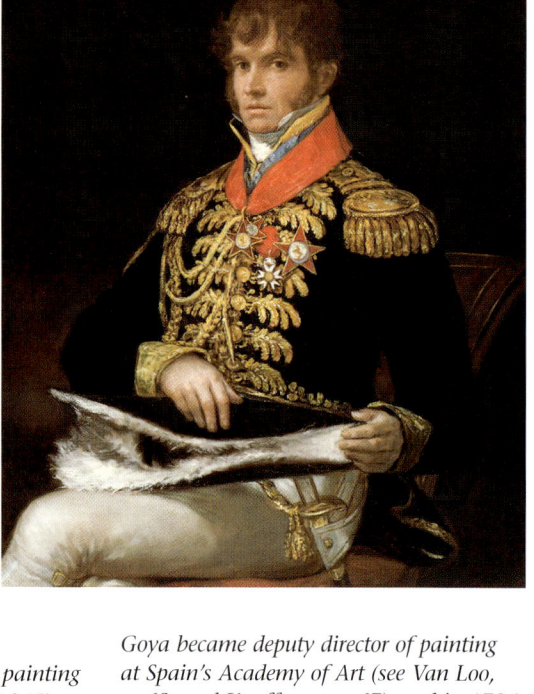

Francisco Goya understood the magic of painting. He believed in the power of art to make ideas visible. Here, in Goya's portrait, General Nicolas Guye's direct gaze arrests the viewer; dashing gold braid and colorful orders of dazzle the eye. The General's tousled hair and relaxed hands lend the painting an almost momentary aura, achieved through Goya's handling of paint. With a brush or a knife (he was also known to paint with his fingers), the artist has loosely applied colorful oils, splashy and sparkling. Textures catch the light: blue and red ribbons; gold-fringed epaulets and corded tassels; enameled medals and a shiny sword-hilt. Guye's hands, face, fur-lined hat, and breeches reflect myriad tints and shades. The portrait displays the reasons for Goya's fame: his deft use of heavy *impasto,* dramatic light and shadow, and brushwork that grows looser and freer as the sizes of his paintings increase. By 1801 he had become known as the Apelles of Spain (see Poussin, pp. 60–61, and Van Loo, p. 63); two years earlier, he had written to a friend, "the King and Queen are crazy about me."

Goya reigned as the court artist for three generations of Spanish kings; he continued to paint under Joseph I, Napoleon's brother who became King of Spain during the French occupation (1808–1814). General Guye, a French military officer under Joseph I, was thirty-seven years old—with twenty years of highly decorated service behind him— when Goya painted this portrait. The General wears the white cross and red ribbon of the French Legion of Honor, the blue ribbon and red star of the Commander of the Order of the Two Sicilies, and the large red ribbon and two stars of the Royal Order of Spain.

Goya, too, belonged to the Royal Order of Spain. Known for his portrayals of European nobility—sometimes searing, sometimes sympathetic—he also painted religious subjects, allegories, and landscapes. But, it was in the private art of his imaginative prints, often dark and satirical, that the artist found expression for "observations for which commissioned works generally give no room and in which fantasy and invention have no limit." An artist of great convictions, Goya never abandoned his belief in artistic freedom.

General Nicolas Guye

An inscription on the back of the painting states that General Guye (1773–1845) was the Governor of Seville and Marquis of Rio-Milanos (both appointments by Joseph I), in addition to his other honors. It also states that Guye gave this portrait to his brother, Vincent, in Madrid in 1810. A portrait of Vincent's five-year-old son, page to Joseph I, is now in the National Gallery of Art, Washington, D.C. Its inscription says that the portrait was a pendant to this painting of the boy's uncle, General Guye.

Goya and the Spanish Academy

In 1774, the Royal Manufactory of Tapestries summoned Goya to paint large-scale oil cartoons for tapestries to decorate royal palaces. He completed sixty-three paintings before he and his collaborator fell ill during the winter of 1792–93. His co-worker died; Goya recovered but had lost his hearing. He abandoned the commission. In 1785,

Goya became deputy director of painting at Spain's Academy of Art (see Van Loo, p. 63, and Kauffman, p. 67), and in 1786 he received an appointment as painter to the King. By 1795, he had become the Academy's director of painting and by 1799, the principal painter to the King.

Goya, Guye, and Guillemardet

Besides General Guye, Goya painted portraits of other French figures, including Ferdinand Guillemardet, the French ambassador to Madrid (1798–1800). While in Spain, Guillemardet purchased a set of Goya's Los Caprichos, *prints that his godson, Eugène Delacroix, later studied (opposite).*

General Nicolas Philippe Guye, 1810
Francisco Goya (Spanish, 1746–1828)
Oil on canvas; 41¾ by 33⅜ inches
Virginia Museum of Fine Arts, Gift of John Lee Pratt, 71.26

Eugène Delacroix
Scene from the Romance of Amadis de Gaule

Eugène Delacroix's painting of Amadis de Gaule and Princess Olga offers a glimpse of the artist's essence: a passionate painter, a lifelong lover of literature, and a leading man of the Romantic movement. Delacroix portrays a scene from an exotic romance, embellished from Spanish and French versions known since the 1300s. The hero in plumed helmet and mail meets the distressed heroine held captive in chains. Choreographed combatants lunge forward and step back beneath the weight of heavy shields and swords. Figures dash down castle steps and tear through gateways. Next to bricks and rubble, "Delacroix 1860" appears on a pile of posts.

His painting technique, once described as a "a river of force which carried everything with it," harmonizes brushwork, color, form, and line so that no single element dominates a picture. Delacroix balances the colors of his palette. Reds and greenish blues unify the canvas, appearing here and there on soldiers, shields, buildings, a background banner, and a foreground cloak. He juxtaposes color—blues and golds of tunic and skirt, reds and greens of soldiers. He places varying tones of a color side by side for the viewer's eye to blend.

Intensity defines Delacroix's art. He painted the human condition in its extremes: the fantasies of romance, the tragedy of wars, the sublime in Shakespeare and Dante. Though his histories and myths may derive from ancient art and the academic tradition, Delacroix imbued his paintings with modern vision, technique, and spontaneity. He has been called the last of Europe's history painters and the first of Europe's modern artists.

Delacroix studied Raphael's form and Veronese's luminosity. He regarded himself as a classical artist like Poussin, and he has been called "the only truly universal artist of the French school after Poussin." He learned about prismatic color, scattered and reflected across a picture, through Titian and Rubens. "Admirable Rubens!" Delacroix exclaimed, as he pushed the boundaries of painting into the modern era. Though he himself preferred a reputation for intellectual rigor, Delacroix is said to embody the French word *fougue* (fiery passion and spirit).

Delacroix and Catlin

The two artists crossed paths in Paris in 1845. Delacroix made sketches of the Ojibwa Indians who traveled with George Catlin (see p. 86), and he designed a poster to publicize their tour of Europe. Delacroix found Romantic exoticism in the cultures of native America, as well as in those of Greece, Morocco, and Algiers.

Painting, Poetry, and Piano

Delacroix left a legacy of 850 paintings and thousands of drawings and watercolors. His journals reveal that he aspired to write before becoming a painter. Poetry fired his imagination and created a "mood for painting." Delacroix also steeped himself in the music of Frederic Chopin and believed that just as a listener had an "ear for music," so a viewer could have "an eye for painting."

Scene from the Romance "Amadis de Gaule": Amadis Delivers Princess Olga from Galpan's Castle, 1860
Eugène Delacroix (French, 1798–1863)
Oil on canvas; 21½ by 25¾ inches
Virginia Museum of Fine Arts Purchase, The Adolph D. and Wilkins C. Williams Fund, 57.1

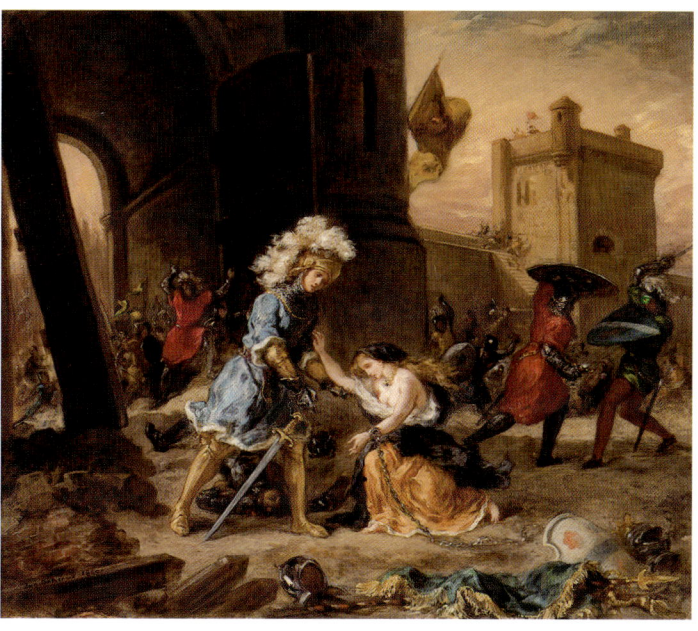

Edouard Manet
On the Beach, Boulogne-sur-Mer

"Pure painting." So Edouard Manet's work is often described. He celebrated the art itself—brushstroke, color, and contrast—while exploring subjects of modern Paris. His images of authors, bohemians, courtesans, and dandies gave the art of painting a new twist, fresh and forthright. Surface rivals story for attention: we look as closely at the paint and the brushwork in *On the Beach, Boulogne-sur-Mer* as we do the figures and the seascape. Manet asks the viewer to see *how* he painted as much as *what* he painted. We may also see traces of Boudin's contemporary seascapes (in the Virginia Museum's galleries).

This picture is one of seven inspired by Manet's mid-career holiday at Boulogne, along the southern English Channel. Though they are small, the paintings mark a turning point in the artist's experiments with loosened brushwork and sharpened contrasts. Among his famous pictures, *Luncheon on the Grass* and *Olympia* had already stirred controversy. His well-known late paintings, such as *Gare St. Lazare, Nana,* and *Bar at Folies Bergère,* were yet to come.

In *On the Beach, Boulogne-sur-Mer,* Manet sketches figures and objects with a swift but calculated brush. A simple stroke or single color suddenly forms a veiled face, the brim of a straw hat, or the roof of a bathing cabin. Black paint, placed against white, beige, or gray, abruptly juxtaposes light and dark. It punctuates the painting by fixing the figures against a neutral ground. Opposing styles coexist: flat shapes and rounded forms, silhouettes and filled-in figures, shadowy images and concrete ones. Scale sometimes varies without rhyme or reason; space from beach to sea to sky seems to recede, and yet it also looks layered. By flattening space and disrupting scale, Manet invites us to see the purity of painting. A picture does not have to represent reality as we might expect.

For this painting, Manet made at least eighteen figure drawings, which he combined into new arrangements in the painting. Each painted group becomes a study in scale, perspective, or technique. Manet inserted a child from one sketch between a parasol-porting woman and child taken from another. He placed a young boy, back-turned, between two playmates from a separate drawing. He transformed one distinctly outlined drawing of three women into a painted blur. Mere hints of bonnets and bows suggest women seated on a bench. Slightly wind-blown from northern breezes, Manet's figures take their places up and down the beach of Boulogne, offering a new, spontaneous way of seeing and painting.

Manet and Art History
Manet understood the long tradition of academic art in Europe. He once wrote that he did not "claim either to overthrow traditional painting or to create a new style" but that he had "simply tried to be himself."

Manet and Impressionism
Often associated with the Impressionists (Monet, Renoir, Sisley, Pissaro, and Morisot, among others), Manet's interests differed from theirs: he concentrated on figures rather than landscapes, he used black paint, and he usually painted indoors rather than in the open air. Nevertheless, from the Impressionists, Manet adopted a lighter palette and they, in turn, adapted his techniques of fresh, unaltered color and forms created by a dab or stroke of color.

On the Beach, Boulogne-sur-Mer,
circa 1868–69
Edouard Manet (French, 1832–1883)
Oil on canvas; 21½ by 34½ inches
Virginia Museum of Fine Arts, Collection of Mr. and Mrs. Paul Mellon, 85.498

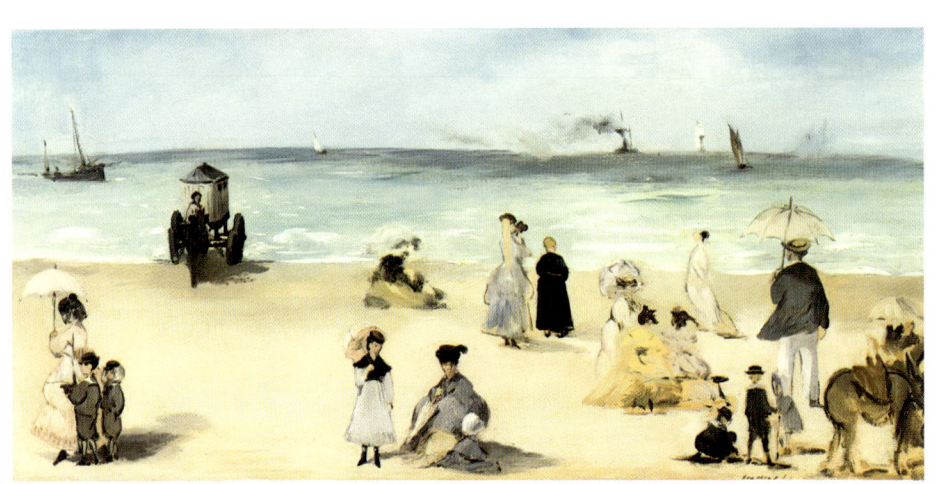

Edgar Degas
Racecourse: Before the Start

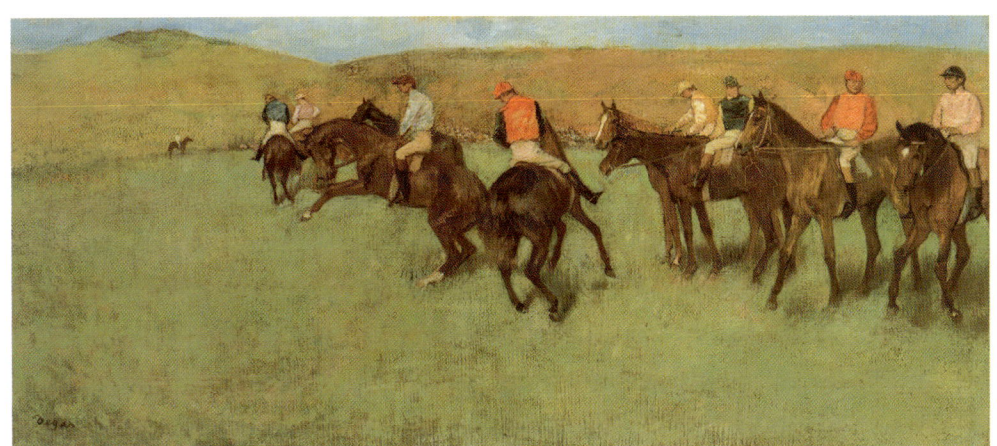

Edgar Degas' *Racecourse* instantly conveys the spirit of his art. He brushes color across the canvas and arrests a world of motion, where thoroughbreds and jockeys restlessly await a call to post. As horses enter our field of vision, others gallop out of sight into the distance. Some nod and stretch; one rears; another veers in response to tugged reins. Three jockeys converse, while a fourth pats his horse's neck. Degas casts wispy clouds against a turquoise sky, lights the hills in gold, and blankets the paddock in soft green. Silks and caps catch our eye: blues, greens, and yellows—shot with orange, lavender, and white—repeat the colors of the landscape.

Degas devoted his life to art. He aspired to freeze the motion of life and to make the ineffable permanent, without a loss of momentum or vitality. He is often regarded as an Impressionist—because of his fleeting subjects, color, and brushwork—yet he railed against the techniques of painters who worked outdoors *(en plein air),* recording their observations directly on canvas. "Painting is not a sport," Degas declared. He followed the classic techniques of European old

masters: he painted in a studio, where composition and lighting could be controlled. Often quoted as saying "no art is less spontaneous than mine," Degas worked from countless drawings and studies. In the tradition of Watteau and Renaissance painters before him, Degas painted figures from his notebook sketches, which served as "pattern books," used again and again.

While the spontaneity of horses and jockeys might seduce the viewer into believing the artist's ease in painting them, Degas has artfully contrived and calculated every step in his quest to "uncover the mystery of the real." From endless sketches of equine anatomy—"to bring thoroughbreds to life"—spirited Bays and Chestnuts emerge in sunlight, their coats and shadows touched with muted green, lavender, and gray.

Degas' informal pictures glimpse "real" life in modern Paris—laundresses, milliners, bathers, portraits of friends and family. Thoroughbred horses and ballerinas became his favorite subjects, his epitome of "exalted movement and grace" (see Degas, pp. 74–75). Yet, his images of

unselfconscious gesture, seen as if through a keyhole or camera lens, are envelopes of introspection: a dancer concentrating on a pose, a horse preparing for a race. Degas catches fleeting external movements—a turned head, a tensed muscle, a drawn breath—and flickers of internal emotion. As horse and rider strike momentary poses and suggest a mood or thought, we see their private world through Degas' eyes.

Degas and Photography

Eadweard Muybridge's photographs of horses in motion—published in Paris in 1874, 1878, and 1887—contributed to the accuracy of Degas' drawing, although the painter's efforts to record motion began much earlier. Degas' angles, perspectives, and casual croppings share much in common with photography's new visual possibilities.

Degas and Art History

Degas enjoyed an extensive visual education in Assyrian, Japanese, ancient Greek art, and the English sporting print. He studied European masters in Italy and at the Louvre. At twenty-one, Degas met the revered Jean-Auguste Ingres, who offered sage advice: "draw lines, young man, draw lines from nature and memory."

Racecourse: Before the Start, circa 1880
Edgar Degas (French, 1834–1917)
Oil on canvas; 15¾ by 35⅜ inches
Virginia Museum of Fine Arts Gift, Collection of Mr. and Mrs. Paul Mellon, 85.496

Edgar Degas
Dressed Dancer at Rest *and* Horse Walking

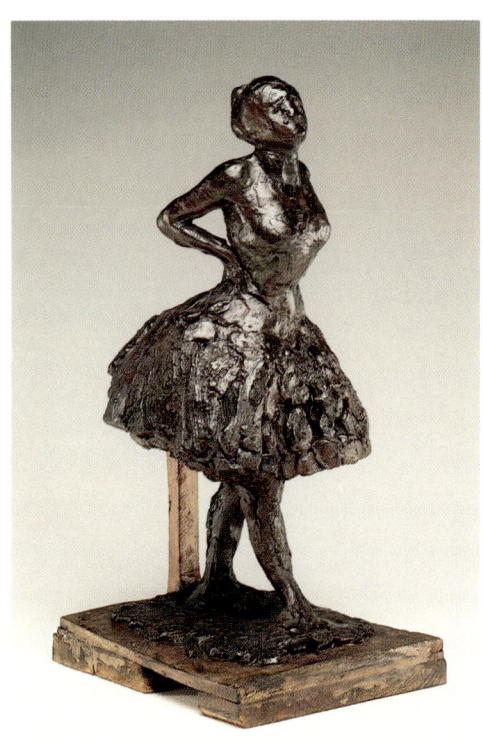

Edgar Degas loved the gracefulness of the ballerina and the thoroughbred. He favored dancers and horses as vehicles for expressing movement in painting and sculpture (see p. 73). His oils and pastels reveal an appreciation of finely tuned bodies and lithe limbs, human— often female—and equine. His waxes show how he worked, restlessly seeking to capture a figure's essence through a pose. He catches quiet moments: training or practicing, getting ready to perform, resting.

Degas experimented with wax figures late in his career: "Why am I throwing myself into sculpture at my age?" he wrote. When he died, he left 150 wax statuettes strewn about his studio. Many of the fragile forms had deteriorated and could not be preserved, but more than seventy were saved and later served as models for sets of bronzes. Here an original wax dancer settles herself. As she stretches, she leans forward slightly, tightening her calf muscles and pressing her hands against her back. The artist has pressed the figure into being; as Degas shaped her head, eyes, nose, breasts, and tutu, he left finger prints and knife impressions in the dark wax.

Degas made his walking horse from a lighter, reddish brown wax. The bronze counterpart, almost a mirror image of the wax, was cast after Degas' death. The two horses raise their heads and open their mouths as if champing at their bits. They strike counterpoised stances; each horse elevates one front and one back leg on opposite sides as if to prance.

Degas built his wax figures around armatures made of flexible wires, so that he could change their poses. He loved the artistic process of beginning over and over again, reworking the wax: "Nobody will see these experiments.... Before my death, all of this will disintegrate of its own accord and it will be just as well." He even experimented with less expensive materials to stretch the costly beeswax and plasticine (a sculptor's paste with a 1897 French trademark). This dancer, in fact, wears a petticoat of wine-bottle corks mixed with wax to form the fullness of her tutu.

The dancer also wears her history: her surface not only records Degas' work but also the restorers', who inevitably left their fingerprints behind as they worked to preserve the malleable waxes for bronze-casting and posterity. Degas may not have intended to make his statuettes in bronze—a material he regarded as permanent and eternal. Still, when Degas' critical colleague, Mary Cassatt, saw the Hébrard foundry's exhibition of the bronze casts in 1921, she succinctly characterized the state of her late friend's sculpture: "It is very rare...that an artist has equal talent for painting and sculpture.... All artists and collectors are indebted to you for the admirable work you have done in reproducing so perfectly these fragile works in bronze."

Walking Horse in Wax and Bronze
These twin horses show the history of their making. The wax horse has a gap in its mane and an extended tail. No gap or hole appears on the bronze horse's neck; its tail is lowered. The bronze may have been cast from a corrected intermediary wax model, made from Degas' original wax figure.

Models and Casts
After Degas' death, twenty-two sets of bronzes were made by founder Adrien Hébrard from seventy-four surviving waxes. The process consisted of making duplicate waxes from the originals, to serve as "wasters" sacrificed and replaced with molten metal in lost-wax casting. The resulting master bronzes then served as the matrix from which the Hébrard foundry made new waxes for subsequent bronze casts, which are smaller and have less surface detail. Of the original twenty-two sets of bronzes casts, A. A. Hébrard's family and foundry kept one group, Degas' heirs another, and twenty sets were sold to collectors and museums.

Degas' *Little Dancer, Age Fourteen*

The wax original was the only sculpture Degas ever exhibited, on view for one month at the Sixth Impressionist Exhibition in 1881. It was shown again, after Degas' death, at the Hébrard Gallery exhibition in 1921. Probably not cast in bronze until 1922, the Little Dancer *now exists in two plaster casts and twenty-eight bronzes, including one in the Virginia Museum's gallery. A nude version of the* Dressed Dancer *also exists in wax.*

Collectors of Waxes and Bronzes

Mary Cassatt (see p. 90) bought a complete set of Degas' bronzes from Hébrard's 1921 exhibition for the Havemeyer collection. Of the original waxes, seventy (including the Little Dancer*) survived the casting process and were stored by the Hébrard foundry. The Norton Simon Foundation acquired the master casts in 1976. In 1955, Mr. and Mrs. Paul Mellon purchased*

sixty-nine Hébrard waxes, some mixed with plasticine and plaster, and have since given waxes as gifts to several museums: The Louvre and the Musee d'Orsay; The Fitzwilliam Museum, Cambridge, England; The National Gallery, Washington, D.C.; and the Virginia Museum of Fine Arts.

A Small History of Degas' Small Sculpture

Degas' fascination with the subject of racehorses began in the 1860s; dancers came later in the 1880s and 1890s. His work in wax dates from the late 1860s to 1917, as his eyesight continued to fail. Some of Degas' wax figures are the same size as his drawn or painted figures. Many scholars see them as complements. Others believe the waxes served as studies, and some think they existed independently of Degas' flat work. In 1977, researchers at the Museum of Fine Arts, Boston, reconstructed the restorers' and the Hébrard foundry's

steps in making the bronzes. Recent scholarship has traced the whereabouts of all known bronzes cast from Degas' originals; the National Gallery, Washington, D.C., has recently been conducting studies of the waxes, which reveal how hastily Degas constructed his armatures.

Dressed Dancer at Rest, Hands Behind Her Back, Right Leg Forward, circa 1895
Edgar Degas (French, 1834–1917)
Wax with cork; 16¾ by 8⅛ by 10½ inches
Virginia Museum of Fine Arts Gift, Collection of
  Mr. and Mrs. Paul Mellon, 93.63

Horse Walking, circa 1866–68
Wax; 9¼ by 4½ by 8½ inches
Bronze; circa 1919–21
Virginia Museum of Fine Arts Gift, Collection of
  Mr. and Mrs. Paul Mellon, 93.57

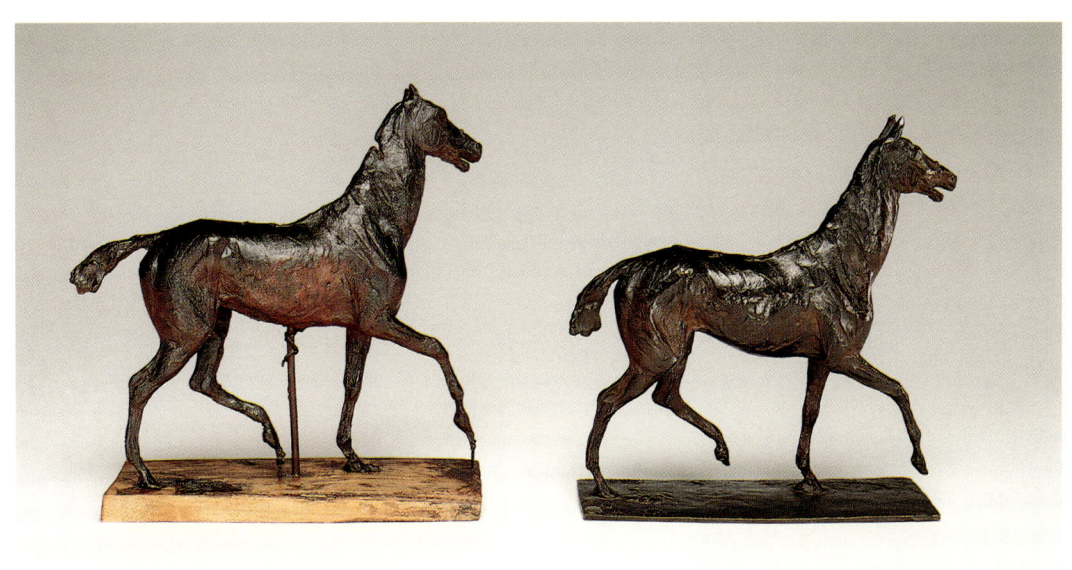

Edouard Vuillard, The Golden Chair

Edouard Vuillard, it has been said, could "paint the pauses in polite conversations." Vuillard turns the spaces of Paris interiors into rich still lifes of quiet moments. His sitters linger in rooms brimming with vases of flowers and floral fabrics, patterned carpets and printed wallpaper. As Vuillard brushes tints and shades into his colors, he hints at the elusive nature of light-filled surfaces and shadowed recesses. In this picture, shades of blue, rose, and lavender shoot through golden chairs and wooden boards; red paint darts across furniture and floor, alights on a screen, and trims a fireplace, flecked with blue and green.

"I was looking at the objects that surrounded me...the molding of the woodwork, the chair with its back of carved wood, the paper on the wall, the knobs of the open door.... I was struck by the abundance of ornament...not one of these inanimate objects had any

connection with another.... All the same there was a vivid atmosphere." So Vuillard describes the wonder of simple scenes, as if seen for the first time and then painted to be contemplated.

The Golden Chair conveys Vuillard's vision, which balances and almost blends animate and inanimate objects. "In the middle of all these objects I was astonished to see Mama enter," he once reflected. "The arrival of Mama was surprising— a living person. For the painter, the differences of shapes, of forms, were interest enough." In *The Golden Chair,* the "living person" very likely takes the form of Vuillard's sister, Marie, and her eight-year-old daughter, Annette. Fond of his niece, Vuillard depicted her as often as he did his mother (see *The Artist's Mother* in the Virginia Museum's galleries). Here, in the background, Annette sits upright with childlike anticipation on the edge of her upholstered seat. Marie casually drapes her arm across the back of a matching armchair and leans her head against her hand. Cropped by the frame and seen from a skewed perspective, a velvet settee and vertical screen fill the back corner of the parlor; paintings, moldings, and mirrors line the walls; a crystal clock, brass candelabra, and painted porcelain decorate the mantelpiece.

Gathering ordinary objects together, Vuillard creates sumptuous interiors that stir comforting and wistful feelings. As if looking at one of Vuillard's paintings, author

Marcel Proust—who knew the artist— describes how memories take shape as mental pictures, emerging from an "elusive whirling medley of stirred-up colors." For Proust, the taste of tea and madeleines summoned remembrances of towns, gardens, and great-aunt's rooms from this "whirling medley." For Vuillard, "stirred-up colors" coalesce into sitters and surroundings graced by notes of nostalgia and poignant recollection.

Vuillard's Variety of Styles
Vuillard is known primarily for his intimate interiors and patterned portraits. He also painted theater sets, large decorative panels for clients' homes and libraries, and small landscapes (one in the Virginia Museum's galleries). Early in his career, in the late 1880s, he joined the artistic brotherhood of the Nabis (Hebrew for "prophets"), with Maurice Denis, Pierre Bonnard, and Vuillard's brother-in-law Ker-Xavier Roussel. Simplified forms, flat patterns, bold colors, and the use of symbols characterize the Nabis style, influenced by Japanese prints and by Paul Gauguin.

Women and Children
Vuillard loved to paint the worlds of women and children in public gardens or private homes, as did other artists of his day— Edouard Manet, Berthe Morisot, Edgar Degas, Mary Cassatt (see p. 90). He saw women as sources of beauty; he saw children, busy and engaging, as sources of charm. Children reappear in Vuillard's paintings; we watch them as they grow up.

The Golden Chair, 1906
Edouard Vuillard (French, 1868–1940)
Oil on panel; 26¾ x 26¼ inches
Virginia Museum of Fine Arts, Collection of Mr. and
  Mrs. Paul Mellon, 84.4

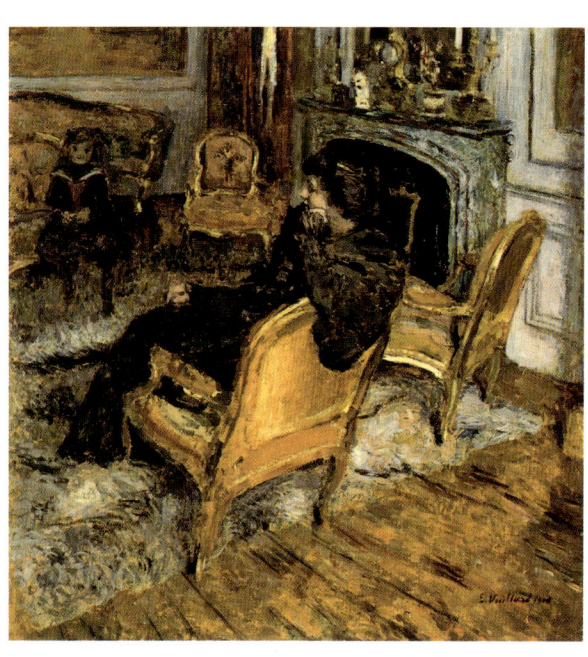

Henri Rousseau, Tropical Landscape—
An American Indian Struggling with a Gorilla

Henri Rousseau's searing red sun draws us into his lush tropical landscape. Although clear and still, the jungle is a wild place where secrets and surprises lurk. Tropics teem with exotic plants from different continents; a man struggles with a gorilla.

The title tells us what we see, and yet the painting baffles us. Rousseau himself offered a hint: "Nothing makes me so happy as to observe nature and paint what I see." Observe nature he did, reading encyclopedias and visiting botanical gardens and zoos in his native Paris. Yuccas, snake plants, giant coleus, eucalyptus, palms, rubber trees, and lotus blossoms thrive in his paintings. Still, Rousseau's pictures do not abide by laws of nature. His world is born of the artist's fancy, which freed him, in his words, to "paint what I see."

Rousseau saw a world of art open to his imagination. His paintings—called "magical counterworlds" where anything is possible—celebrate a new epoch of modern painting. Known as a "naive" or "primitive" painter, both admired and ridiculed by his fellow artists and critics, Rousseau broke with European traditions of rendering space, scale, and perspective. Overgrown plants dwarf man and gorilla; leaves and blossoms do not recede from the viewer but, instead, flatten against the canvas. Carefully painted, as if to be more clearly understood, each feather, petal, leaf, and face receives the artist's equal attention.

In Rousseau's world, figures and settings exist in balanced harmony. The same sun-warmed orange, tinted with yellow ocher, bathes man and lotus blossom alike. Dense vegetation grows across the painting like tropical scaffolding. Rendered in more than fifty shades of green, Rousseau's unifying grids of jungle foliage

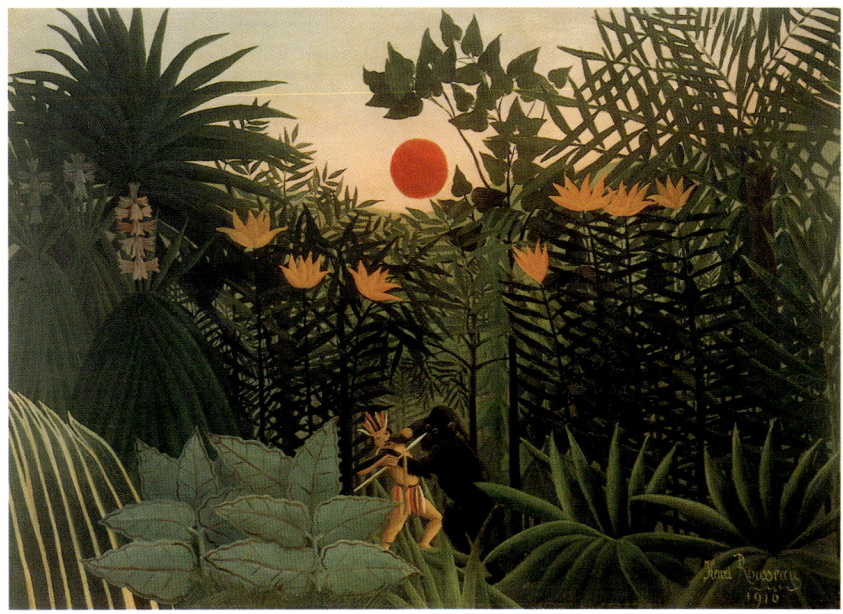

show variety in each plant. He defines a spikey frond here, a flower stalk there. Rousseau gathers the full range of his palette into the feathers of a fanciful headdress and loincloth: red, orange, ochers, greens, and whites. Seen up close each brushstroke carries a slightly different tint or shade. At a distance the painting seems smooth and seamless, with undetectable transitions from the lightest blue-green to the palest pink-orange sky. Playful and eerie, Rousseau's dreamlike tropics may seem uncomplicated; their recesses, however, are as fertile and as puzzling as the human imagination.

Rousseau's Myths and Paradoxes
He announced at Picasso's famous banquet that he and his host were "the greatest painters of our time." He was called a simpleton, a naive, a dreamer, and a genius. He is known as the douanier *(customs*

official), although he collected municipal tolls in Paris. Never having traveled to America, he held a romantic view of the wild west in the era of George Catlin (see p. 86). He shared Cézanne's belief in painting as nature's equal, not its imitation; Gauguin's passion for exotic lands; Picasso's fascination with a subject's underlying structure. He exhibited with Matisse. All this, and he claimed to have started painting in his forties. Rousseau's first tropical landscape is dated 1891 and his last in 1910, the year of this picture.

***Tropical Landscape—An American Indian Struggling with a Gorilla,** 1910*
Henri Rousseau (French, 1844–1910)
Oil on canvas; 44¾ by 64 inches
Virginia Museum of Fine Arts Gift. Collection of
  Mr. and Mrs. Paul Mellon, 84.3

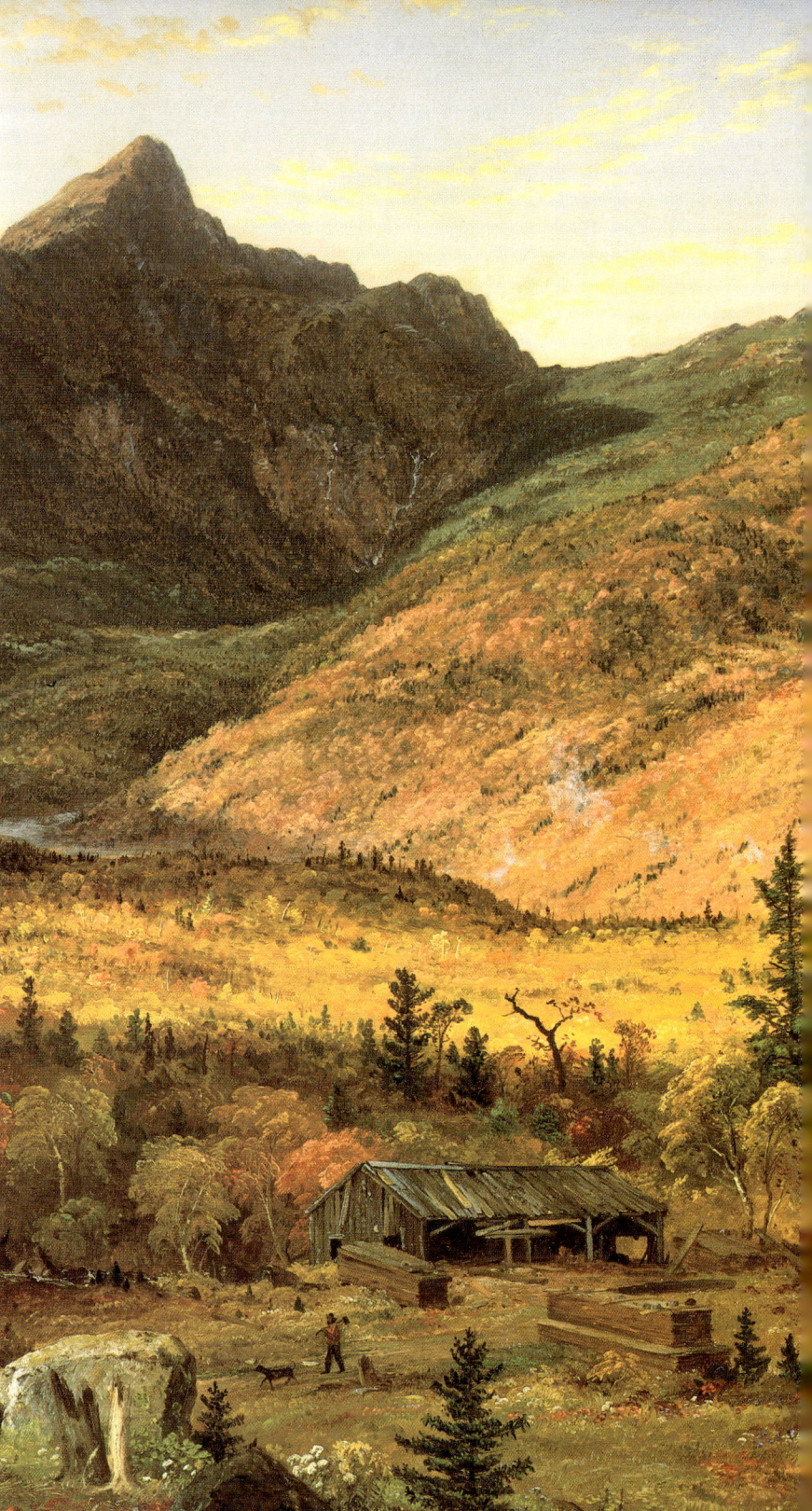

CHAPTER 7

American Art

1700s

1800s

1900s

Japanned High Chest

As delicate as it is delightful, this *Japanned High Chest* offers a rare opportunity to experience the William and Mary style from colonial Boston, the center of American "japanning." Painted black to simulate Asian lacquer, the storage chest serves as a dramatic background for lively gilded "chinoiserie," fanciful combinations of Chinese, Indian, and Japanese motifs. On this piece, an imaginary landscape unfolds—a world of weeping willows, elephants, and dragons. Flowers, reeds, and ribbons decorate every corner of the surface. Birds fly and horses gallop between peopled pagodas, bridges, and boats.

"Japanners" typically painted "flat" ornaments over designs inscribed on the surface of the wood. The more prominent motifs were treated as "raised" ornaments, molded of gesso in shallow relief. Layers of reddish-brown stain, sizing, gilding, brushed details, and varnish create the finished decorative effect, treasured for its fragility.

The chest itself, made in two sections, provides sturdy support for the precious painted decoration. The chest is made primarily of white pine; maple is used as a secondary wood. Typical of Boston's japanned-style high chests, an architectural cornice and flat top crown this piece. It stands on unusual legs, however, carved with "English-style" facets. Named for England's William of Orange and Mary Stuart—who followed the fashion for oriental-style wares inspired by French and Dutch artisans and created by English craftsmen around 1690—the William and Mary style traveled to the colonies to be crafted in furniture between 1690 and 1730. A *Treatise of Japanning and Varnishing*, published in Oxford in 1688, served English artisans, who then influenced the dozen or so "japanners" active in Boston in the early 1700s.

Among them were William Randle and his son-in-law Robert Davis, whose talents may be seen in this *High Chest*.

William and Mary-Style Furniture

The period from 1690 to 1730 produced a taste for tall and sculptural furniture—high chests and tall-back chairs—as well as dressing tables, secretaries, and gate-legged tables. Energy and ornament characterize these pieces. Cone-shaped turnings, curves and scrolls, and foliate detail enliven wooden surfaces, as did the art of "japanning."

Cabinetmaking

Design, wood, and the language of furniture-making changed with the William and Mary style. Dovetailing and veneering replaced techniques of joining and pegging. Instead of panels—often oak—attached within frames, thin veneers of walnut and ash burl were glued to lighter-weight pine panels. The construction offered new design possibilities, especially for taller furniture. Artisans evolved from old-fashioned "joiners" of wooden panels into highly skilled "cabinetmakers." Born into a family of Boston joiners whose trade had evolved into cabinetmaking, John Scottow made this Japanned High Chest.

Eastern Imagery in Western Art

"Japanned" motifs on the High Chest *may seem familiar from patterns in the blue-and-white ware of Chinese porcelain. Asian influences surface throughout the collections of Western art in the Virginia Museum of Fine Arts; Far Eastern motifs may be found in American and European art from the 1700s through the 1900s, including this work by Randle and Davis, the Herter Brothers (see p. 89), Mary Cassatt (p. 90), Hector Guimard (p. 98), and Eileen Gray (p. 104).*

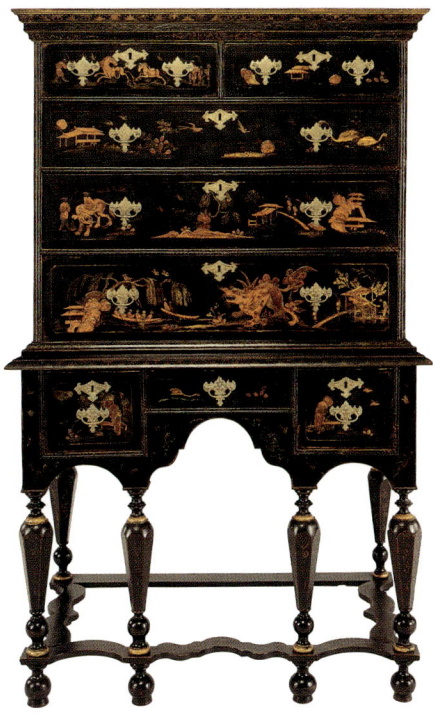

Japanned High Chest, 1720–30
Cabinet by John Scottow (American, 1701–1790)
Japanning attributed to William Randle and Robert Davis (American, active 1720–circa 1735)
Painted and gilded white pine with maple drawer fronts; 64¼ by 40¾ by 22½ inches
Virginia Museum of Fine Arts Purchase, The Adolph D. and Wilkins C. Williams Fund, 91.8a/b

Charles Willson Peale
William Smith and His Grandson, Robert Smith Williams

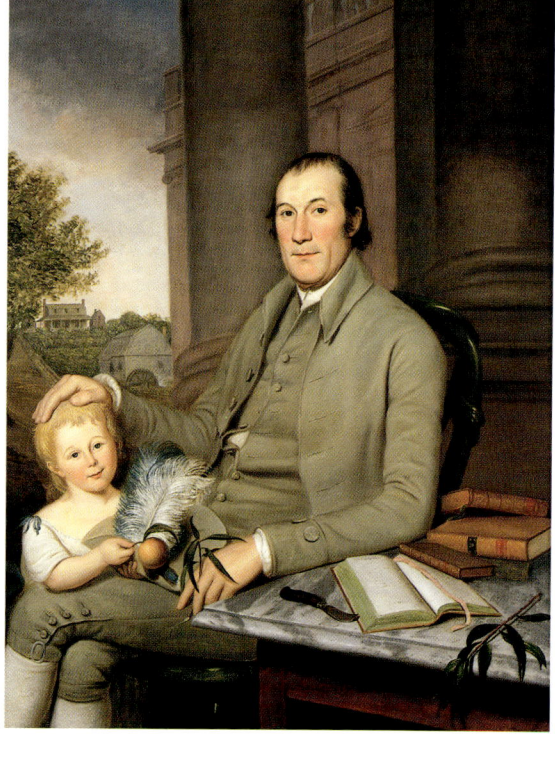

In this pastoral setting, ripe with peaches and poetry, soft light falls on the faces of Smith and his grandson, illuminating a scene of casual elegance and high social position. Rosy cheeks, loosened vest, and tousled hair—free of period wigs—project an image of leisure at the family home. Trappings of country life surround the pair. The grandson holds an ostrich-plumed sunbonnet and proffers a freshly picked peach. A pruning knife rests on the marble-top table beside the grandfather, next to an open book on gardening, turned to share its lessons with the viewer. The unpretentious painting conveys good health and good citizenship. Charles Willson Peale's portrait of the Maryland Congressman, his young heir, and his family legacy and land, maps out the idealism of a new Federalist nation.

Peale paints crisp forms, smooth surfaces, and sharp details of button, buckle, and bow; light, color, and brushstroke are unobtrusive and understated. Peale nods to patriotism, placing the sitters in the foreground of their country estate at Eutaw Springs, the site of a decisive Revolutionary War battle led by the boy's father. The artist then alludes to classical virtues by seating the grandfather—dignified, solid, and forthright—in front of classical columns and pediments. Smith, a wealthy Baltimore flour merchant, asked that his grandson join him for the sitting (which actually took place at his townhouse). Blessing the boy, the grandfather affectionately places his hand on the child's head, to form the picture of family devotion and domestic harmony considered essential to a republic's well-being. The imaginary backdrop connotes wealth, prosperity, and idyllic retreat: a country house to be filled with burgeoning

American arts; orchard, mill, and waterwheel to reap the rural rewards of a young nation.

William Smith is a well-read Congressional embodiment of republican duty. Peale's simple and direct likeness suggests the honest and trustworthy nature of his sitter (though Smith was not without political detractors). The artist's teacher Benjamin West, a founding father of American painting, would later write to him that "correctness of line" and "justness of character" are the truths for which a portrait painter should strive. Peale's own vows to remember only the virtuous in painting—"never paint the portrait of a bad man"—inspire this image.

Peale, Portraiture, and Patriotism

Peale preserved history as it was being made. He painted the founding fathers— George Washington, Thomas Jefferson, and John Adams—who praised him for his ingenuity. A "founding father" himself, he established the first U.S. portrait gallery and natural history museum, to bring "into public view the beauties of nature and art," he proclaimed. Peale's zeal for art and science—patriotic portraiture and wildlife taxidermy—led him to propose to an audience of founding fathers that not only their likenesses but also their actual remains be preserved for posterity. (He lamented his failure to "prevail" upon his friend Ben Franklin in time to do so.) An artist, soldier, and naturalist, Peale left

a legacy through his art, inventions, and seventeen children, named for his favorite scientists and for painters Titian, Rembrandt, Raphaelle, Rubens (see p. 58), and Angelica Kauffman (p. 67).

Emblems of Enlightenment
In this painting, spines of books stamped Milton, Beattie's Essays, Thompson's Seasons, *and a page casually turned to* "Gardening" *reveal this family's education in the arts and sciences. Pragmatic Americans admired James Beattie's Scottish "common sense" philosophy;* The Seasons *imitated classical Latin idylls, extolling the virtues of country life.*

William Smith and His Grandson, Robert Smith Williams, 1788
Charles Willson Peale (American, 1741–1827)
Oil on canvas; 51¼ by 40⅜ inches
Virginia Museum of Fine Arts Purchase, The Robert G. Cabell III and Maude Morgan Cabell Foundation and The Arthur and Margaret Glasgow Fund, 75.11

Paul Revere, Teapot and Stand

This striking silver teapot and stand reflect the high style and practicality of American hospitality during the Federal period, 1785 to 1825. This elegant vessel graced teatime in Boston; its base stood poised to protect a fine wooden sideboard or table. Together they form a fitting tribute to their creator.

The name "Paul Revere" triggers patriotic reveries—the Sons of Liberty, the Boston Tea Party, lantern-lit midnight rides. Yet the man himself was best known in his day as a silversmith. When a Boston newspaper published the obituary for Paul Revere II, it praised his acts of "benevolence or general utility." "Cool in thought, ardent in action," Paul Revere possessed honesty, integrity, and adaptability, which led to his success as craftsman, businessman, and patriot.

Here he shaped and soldered this stylish Neoclassical set from a rolled silver sheet. The stand's dainty ribbed feet and scalloped edge echo the fluting of the teapot's oval body, to create a harmony of surfaces from bottom to top. A carved wooden handle on one side repeats the curves at play around the pot, balanced on the opposite side by a straight, long spout, sporting an engraved acorn. A pinecone finial crowns the hinged cover, to invite a peek at the teapot's contents. The surface sings with classical motifs: swags and sashes, tassels and trimmings, finished by two ribbons of scrolling leaf patterns. The engraved motifs create shallow grooves that sparkle as they catch the light, revealing Revere's "bright-cut" technique.

The son of French goldsmith Apollos Rivoire, who emigrated to the colonies to become Paul Revere I, Paul Revere II first worked as an apprentice metalsmith in his father's shop. He also trained as an engraver of prints and bookplates, then embarked on successful ventures in metal-casting, copper-rolling mills, and silversmithing. In 1790, he featured the first of his "Silver fluted and Engraved teapots," which would become hallmarks, treasured today, like his patriotism.

American Silver

Silver grew in popularity after the American Revolution as a tasteful expression of wealth and a practical investment. Rolling mills produced sheet silver of a uniform gauge, which saved the silversmith time, reduced costs, and increased inventory. No assay office existed in the young nation to certify metal, so the guaranteed quality of a given piece depended upon the silversmith's integrity and materials. Success as a silversmith rested on personal pledges, and so Paul Revere, whose sterling character inspired trust, achieved success in his trade.

Neoclassicism

The Neoclassical style, with roots in the classical art of ancient Greece and Rome, became fashionable in the young republic during its formative years, 1780s–1790s. Inspired by Roman artifacts unearthed at Herculaneum and Pompeii in the 1740s and 1750s, the style is one of symmetry and restrained ornament—garlands, festoons, and fluting—as expressed in Paul Revere's teapot and stand.

Pineapples and Pinecones

Identified as pineapples or pinecones, and sometimes even as artichokes or acorns, conical finials with prickly leaves derive from the arts of antiquity. Whether cast on a small scale in silver or carved from large stone blocks (one sits above the original entrance to the Virginia Museum), these spiny forms are regarded as symbols of American hospitality.

Teapot and Stand, 1790–95
Paul Revere II (American, 1735–1818)
Silver, wooden handle; Teapot: 6¼ by 11¾ by 3⅝ (diameter) inches; Stand: 1 by 7⅜ by 5¼ inches
Virginia Museum of Fine Arts, Gift of Daniel D., Lilburn T., and Edmund M. Talley in memory of their mother, Anne Myers Talley, and Museum Purchase, The Arthur and Margaret Glasgow Fund, 91.392a/b

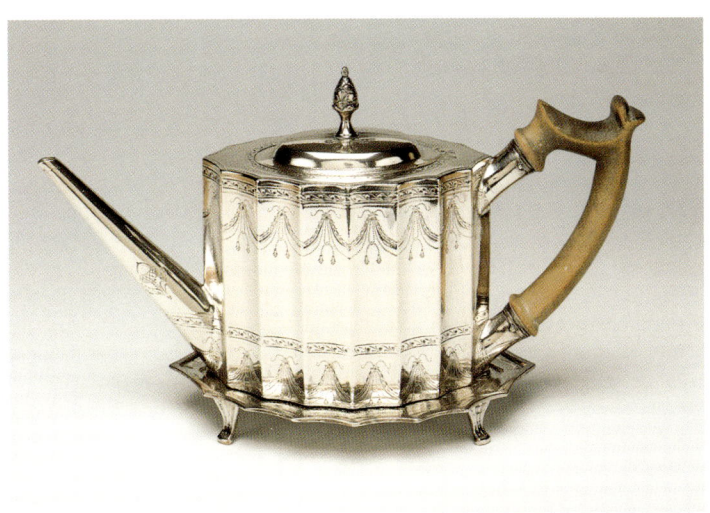

Federal Style Shield-Back Armchair
Empire Style Lyre-Base Card Table

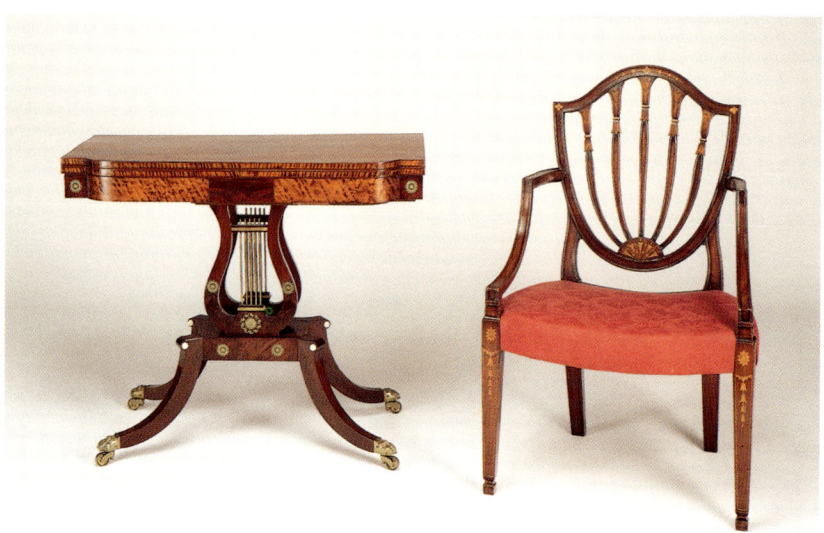

The simple beauty of this lyre-base table and shield-back chair leads the viewer into the world of southern living in the young United States. Both share roots in Virginia. The chair hails from the northern part of the Old Dominion; the table, one of a pair from Philadelphia, served family and friends in a Virginia home during the mid 1800s.

The revived interest in the arts of antiquity, which inspired American furniture-makers after the Revolutionary War, pervades both chair and table. Each expresses a love of fine, rich wood—primarily mahogany—carved into a perfect sculptural balance of simple curves, straight lines, and open spaces. Dainty ornamental designs, based on antique decorative details, present subtle surprises. Inlaid wood provides touches of color. A fan of tulips springs from the base of its shield-shaped back. Flowered traceries cascade across the shield's crest and down the legs. The table is enlivened by

maple veneer. Beaded pinwheels provide brass counterpoints to dark wood, while turned ivory buttons punctuate the platform as it splays into legs. Brass lyre "strings" and "lion's-paw" feet complete the detail.

The Federal-style chair and the Empire-style table bracket forty years of fashion in American furniture. Up and down the East Coast, artisans of the new nation created unique interpretations of imported English and French traditions. Centers for American crafts flourished in Boston, New York, and Philadelphia, as well as Baltimore, Norfolk, and Charleston.

Cabinetmakers and furniture designers—the Englishman George Hepplewhite and later, under his influence, the American Duncan Phyfe—set the standards for interior decor. Hepplewhite-style furniture grew in reputation after the designer's death, when his widow, Alice, published an influential pattern-book of the firm's designs, *The Cabinet-Maker and Upholsterer's*

Guide (London, 1788). To make this chair, the Virginia artisan apparently found a pattern in the *Guide*. He improvised by adding a saddle seat in Philadelphia's Federal style. Today this chair is one of only two known examples of its kind.

A generation later, the furniture-maker in Philadelphia based his table on the work of Duncan Phyfe (1768–1854), the New York cabinetmaker famous for his adaptations of the French Empire style. Classical motifs favored in chairs, card tables, and sofas from Phyfe's workshop—the ever-popular Greek lyre shape, concave legs, claw feet, and metal mounts (applied ornaments)—lend a graceful air to this card table.

The Fine Art of American Furniture

Classical revivals created a taste for delicacy and lightness, expressed in contrasting veneers or detailed, coloristic inlays of wood. Furniture in the Hepplewhite style often consists of straight though tapering legs, serpentine lines, and chairs with backs in the shape of a shield, a heart, or an oval. Empire furniture, named for the Napoleonic era in France, often features lyre and wing motifs, pawed feet, scrolled backs, and concave legs.

Shield-Back Armchair
Northern Virginia, circa 1790–1800
Mahogany inlaid with holly, yellow pine; 36½ by 24 by 20 inches
Virginia Museum of Fine Arts Purchase, The Floyd D. and Anne C. Gottwald Fund, 95.81

Lyre-Base Card Table
Philadelphia, circa 1830
Mahogany, brass, and ivory; 29½ by 35 by 17⅛ inches, closed
Virginia Museum of Fine Arts Purchase, The Mary Morton Parsons Fund for American Decorative Arts, 78.5.1/2

Junius Brutus Stearns
Washington Addressing the Constitutional Convention

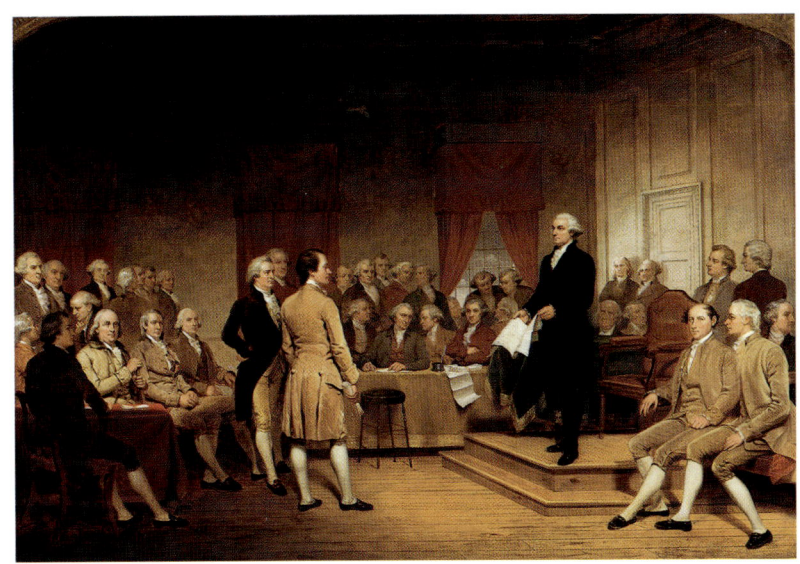

Posed like actors on a stage, renowned statesmen gather before us in Philadelphia at the Constitutional Convention of 1787 under the persuasive powers of George Washington. Urging the delegation to draft the constitution for the American government, he now waits, ignoring whispers and furtive asides. Quill pens in ink pots stand ready to deliver signatures.

Junius Brutus Stearns re-created this scene one year after Washington's "mighty moral influence" had been so described in a publication of 1855. That same year, on the anniversary of Washington's birthday, the Assembly Room in Philadelphia's Independence Hall—the site of the convention—had been declared a national shrine. Called the "father" of his country, as states formed a national identity, Washington had acquired an almost godlike image by the 1850s as the "sun" around which a "whole system" revolved. Indeed, in Stearns' painting, Washington commands the center of

attention at this turning point in the new nation's history.

Stearns surrounds Washington with a few touches of Federal-period interiors—cornice moldings, paneled walls, multi-paned windows, valences, curtains, and worn wood floors. In truth, this Assembly Room no more resembles the site as it appeared in 1787 than it does the chamber that Stearns would have seen almost seventy years later, in 1856. In Stearns' day, the room was lined with paintings by Charles Willson Peale (see p. 80).

Yet while Stearns' setting is largely imaginary, his likenesses are accurate. Of the delegates present at the Statehouse that day, fifteen may be identified in this painting. The most prominent figures sit in pairs and catch our eye: Pennsylvania's Benjamin Franklin and Virginia's James Madison; Abraham Baldwin of Georgia and Rufus King of Massachusetts. New York's Alexander Hamilton stands with his back turned to the viewer.

Stearns' drama romanticizes Washington as a steady statesman devoted to a nation's ideals. By staging an exemplary moment in the country's development, Stearns is true to the often edifying nature of earlier American art, created in service of a national character.

The History of the Painting
This painting and three others by Stearns— Washington as Captain in the French and Indian War, The Marriage of George Washington, *and* Washington as a Farmer—*depict the first president as statesman, soldier, husband, and planter. The Virginia Museum of Fine Arts received the series as a gift in 1950 on Washington's birthday, February 22. In 1987, in honor of the U.S. Constitution's bicentennial, the painting was displayed at the U.S. Supreme Court. It ranks among the most often reproduced paintings in American art, featured in textbooks, film strips, and encyclopedias.*

American Paintings and Prints
Because of new developments in lithography during the 1800s, Stearns' four paintings of Washington were produced as affordable prints almost as soon as he finished painting them. An early set is now preserved in the Virginia Museum.

Washington Addressing
the Constitutional Convention, 1856
Junius Brutus Stearns (American, 1810–1885)
Oil on canvas; 37½ by 54 inches
Virginia Museum of Fine Arts, Gift of Edgar William
and Bernice Chrysler Garbish, 50.2.1

Jasper Francis Cropsey
Mt. Jefferson—Pinkham Notch, White Mountains

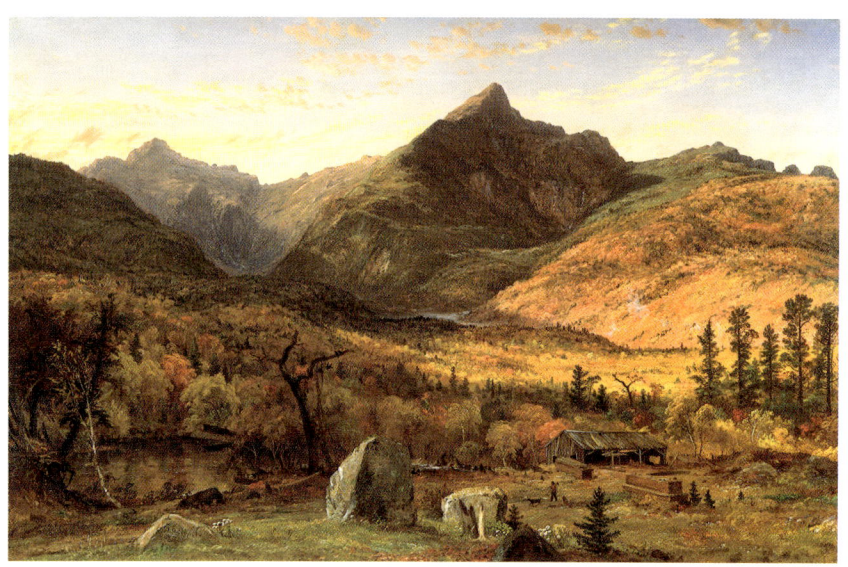

Jasper Francis Cropsey sets the rugged White Mountains of New Hampshire ablaze in autumn color. Under a buttermilk sky, he gathers the grandeur of the American wilderness into one breathtaking view, then casts it in a fall palette of fiery red, orange, and golden-yellow. From foreground to background, Cropsey registers the effects of light, atmosphere, and distance. Up close, white autumn blossoms, green baby pines, and dark aging tree trunks display intense hues. As the terrain climbs to distant mountaintops, woodland details fade; light and color soften into rose, gold, and green foliage, touched by shadow. As space recedes, tree leaves and evergreen needles merge into groves, then into treetops only, painted with quick dabs of color. A mountain stream reflects the reds and greens of overhanging trees; foothills trap valley mists as they rise to Mt. Jefferson's crown.

A favorite natural haunt for painters at the time, the White Mountains offered inspirational views of peaks and valleys in changing seasons. In the mid 1800s, the American landscape painter's "sacred mission," as one critic called it, was to record the unspoiled land of a new republic before advancing civilization claimed it.

Like his fellow landscapists—who came to be called the Hudson River School (1830s–1870s)—Cropsey sketched dramatic scenery outdoors, painted his pictures in the studio, and sold them to an urban audience. He often derived his landscapes from composite views. Here, he suggests the breadth Nature by combining disparate vistas from different locations into one all-encompassing painting. This terrain is not entirely untouched, however: a lone, ax-wielding lumberjack strides past a ramshackle sawmill. His presence embodies an American paradox: the advancement of industrial society and the destruction of the wilderness. "The ax of civilization is busy with our old forests," Cropsey warned, as he recorded the changing American landscape in his paintings.

American Leaves in London
Known as a master of American autumn paintings (see Durrie, opposite), Cropsey painted a group of landscapes, including this picture, while in London. Made from sketches of New Hampshire, it is one of two images that stunned English audiences with its brilliant color. Comments, including those of critic John Ruskin, ranged from "unbelievable" and an "exaggeration," to "radiant truth." British and European viewers then saw the American autumn for themselves when a display of actual American autumn leaves went on view in London.

American Landscape Painting
The landscape matured as an essential type of American painting during the first decades of the 1800s. Its development may be seen in the Virginia Museum's collection, from country estates used as backdrops in portraits by Charles Willson Peale (see p. 80) to colorful vistas—displayed as worthy subjects in their own right—by John Kensett, Frederick Church, and Martin Johnson Heade (in the galleries). Today, Cropsey's painting hangs in pristine condition in its original frame, attesting to why landscapes of its type were the first to enjoy a large market.

Mt. Jefferson—Pinkham Notch, White Mountains, 1857
Jasper Francis Cropsey (American, 1823–1900)
Oil on canvas; 31½ by 49½ inches
Virginia Museum of Fine Arts Purchase,
 The J. Harwood and Louise B. Cochrane Fund for
 American Art, 96.35

George Henry Durrie
Winter in the Country: A Cold Morning

"Trees sparkling with icy limbs made the scene almost enchanting….the weather…cold, blustering….The ground…covered with ice, glittering." George Henry Durrie's own musings on the beauties of winter invite us into the frosty world of snow scenes for which he is famous. Freshly fallen snow blankets the ground, layers the barn roofs, and dusts the tops of tree branches, stone walls, and haystacks. Low clouds cast lavender shadows across snow and sky, scattering the pink reflections of a morning sun. Travelers make their way, on foot and by sleigh, to the shelter of a country inn. Its golden clapboard frame and curling chimney smoke entice visitors to draw near, attracted by a red signboard and the promise of a warming fire indoors. Durrie's own appreciation of family, hearth, and home enhances the feelings of comfort that his picture might stir. "It is happiness to spend evenings at home with my wife….My little boy…lies in bed sleeping. All is peace, contentment, and enjoyment." Such are the pleasures offered by his cozy country inn on a cold winter morning.

Durrie's "snowpiece," a New England genre painting, is touched by nostalgia for old-fashioned country life, a yearning for simpler times. If images from Currier and Ives come to mind, it is because the American printmakers reproduced Durrie's country scenes as he painted them. Durrie's now familiar mills, homesteads, barnyards, and woodlands—by way of paintings, prints, porcelain platters, and greeting cards—forever freeze the winters of a vanishing age within the lexicon of American imagery.

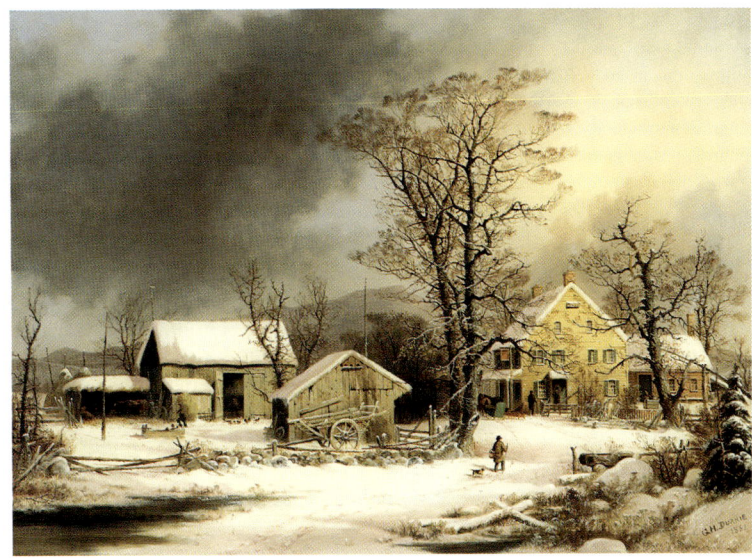

From Likenesses to Landscapes

Durrie, a native of New Haven, Connecticut, began painting his snowpieces for an increasingly appreciative audience and profitable market in the late 1850s (see also Cropsey, opposite). At that time he abandoned his work of nearly fifteen years as a professional portrait painter, which had included a residency in Petersburg, Virginia, during the fall, winter, and spring of 1845–46.

Currier and Ives

Technical advances in printmaking during the 1800s spawned new possibilities for graphic arts, particularly steel engraving and the new art of commercial lithography. Making fine-quality images available to wider audiences, New York's leading lithographic firm of Nathanial Currier and James Merritt Ives published ten of Durrie's rural scenes, including this painting, during the 1860s.

Durrie's Landscapes as Social Backdrops

Durrie, a master of the winter landscape, captures a social history even as he romanticizes the dignity and simplicity of northern country life. His paintings of rural havens and homecomings—sparkling with color, light, and atmosphere—appealed to his patrons, witnessing the country's vast territorial expansion, technological progress, rapid industrialization, and rumblings of civil war.

Winter in the Country: A Cold Morning,
1861
George Henry Durrie (American, 1820–1863)
Oil on canvas; 26 by 36¼ inches
Virginia Museum of Fine Arts Purchase,
  The J. Harwood and Louise B. Cochrane Fund
  for American Art, 92.124

George Catlin
Ba-da-ah-chon-du (He Who Outjumps All)

"I have painted him as he sat for me, balanced on his leaping wild horse with his shield and quiver slung on his back, and his long lance decorated with the eagle's quills." So George Catlin, writing one evening as a guest of the Crow and the Minnetaree on the upper Missouri River, describes his portrait of Ba-da-ah-chon-du, a Crow chief. Catlin's quest—to make visual and written records of vanishing Native American cultures—had led him north from St. Louis on a two-thousand-mile steamboat trip in 1832. In this particular evening's epistle (No. 24), Catlin explains his artistic mission: "the world…will learn vastly more from lines and colours than they could from oral or written delineations." His reflections not only define the lines and colors of the Crow chief's portrait, but also illustrate the passions and perceptions of the artist himself.

"His shirt and his leggings, and moccasins, were of the mountain-goat skins… their seams everywhere fringed with a profusion of scalp-locks taken from the heads of his enemies.…His long hair, which reached almost to the ground whilst he was standing…was now lifted in the air, and floating in black waves over the hips of his leaping charger. On his head…he wore a magnificent crest or head-dress, made of the quills of the war-eagle and ermine skins; and on his horse's head also was another…precisely the same in pattern.…"

Depicted in Catlin's characteristically fresh color, Ba-da-ah-chon-du and his horse face the limitless plains of what is now North Dakota. Catlin washes the prairie sky and landscape in soft blues, greens, and golds, then picks out colorful flowers, feathers, and embroidery in reds, blues, blacks, and whites.

Imagination and empiricism, Old World romanticism and New World determination mingle in Catlin's first-hand view of the "plumes and trappings" of a Crow war-parade, a celebratory show of power "to produce a pleasing and thrilling effect" at a reunion with the Minnetaree. Catlin's words convey his vision: "The history and customs of such a people, preserved by pictorial illustration, are themes worthy of the life-time of one man."

Catlin's Lifetime

Catlin abandoned an East Coast law career for portrait painting. Then, with little training in art or ethnography, he devoted a lifetime to painting the native cultures he encountered on his North American travels up the Mississippi, Missouri, Platte, Colorado, and Snake Rivers, and later on a South American journey down the Amazon. He organized one collection of images— many painted quickly in thinly applied oils on portable canvases—into a catalogue of 494 entries in 1837. He published his Letters and Notes in 1841. His paintings and notebooks describe the Minnetaree, Mandan, Crow, Blackfoot, Pawnee, Comanche, and Ojibwa, among the 146 Native American cultures that he visited. Forced to sell the collection in 1852 to avoid bankruptcy, Catlin later re-created this painting, among others in the 1860s, from memory and from surviving drawings.

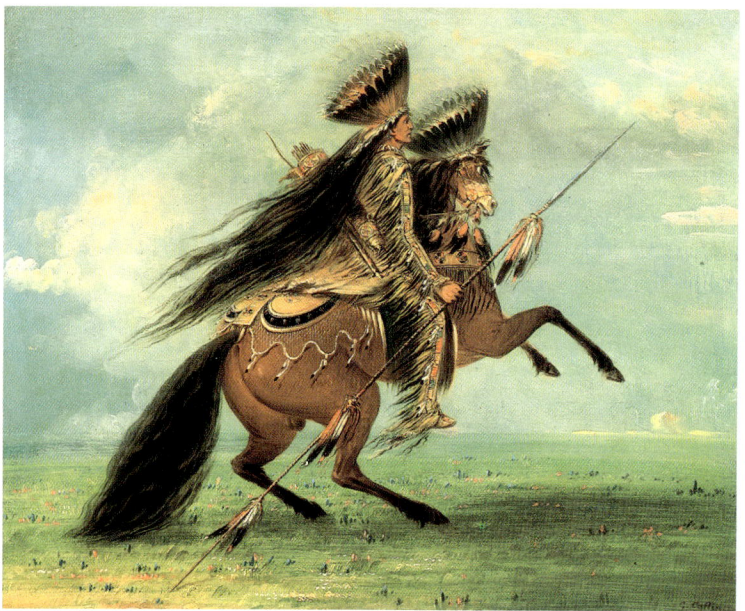

Ba-da-ah-chon-du (He Who Outjumps All), a Crow Chief on Horseback, circa 1865–70
George Catlin (American, 1796–1872)
Oil on canvas; 21⅜ by 26¾ inches
Virginia Museum of Fine Arts, The Paul Mellon
  Collection, 85.609

Eastman Johnson
A Ride for Liberty—The Fugitive Slaves

"A veritable incident in the Civil War seen by myself at Centerville on the morning of McClellan's advance to Manassas, March 2nd, 1862. Eastman Johnson."

These words on the back of Eastman Johnson's painting identify the time and place of this event. Three versions of the image exist, based on an incident witnessed by the artist during the Battle of Bull Run (Manassas). Through Johnson's eyes, we see four fugitives fleeing on horseback. Although isolated against the landscape, they seem to fear they are not alone. The woman, holding a baby close to her breast, glances over her shoulder in search of pursuers; the man tightens the reins as he wraps a protective arm around a small boy who clutches the horse's mane. Sun begins to light a distant eastern sky through the blue morning mist, silhouetting the refugees. They are riding north.

The *Ride for Liberty*—a desperate race to escape southern enslavement—reflects the directness and energy for which Johnson is known. Primarily a portraitist, he began to paint genre scenes at mid-career (1860s–1880s). One of the earliest scene painters, Johnson often selected moments from the everyday lives of his subjects. In his travels around the country, he portrayed its cultural diversity in drawings and paintings of the Chippewa of Lake Superior, Union soldiers on the Potomac River, and African Americans in Virginia and Washington, D.C.

Johnson's style reflects a transitional age in American art. His pictures range from finished genre pieces of children hunting eggs in chicken coops, to sketchy, impressionistic scenes of women conversing by the shore. Art critics in 1876 admired Johnson for his snippets

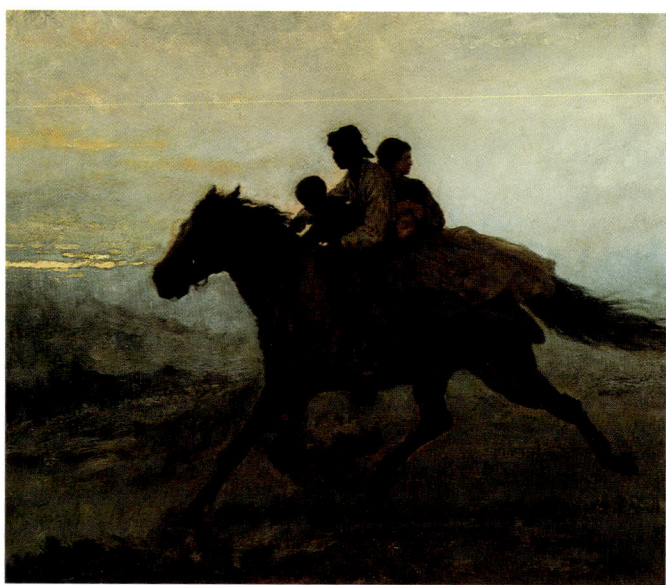

of American life: canoeing, corn-husking, fiddling, sugar-making, cranberry-picking. His expression of feeling won praise, though his "uncertainty" of form is also noted. In this painting, he places the fleeing slaves in the center, suggesting their contours with indistinct line, traced against sketchy terrain. He applies subtle color, modulating tones of blue, white, gray, copper, and brown to add atmosphere rather than to decorate.

Deceptively straightforward, Johnson's scenes provoke complex reactions. Praised for his renderings of courage, sacrifice, and devotion—set against conditions of poverty, slavery, and war—he has also been criticized for stereotypic imagery. Still, the humanity that underlies his best work resides here, in a testament to the strength of the human spirit, recorded by Johnson in the fugitives' ride.

Johnson's Portraiture

The son of Maine's Secretary of State and a portraitist in Washington's Capitol Building by the age of twenty, Johnson drew and painted many of the nation's leaders during his lifetime. His portraits parade the "Who's Who" of nineteenth-century America—John Quincy Adams, Dolley Madison, Grover Cleveland, Daniel Webster, Ralph Waldo Emerson, Henry Wadsworth Longfellow—though today he is better known for his genre scenes.

A Ride for Liberty—The Fugitive Slaves, 1862
Eastman Johnson (American, 1824–1906)
Oil on wood; 21½ by 26 inches
Virginia Museum of Fine Arts, The Paul Mellon Collection, 85.644

John Henry Belter, Sofa

An ornate sofa, one of a pair, welcomes us into the Gilded Age of Victorian parlors in America, where gilded furniture actually was rare. The style is more precisely called Rococo Revival, the style of John Henry Belter. Rosewood curves into a profusion of cornucopias, vines, and leaves; a basket of flowers forms the center crest of the three-part frame, flanked at each corner by bouquets of roses and tulip-shaped flowers. Grapes, acorns, and gourds cluster along tendrils that twist into spiral fluting. Undulating legs are supported by "knees" of roses and "feet" of leafy volutes. Like a painting, Belter's sofa surrounded the sitter with a gilded frame, while transforming furniture into freestanding sculpture, to be appreciated from all sides.

The elegance and grace of Rococo Revival-style furniture account for its popularity during the mid 1800s. The prestige of Belter's New York workshop equaled Duncan Phyfe's in the preceding decades. Belter not only became a master of parlor design, but he also perfected the technique that made his furniture possible. He is actually known as the "father of plywood." Although he did not invent it, he did refine and patent it, bringing secrets from his native Germany to the United States. His secrets rested in his lamination and bent-wood processes. Belter recommended using rosewood, his favorite, as the exterior veneer to cover up to twenty-one layers of more pliable wood, often oak, hickory, or black walnut. The layers were probably steam-bent in molds, removed, then glued together—the grain of one set at right angles to the next—then placed again in molds, possibly under heat. Once the glue had dried, the mold clamps were released and the wood was ready for veneering, carving, and gilding.

Belter lived in an era of patent-applications for pressed- and bent-wood techniques, but even so his developments could never be entirely protected. The myth tells us that he destroyed his tools, designs, and molds in a state of despair over the "theft" of his ideas before he died, but the success of his workshop and showrooms actually survived him by several years.

A Belter Attribution
Belter claimed to make "all kinds of furniture," but mostly parlor sets survive. Although not every piece bears his maker's mark, Belter's furniture can be attributed on the basis of design patterns and materials that characterized his work throughout his twenty-year career.

Belter's Rococo Revival Style
European Rococo—a light, frothy style that strews flowers, ribbons, shells, and scrolls about paintings, furniture, and architecture—actually evolved in the 1700s. Its revival in American furniture (1840–1900) saw the intermingling of English, German, and French influences—Louis XV, Empire, Biedermeyer. Belter also may have borrowed flower baskets, grapes, roses, and scrolling vines from French engravings of the 1600s.

The History of Plywood
Belter's woodworking procedures were unequaled (Dun and Bradstreet's financial reports on businesses called Belter a good risk, but the quality of his furniture too high to be profitable). Plywood had a history before Belter, however: in the three-layered veneers linked to Robert Adam's eighteenth-century designs and in the laminated wood traced to ancient Egyptian coffins.

Herter Brothers, Center Table

Tabletop mosaics of light-colored wood mimic the fragile beauty of blossoming cherry branches. Ebony-colored wood surrounds them and continues below in a stretcher of carved chrysanthemums. The style is vintage Herter Brothers, America's leading interior design firm and premier taste-makers of the late 1800s. Through artistic hallmarks such as this table, Christian Herter, Gustave's younger half-brother, established himself as standard-bearer of Aesthetic Movement craftsmanship in the United States. From Italy, France, and their native Germany, Herter Brothers imported the technique of marquetry (a veneer of intricately patterned, thin wooden pieces), and they perfected the technique of ebonized wood (blackened with layers of dark varnish).

This table originally stood in the mansion built by Mark and Mary Sherwood Hopkins on Nob Hill in San Francisco. The mansion was destroyed as a result of the 1906 earthquake; the Mark Hopkins Hotel now stands on the site. The table, removed in 1891, is one of the few pieces from the Herter Brothers' interior to have survived. The design intermingles exotic Greek, Moorish, and Japanese motifs with an English rectilinear form. The style became known as "Anglo-Japanese," the Herter Brothers' signature. The Far Eastern cherry blossoms repeat the marquetry designs that once decorated the door panels and dado of the salon. The legs taper to "hocked" feet in a modern, stylized version of ancient Orientalized griffin- or lion-legged furniture. Each leg then assumes the form of a large Oriental folded fan: the narrow edges end with pleat-like molding ("reeding") trimmed in red; the flat surfaces are carved in low relief with floral motifs and incised with gilded Greek keys (meander-patterns) and asymmetrical fan motifs. Spindles add a Moorish touch, gilt-bronze fixtures an exotic finish. These motifs are gathered into an exquisite whole, to form a table intended, like freestanding sculpture, to be seen from all sides.

The Herter Brothers' Style

The Herter Brothers' name is synonymous with the fine art of cabinetmaking. Gustave, considering himself a sculptor, specialized in ornate forms: carved lions, harpies, palmettes; Christian preferred flattened patterns: inlays of Greek vases, birds, flowers. At the height of the Aesthetic Movement, Herter Brothers orchestrated an array of luxurious styles into unified interior designs. They advertised: "Rich and Plain Furniture, Curtains…Wood Mantels, Looking-glasses, Frames, Cornices, and Clocks…Mosaic and Marquetterie… Wall Decorations." Patronized by clients such as J. Pierpont Morgan, William H. Vanderbilt, and the White House, a new style of complementary architecture and interior design had been born (see Guimard, p. 98, Mackintosh, p. 99, and Gray, p. 104).

The Gilded Age of American Designers

When Christian joined the Herter firm in 1865, Gustave's business was located in a New York neighborhood with other rising designers of the Gilded Age: John Henry Belter (see opposite) and Tiffany & Co. In fact, both brothers had worked for Charles L. Tiffany; when Christian Herter retired in 1880, the torch of American interior design passed to Tiffany's son Louis Comfort (p. 100).

Center Table, 1877–78

Herter Brothers, American (Firm active 1865–1906)
Gustave Herter (born in Stuttgart, Germany, 1830–1898); Christian Herter (born in Stuttgart, Germany, 1840–1883)
Carved, ebonized, inlaid, and gilded maple; gilded bronze fittings; 30¾ by 56 by 35 inches
Virginia Museum of Fine Arts Purchase, The Adolph D. and Wilkins C. Williams Fund, 90.30

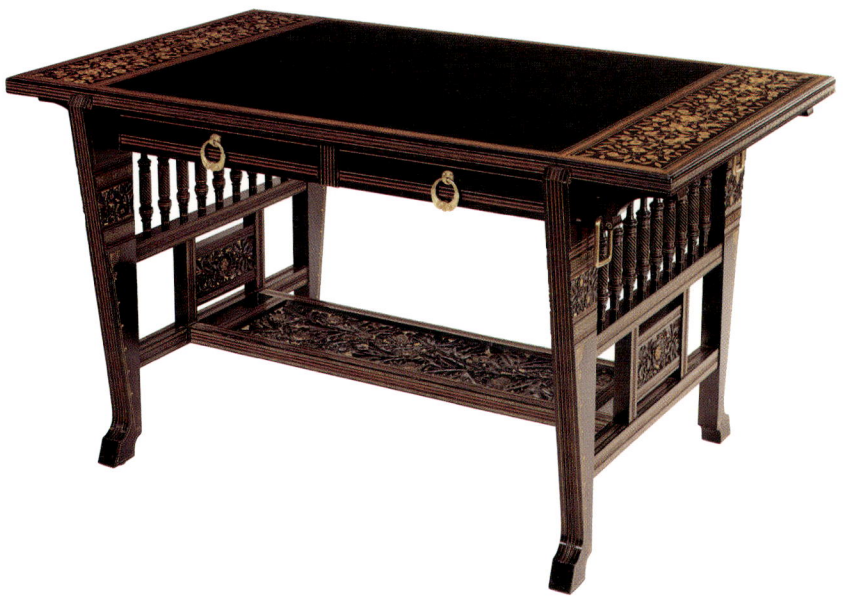

Mary Cassatt, Baby Reaching for an Apple

A mother gently lowers a branch so that her child might pick an apple. Their simple gestures, set in a fresh bower of pinks and greens, open a world of pure wonder as inquisitive young eyes investigate the golden fruit. Safe within the crook of the mother's arm and propped against her hip, the little one reaches into the air.

Mary Cassatt, an American Impressionist in Paris, tempered the tenderness of her favorite subject—mother and child—with the convictions of her art. Gauguin remarked that Cassatt "has much charm, but she has more force." She studied her subjects: mothers and

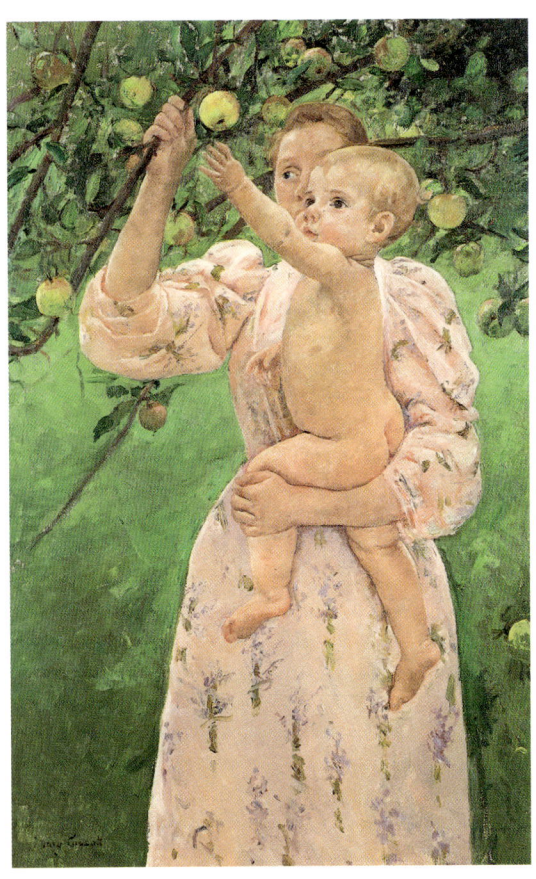

daughters, fathers and sons, babies, brothers, and sisters. Children are bathed, hair is combed, books are read, sewing is completed. Focusing on figures, Cassatt explored the endless possibilities of line, color, pattern, and composition. Perspectives shift as we view gardens and interiors, seen from above or cropped by the frame. Here, Cassatt places the mother and baby slightly off-center and brings them close to us, to seal the intimacy of the moment.

This painting relates to Cassatt's twelve-foot-high mural of *Modern Woman,* created for the 1893 World's Fair in Chicago. The artist created both the mural, now lost, and this canvas in her French country studio.

Cassatt counters warmth and sentimentality with her keen eye and even sharper technique. Minimizing detail, she renders mother and child with assured line, balancing the patterns of the composition: floral print against fabric, plump fruit against foliage. Large and unidealized figures, shallow space, and active brushwork contribute to Cassatt's direct style, here more impressionistic than most of her forcefully drawn images. Degas admired her draughtsmanship ("I will not admit that a woman can draw so well") and the genuineness of her art; he had invited her in 1877 to join the group later known as the Impressionists.

Cassatt's Outlook

Cassatt, relentlessly self-disciplined, worked in oils and pastels from morning until dusk; she often devoted her evenings to graphics. "There are two ways for a painter, the broad and easy one or the narrow and hard one." Cassatt spent her childhood in France and her teens in Philadelphia, where she studied at the Pennsylvania Academy of Fine Arts. She returned to France in 1866 to pursue a sixty-year career in painting. She lived an orderly life, dedicated to her art and to her parents, siblings, nieces, and nephews, and intolerant of other artists' bohemianism.

Cassatt and Degas

Cassatt and Degas weathered a stormy forty-year friendship, bound by a mutual respect for one another's art, by high artistic standards, and by forthright criticism of the art world. Both valued the necessity of drawing over the Impressionists' dissolution of form in color and light; both were fascinated with capturing figures in intimate moments seen with artistic detachment; both shared an interest in the flattened patterns, strong lines, and asymmetry of Japanese prints (see Degas, p. 73).

Apples in the Air

Apples abounded in French art during Cassatt's lifetime, as did maternal subjects. "With an apple, I wish to astonish Paris," Cézanne had proclaimed in 1895, having struggled since the 1870s to perfect its painted shape. At the turn of 1896, Degas purchased three Cézannes, including two apple still lifes. Mary Cassatt owned two of Cézanne's "astonishing" apple paintings.

Baby Reaching for an Apple, 1893
Mary Cassatt (American, 1844–1926)
Oil on canvas; 39 by 25½ inches
Virginia Museum of Fine Arts, Gift of Ivor and Anne
  Massey, 75.18

John Singer Sargent
The Sketchers

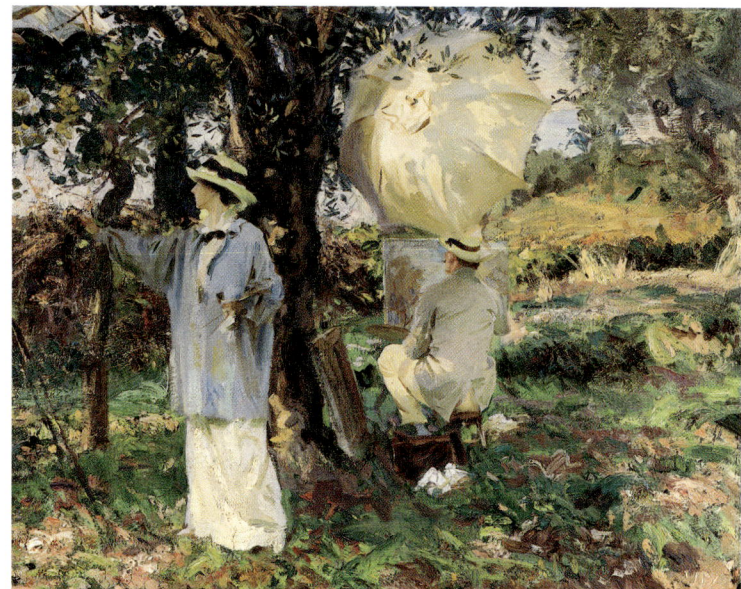

John Singer Sargent arranges and records sweet moments of life: companions painting in Frascati, reading in Corfu, napping in Canadian mountain meadows. Here, he paints the serene "sweetness of doing nothing" (*dolce far niente* in Italy, his place of birth). He sets a sun-drenched olive grove before us; a pleasant drowsiness fills the air as his friends sketch in midday light. Active brushwork depicts their forms. Color sparkles in the painting, more than can even be seen in the muted golds and silvery greens of actual sunlit Mediterranean landscapes. Swaths of greens, browns, and golds create distance from foreground to background. Dashes of pinks, reds, and orange enliven the grove, while swirls of plums, lavenders, and whites add to its atmosphere. Although he often blurred edges under the influence of French Impressionism, Sargent never dissolved form. He insisted on black pigment long after the French Impressionists had given it up. Fascinated by the way that sun-washed surfaces reflect pure color, visually altering the surfaces themselves, he used color to build, rather than shatter, his imagery. Blues, ivories, blacks, and grays define facets of the friends who posed for him: painters' smocks and straw hats, a parasol's ribs, a classic profile.

Sargent called such paintings his "subject pictures." His cousin called them his "painted diaries." Often threatening to forsake his portraits of high society (see *Mrs. Albert Vickers* in the Virginia Museum's galleries)—by which he gained his fame and fortune—the artist sought refuge in his travels. "I want now to experiment in more imaginary fields." Friends, sisters, nieces, and nephews accompanied him on holidays to Palestine, Italy, Switzerland, Spain, Portugal,

and Turkey. Their letters from the early 1900s recall days spent out-of-doors posing and watching him paint, afternoons of walks and siestas, evenings of chess and music.

Sargent's painted diaries offer sensuous surfaces to contemplate, without an urgency to delve for deeper meaning (he cautioned against over-interpretations). For Sargent, meaning rested in the world of appearances. Whether in a portrait or a landscape, he sought the aesthetic play of paint—color, light, and texture—on a canvas. He excelled in portraiture, but he also cultivated, savored, and transformed poetic moments—friends sketching in the light of day—into painted ones.

Sargent At Home and Abroad

Sargent was born in Florence to American parents on a tour of Europe that lasted a lifetime. He was raised in Rome, summered in Switzerland, and painted with Academics and Impressionists in Paris and London. He spent only a total of eight years in the United States.

Sargent's Portraits

Sargent's work inspires phrases such as "scintillating light" and "bravura brushwork." By 1900, he had earned the reputation as the Van Dyck, Velázquez, and Frans Hals of his day. Occasionally criticized as facile and formulaic, Sargent's portraits, at their finest, are fresh and direct, his brushwork seemingly effortless. Henry James described Sargent's portraits as "pure tact of vision" and modeled several characters after him in the early 1890s. The "sweep and dash of the brush on the canvas" in Oscar Wilde's Picture of Dorian Gray *(1891) gives a nod to Sargent. Wilde had aptly inscribed a book of poetry for the painter: "nothing is true except the beautiful."*

The Sketchers, circa 1913
John Singer Sargent (American, 1856–1925)
Oil on canvas; 22 by 28 inches
Virginia Museum of Fine Arts Purchase, The Arthur and Margaret Glasgow Fund, 58.11

Edward Hopper
House at Dusk

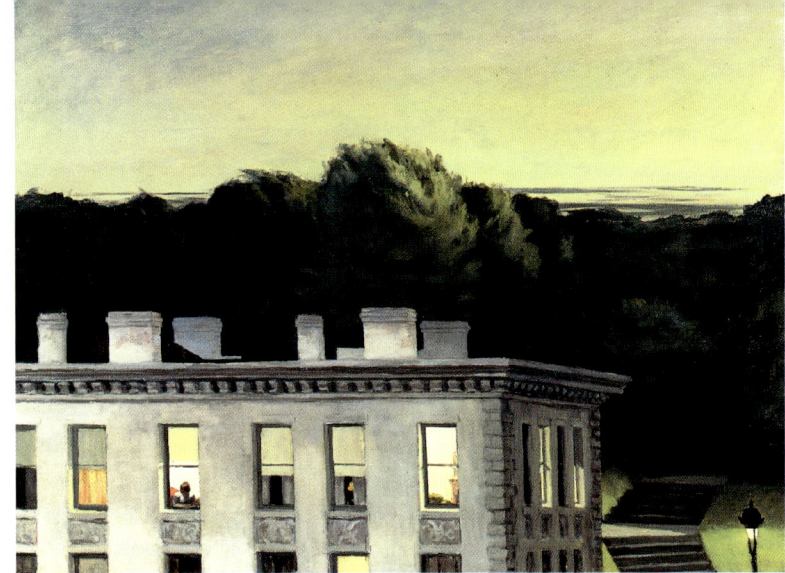

Dusk: "an exquisite hour." Edward Hopper was fond of quoting the poet Paul Verlaine on the subject that he painted many times. As dusk falls and natural light dims, electric light begins to glow. The vanished sun leaves a sky touched with yellow and streaked low by wisps of soft violet clouds, catching its last rays. Creeping shadows start to shroud the building, stone steps, and treetops. A lamppost illuminates a path; a ceiling light, a room; and a floor lamp, a corner.

Through fictive windows and doorways, Hopper invites us to enter houses, automats, theaters, and restaurants, where solitary figures often dwell, unaware of our presence. Here, as we look into private spaces lit behind half-drawn shades, a woman leans upon the sill, looking out. Indoor light escapes to strike the window frame, reflecting green trim against the violet-gray building as daylight fades. Chimneys line the rooftops; inside, the edge of a fireplace mantel can be seen. Cornices and quoins trace the building's lines: dentil molding, rusticated blocks, and scroll-like reliefs punctuate its spaces. Hopper casts the house itself—or, rather, its looming upper floors—in relief against the darkening green trees.

The quiet drama in Hopper's paintings lies, it is said, in the spaces he leaves vacant—between cityscape and nature, one window and another, the people in his pictures. His paintings pose dilemmas for the viewer: between looking and intruding, glancing and staring, fascination and discretion, emotion and detachment. Evidently a man of profound silences—"if you could say it in words, there'd be no reason to paint"—Hopper spoke of painting as hard work. He wrote about his hope to grasp nature's surprises, accidents, and moods through art, in his search for renewed wonder. He carried a quote from Goethe in his wallet that reflected his artistic strivings: "To reproduce the world that surrounds me by means of the world that is in me."

Hopper's strong style—with which he taps the most fragile and ephemeral of feelings—finds expression in scenes constructed like stage sets; in the mystery of obliquely angled buildings; in a clarity of light that reveals the surfaces and the character of his subjects; and in the spaces he creates between painting and viewer. As we look at *House at Dusk*, we become part of its silent drama. His essential image exudes a stillness to contemplate without the distractions of activity or story. But Hopper refrains from offering interpretations: "The most important element in a picture cannot be explained." Hopper's *House at Dusk*—caught between the light and the dark—captures an ambiguity as elusive as twilight itself.

Hopper's Background

Edward Hopper studied with Robert Henri at the New York School of Art in the early 1900s (see Stuart Davis, opposite). Fellow student Rockwell Kent pronounced Hopper the "John Singer Sargent" of the class, for his brilliant drawing (see Sargent, p. 91; see also paintings by Robert Henri and Rockwell Kent in the Virginia Museum's galleries). Trained as a commercial illustrator, Hopper began painting full-time at age forty-one, producing two or three pictures a year. After traveling to Europe (1906–1910), he worked largely from his New York City studio for fifty years, summering in Cape Cod. Hopper considered himself a loner rather than an "American scene" painter; while he talked of painting the "facts" of what he saw, he described the process as "gestation," in which he combined "impressions of nature" with sensations, emotion, and imagination.

Dusk and Dawn

Hopper painted transitional times of day, studying light as it intensifies or fades: Railroad Sunset, Early Sunday Morning, Nighthawks. *"Thoughtful light at the edges of the day"—John Updike's simple eloquence matches Hopper's.*

House at Dusk, 1935
Edward Hopper (American, 1882–1967)
Oil on canvas; 36¼ by 50 inches
Virginia Museum of Fine Arts Purchase, The John
  Barton Payne Fund, 53.8

Stuart Davis, Little Giant Still Life

American art changes with Stuart Davis, the New York Sun's "ace of American modernists." Davis leads us from the realm of portraits by Charles Willson Peale or landscapes by Jasper Francis Cropsey into the arena of abstraction. "Art is a sign of life," proclaimed Davis and his fellow artists, advancing the cause of abstraction in a society accustomed to scenes, not signs, of life in art. Davis's prolific paintings and writings are passionate signs of his life—serious yet witty, calculated, and colorful.

Here, "Champion" flashes orange. Three blue-green diagonals cut across three letters. Below, an orange "Stuart Davis"—about as wide as the distance between the two diagonals above it— scrolls its way across the canvas. White and light-blue fields fill the spaces between and around the large and small letters. Green diagonals criss-cross; bright blue and yellow colors form fanciful triangles, rectangles, and curves. Strips of blue on one side and green on the other border the lively activity, while light red—warmed by a touch of yellow— surrounds and supports it.

"Art is a dynamic event," Davis declared. Set side by side, colors play off one another. Painted letters may be read as words, but they may also be perceived as simple shapes. Space compresses into layers (white on blue on red), but it also flattens into a single plane when certain colors abut (green and yellow, yellow and red, red and blue). Background becomes border, color becomes shape, shape becomes space.

Davis called "Champion" the "subject matter" of his painting. When asked, he displayed his consuming devotion to visual art by talking more about how the letters and diagonals looked than about what they might mean. Although he recognized that words trigger different associations in different viewers, Davis

painted words largely for their artistic challenges. "All of my paintings," he explains, "are derived from specific subjects....I always start with something I have just seen...or something that is immediately in front of me....It could be a box of matches...it could be a recording that Fats Waller made." Here, he abstracts and transforms "Champion, America's Favorite Spark Plug"—an advertisement printed on a matchbook—into art, a sign of modern life.

Davis and American Scene Painting

"I am an American, born in Philadelphia of American stock...I paint what I see in America, in other words, I paint the American scene." Schooled in New York City under Robert Henri, a member of the "Ash Can" school who sent students into city streets to observe life, Davis created visual equivalents of urban sights and sounds. Photographs of Davis's studio show ordinary objects—cigarettes, matchbooks, batteries, soup cans, jazz recordings— all awaiting transformation. "The act of painting is not a duplication of experience...; [it is] the extension of experience..." in balanced color, line, space, light.

Jazz

The words in Davis's paintings have been called his brand of jazz "jive talk." Davis admired the precision and the freedom of expression in this distinctly American music, orchestrated or improvised, within a framework. Davis found jazz, like his paintings, full of surprise and continuity at the same time.

Little Giant Still Life, 1950
Stuart Davis (American, 1894–1964)
Oil on canvas; 33 by 43 inches
Virginia Museum of Fine Arts Purchase, The John
  Barton Payne Fund, 50.8

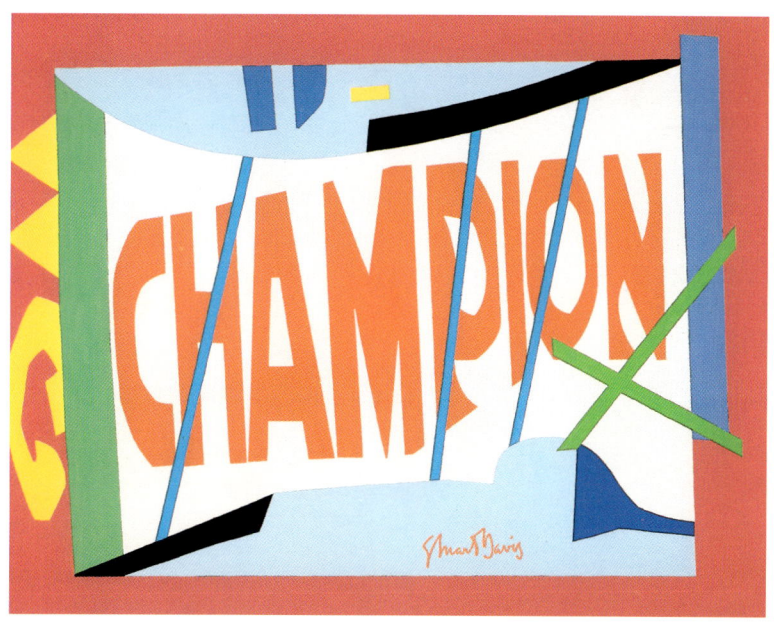

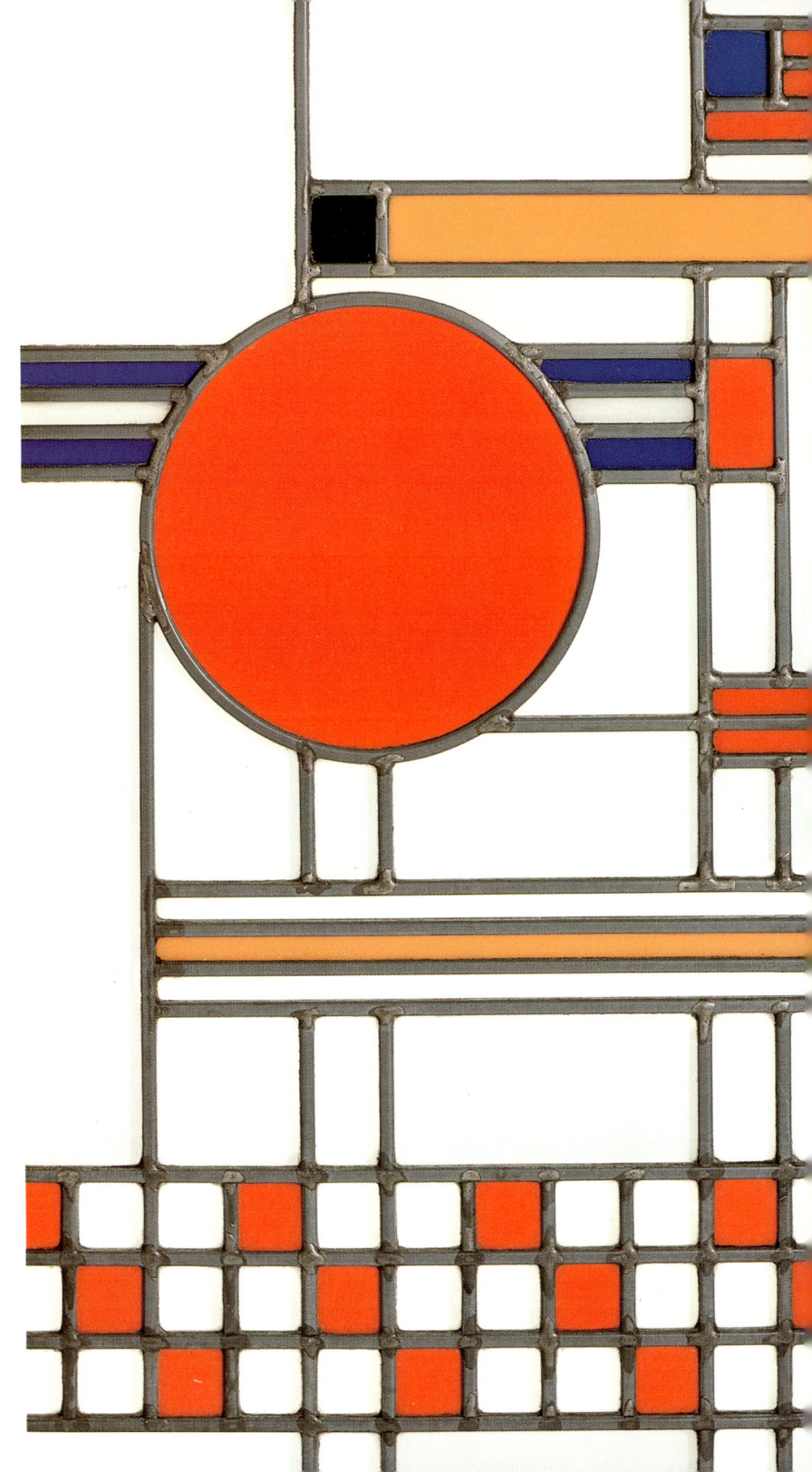

CHAPTER 8

19th and 20th Century Sculpture and Decorative Arts

Russian

English

American

Art Nouveau

Art Deco

Post-1950

Peter Carl Fabergé
Imperial Czarevich Easter Egg

Czar Nicholas II gave this lavish egg of gold and lapis lazuli to his wife, the Czarina Alexandra Feodorovna, on Easter Sunday in 1912. Earlier, during Holy Week, the royal commission would have been available for public viewing in St. Petersburg at the Fabergé Workshops. There, Peter Carl Fabergé's best workers had carved and joined sections of deep blue stone to form the egg, embellished by elaborate gold floral baskets and swags of bell-shaped flowers, cornucopias and canopies, winged eagles and figures. Diamonds mark the egg at its top and bottom. Like the other four Imperial Easter Eggs now in the Virginia Museum's collection—made either for the Czar's wife or for his mother—the Czarevich Egg was intended as a token of royal affection and appreciation.

Each Imperial Egg holds a surprise inside. The Czarina would have opened the top of this one to lift out a miniature portrait of the Czarevich Alexis, the Romanovs' only son and heir to the throne. A diamond-encrusted frame, in the shape of the family's double-headed eagle, surrounds the painting of Alexis, who wears a favorite sailor suit, seen often in boyhood photographs.

The House of Fabergé created luxurious objects—enameled candy boxes and cigarette cases, jeweled parasol handles and picture frames—for the last three Russian czars. Gustave Fabergé established the St. Petersburg firm in the early 1840s; in the early 1870s, his son Peter Carl took over the business and eventually expanded it with shops to serve aristocratic clients in Moscow, Odessa, Kiev, and London. He supervised a huge staff of artisans. These men and women, excelling in skill and patience, crafted the intricate objects of beauty that bore the mark of Fabergé. Though often small in size, a true Fabergé piece is always grand in stature. Upholding a long European and Imperial Russian tradition of giving jeweled eggs as Easter gifts, Fabergé perfected the art form under Czar Nicholas II. After the Romanov rule met its demise with the Russian Revolution of 1917, the Bolsheviks closed the House of Fabergé in 1918. Fabergé settled in Switzerland, where he died. His ashes were interred in France; his tombstone reads: "Carl Fabergé, Jeweler of the Russian Court."

Fabergé's Russian and European Heritage

Fabergé was born in St. Petersburg to a French father and a Scandinavian mother. His extravagant creations were in part inspired by the opulence of Russian palaces, such as the Hermitage, built along the banks of the Neva River in St. Petersburg under Catherine the Great. The doors of the Hermitage opened to the public in 1852. Its ornate exterior, influenced by the Baroque and Rococo architecture of Europe, serves as a grand shell in which to house great art treasures—among them, rooms of lapis lazuli and malachite, racks of paintings by Rubens, and cases filled with Fabergé treasures.

Lillian Thomas Pratt's Collection

The Lillian Thomas Pratt Collection of Fabergé was bequeathed to the Virginia Museum in 1947. It is one of four prominent Fabergé collections in the United States, gathered at mid century.

Fabergé's Workmasters

The Imperial Czarevich Easter Egg is engraved Fabergé and bears the initials of head workmaster Henrik Emanuel Wigström (1862–1923). Other artisans whose initials appear on the objects include Mikhail Perkhin (1860–1903), Erik Kollin (1836–1901), Anders Nevalainen (1858–1933), Victor Aarne (1863–1934), and Hjalmar Armfelt (1873–1959). François Petrovich Birbaum, who had long been with the firm, tells much about its history and offers many anecdotes in his Memoirs of 1919.

Imperial Czarevich Easter Egg with Miniature Portrait, 1912
Peter Carl Fabergé (French, born in Russia, 1846–1920)
Lapis lazuli, gold, diamonds, platinum or silver; 4 5/16 by 3 1/2 inches
Virginia Museum of Fine Arts, Bequest from the Estate of Lillian Thomas Pratt, 47.20.34

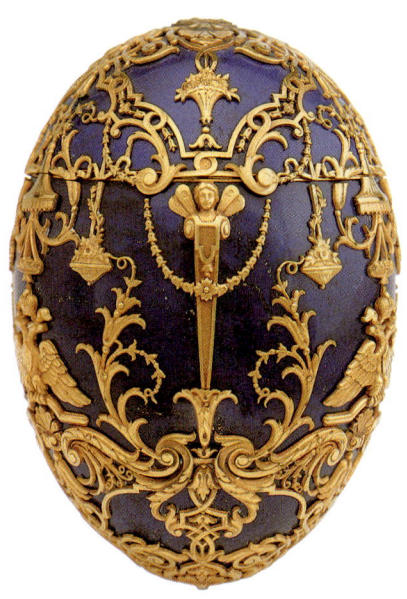

Paul Storr
Hebe Sculpture

Hebe, daughter of Zeus and Hera, personifies youth. According to ancient Greek mythology, she served nectar to the Greek gods and danced with the Muses on Mt. Olympus. The gods celebrated eternal life with her at her marriage to Herakles, who had completed his earthly labors to become divine. Paul Storr's statuette of Hebe, pouring the waters of life from a ewer into a goblet, shines with classical beauty and everlasting youth.

Hollow-cast in silver, Hebe floats on a cloud. She is the vision of an idealized classical figure, partly nude: elegant profile, fillet-bound ringlets, breasts revealed. Her skirt, gathered at her waist, falls into fine pleats that swirl as though stirred by a soft breeze. Posed like the virtue Temperance (see Molenaer, p. 59), she lifts a pitcher in one hand and lowers a cup in the other. Storr separately cast both vessels, decorated with classical friezes of beads and leaves. A fluted pedestal set upon stepped moldings supports her seemingly weightless form.

Hebe enjoyed great popularity among English silversmiths in the early 1800s. Her image graced handles on table bells, as well as stoppers on Scotch whisky bottles (the word "whisky" is said to derive from the Gaelic *uisge beatha*, meaning "water of life"). Storr's silver statuette of Hebe—a small-scale version of one of Antonio Canova's large marble sculptures of the goddess—brightened the home of the Duke and Duchess of St. Albans. Sir Francis Burdett, friend of the Duchess, had given the silver Hebe to the Duchess as a gift, honoring the former actress with Hebe's eternal beauty and youth.

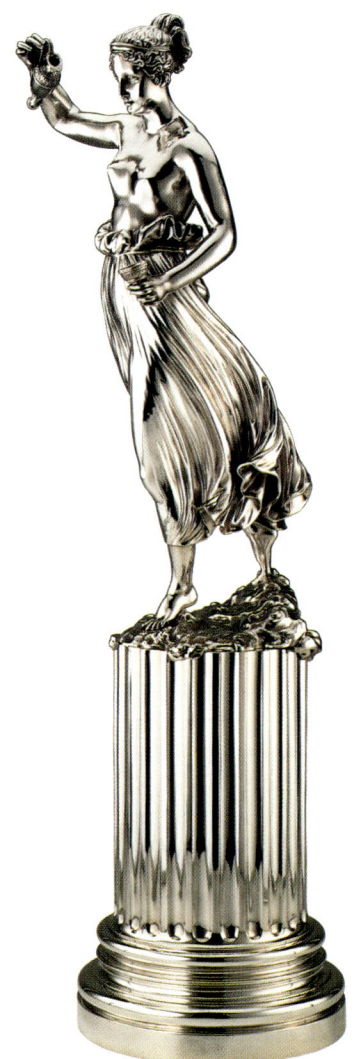

Paul Storr

Storr followed his father's trade, working as a metalsmith in London between 1792 and 1838. He had shops in Soho and Picadilly before becoming the head of the Dean Street manufactory of the royal goldsmiths Rundell, Bridge & Rundell. With these partners, he formed the firm Storr & Company, specializing in centerpieces and Neoclassical sculpture made of fine metals.

The Duchess of St. Albans

Actress Harriet Mellon (circa 1777–1837) became Duchess of St. Albans upon her marriage to William Aubrey de Vere, the ninth Duke of St. Albans (1801–1849). She willed Hebe *to the Duke, her second husband twenty-four years her junior.*

Neoclassicism and English Silversmiths

By 1800, Neoclassical motifs had become a fashionable component of the silversmith's repertory in England and America (see Paul Revere, Teapot and Stand, *p. 81). British goldsmiths sought sculptors to design Neoclassical-style racing trophies, the occasional mythological figure, and royal portraits, including statuettes of George III and Queen Victoria, all made of silver. In the Virginia Museum's galleries, see Storr's classical* Cups and Covers, Tea Urn, Zodiac Salver, *and* Theocritus Cup *in the form of a Greek crater (see the* Symposium Vessels, *pp. 4–5).*

Canova's Sculpture

The Italian artist Antonio Canova (1757–1822) is best known for his tomb monuments and Neoclassical figures, including a life-sized marble sculpture of Napoleon's sister, Maria Paulina Borghese, as Venus. With her classic profile, hair piled high, and garment draped about her lower torso, she, in turn, also inspired Storr's silver Hebe.

Sculpture, "Hebe," figure, 1829–30; base, 1837–38
Paul Storr (English, 1777–1844)
Silver; statuette, 23¼ inches high; pedestal, 13¾ inches high
Virginia Museum of Fine Arts Gift, The Jerome and Rita Gans Collection of English Silver, 97.59

Herbert Haseltine
Suffolk Punch Stallion: Sudbourne Premier

Herbert Haseltine's sculpture of *Sudbourne Premier* charms the viewer, just as the artist's memoirs about making the statue engages the reader. Haseltine's reflections on how he fashioned a bronze horse, by studying a live model, reveal the sculptor's dedication, frustration, and amusement as he created a series of British champion animals. The artist had been working on animal sculptures in his Paris studio when he decided to model the breeds "of those I had seen at the shows of the royal Agricultural Society of England."

Encouraged by the editors of the English journal, *The Field*, who provided letters of introduction, Haseltine began to scour England for specialists in sports and agriculture who could lead him to champion sheep, pigs, dairy and beef cattle, draft horses, jumpers, and race horses. His meeting with the chestnut Sudbourne Premier inspired him.

The resulting bronze captures the classic qualities and intelligent expression of the champion draft horse that so arrested the artist. From a plasticine model (a malleable material developed in France in the late 1890s; see Degas, pp. 74–75), Haseltine had the bronze horse cast by the lost-wax process. The reddish brown patina, over a mercury gilt surface, recollects the stallion's chestnut coat; the onyx eyes, set in ivory, recall his sensitive expression noted in Haseltine's account. As though preparing for a show, the stable groom had braided Sudbourne Premier's mane and tail, which the artist then modeled with ribbons of Persian lapis lazuli, created by Cartier of Paris. Echoes of Art Deco resound in Haseltine's style; the years he spent copying ancient Egyptian, Assyrian, Greek, and Chinese sculpture are evident. His reserved work attempts to extract the essential nature of each of his subjects, while remaining true to the block-like form of stone or finely chased and polished bronze.

Sudbourne Premier was one of three "animals in motion" that Haseltine was to make for the series. Setting up his stand outdoors in the middle of an open space while the stallion walked around him, the sculptor worked on the model for five days. It was December, and Haseltine complained—about being forced outside because the stall was too dark, about having to work in cold too bitter to model a horse, much less to rest to eat a sandwich and drink a beer. Still, through his tenacity, the artist turned a champion draft horse into a stylish art form.

Haseltine's Set of British Champion Animals

Born in Rome to Helen Marshall and the American painter William Stanley Haseltine (1835–1900), Herbert Haseltine had a pedigree that may be traced to Philadelphia (see Peale, p. 80; Cassatt, p. 90; Sargent, p. 91; Davis, p. 93). His sculpture combines art and natural history. Marshall Field contracted to buy the complete set of British champion animals in 1925, for the Field Museum of Natural History, Chicago. By 1933, Haseltine had completed nineteen, which were delivered in 1934. The set—bulls, pigs, sheep, and steeds, each one-fourth life-size with a personality as sparkling as its surface—came to the Virginia Museum in 1986.

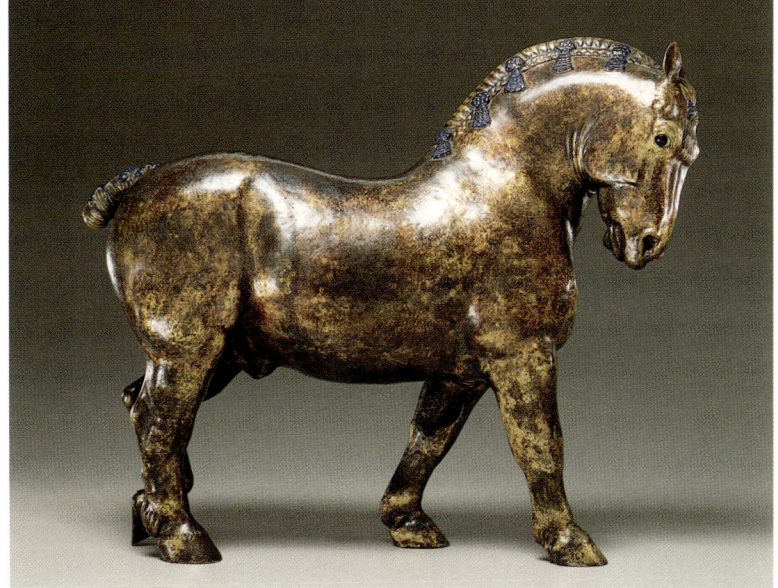

Suffolk Punch Stallion:
Sudbourne Premier, after 1922
Herbert Haseltine (American, 1877–1962)
Bronze, gold plate, lapis lazuli, ivory, onyx; 21½ by 24½ by 6½ inches
Virginia Museum of Fine Arts, The Paul Mellon Collection, 86.133

Hector Guimard, Cabinet

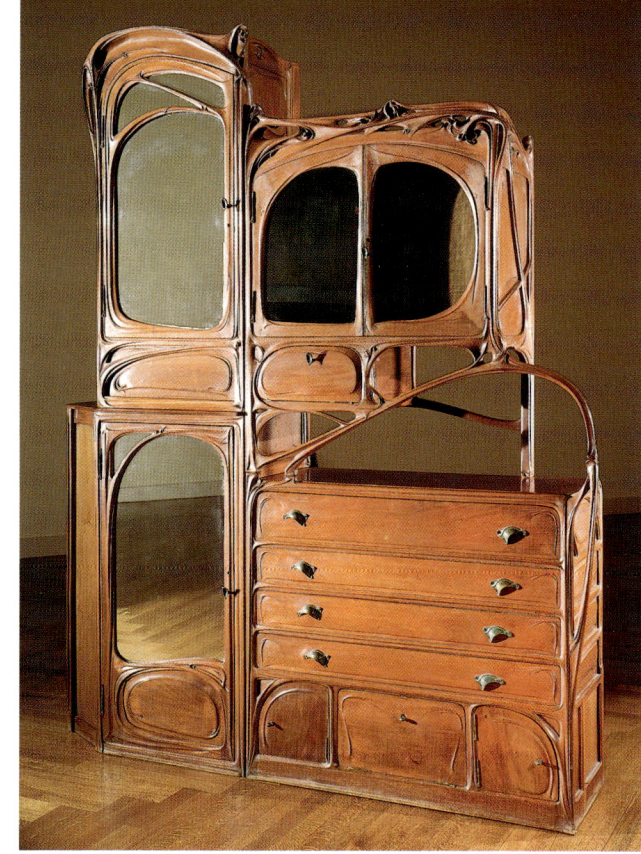

Architect and designer Hector Guimard ushered in an era of new art, embellishing places in Paris in time for the 1900 World's Fair. Among the many Art Nouveau styles flowering in Europe at the turn of the century was *Le Style Guimard.* Guimard named the style after himself, and his designs have come to be viewed as taproots of the Art Nouveau movement. By 1899 he had won the competition for the best facade in Paris with the Castel Béranger, one of a group of apartment buildings that Guimard created between 1894 and 1910. By 1900, when the Paris Metro opened to transport crowds to and from the Fair, Guimard had adorned the subway entrances with a lively interplay of cast-iron handrails, balustrades, and lampposts, set beneath glass awnings and stylish signs that to this day evoke the atmosphere of Art Nouveau Paris.

Guimard's endless curves of carved wood and cast iron spring from his efforts to capture an abstracted form of nature in art. His vision of nature—a universe of asymmetry and uniqueness, in which all living things are part of an organic whole—inspired his designs for this cabinet, as well as desks, stained glass, and stairwells (his *Office Suite* and *Picture Frame* are in the Virginia Museum).

Guimard's cabinet of twisting lines and hollowed spaces once graced an apartment in the Castel Béranger, as part of a dining-room suite. His vision once pervaded every element of his building. Custom-designed furnishings—buffets, benches, cupboards, and wallpaper once filled the interiors. Cast-iron masks and swirling sea-horses still decorate the building's exterior balconies.

This cabinet seems to grow upward, made of ash and pear, a supple wood suited to the lines of Guimard's designs. From the bronze-handled drawers to the mirrored cupboard doors, the solid and open spaces of this piece create a play of light and dark, shadow and surface. Wood changes form; its broad planes narrow to attenuated lines that seem to be drawn out of thin air. Deep ornamental carving snakes its way from bottom to top. Branches, tendrils, and trumpet-blossoms of fruitwood climb under, over, and around each nook and cranny. Guimard's art unites form and content: the structure of the cabinet is inseparable from its decoration. The carving, like a woodland vine, at once enfolds the cabinet and defines it, as if rooted to its very core.

Art Nouveau and Art Deco in a Nutshell
"At the 1900 World's Fair, it was the triumph of the coil, the twist, the ornament. Now. . .nobody talks about anything but straight lines, essentials, construction."—Auguste Perret, Architect, 1925.

Modern Architecture and Design
Guimard was part of a new breed of architect and designer who believed in unified creative expressions: "The lines of the most humble furniture should reflect the character of the whole dwelling." During the late 1800s and early 1900s, artists, designers, and architects in the forefront of the Aesthetic, Art Nouveau, and Art Deco movements harmonized their decorative and fine arts styles and designs (see Mackintosh, opposite, and Gray, p. 104).

Cabinet, circa 1899
Hector Guimard (French, 1867–1942)
Pear, ash, bronze, mirrored glass; 117 by 93½ by
   19½ inches
Virginia Museum of Fine Arts Purchase, The Sydney
   and Frances Lewis Art Nouveau Fund, 72.12

Charles Rennie Mackintosh, Chair

This armchair by the preeminent Scottish architect and designer Charles Rennie Mackintosh represents Art Nouveau in Glasgow. In 1896 the established Arts and Crafts Society of London dismissed Mackintosh's designs; its members linked him to the emerging, and equally disdained, Art Nouveau artists in Europe. Mackintosh represents a fiercely independent vision, however, and his art has little in common with that of the French architect and designer Hector Guimard (opposite). Mackintosh's chair seems to counter every curved line of Guimard's cabinet with a perpendicular one. For every unexpected bend in Guimard's honey-colored furniture, each angle of Mackintosh's dark-stained wood asserts the integrity of its hard surface. The two designers' styles diverge along different branches—one sinuous, one straight—though the artists shared a quest for unified interior designs that encompassed walls, windows, wallpaper, screens, panels, and furniture (see Gray, p. 104).

Purity and simplicity define Mackintosh's style. His armchair displays his love of rhythmic geometric patterns, dark-stained wood often set against neutral-colored walls, and the interplay of positive and negative spaces. Slender, vertical slats stretch from the top to the bottom, to form the chair's high rectangular back. To counterbalance the height, a solid square seat rests above a square base, its space sliced by horizontal slats. Framed ovals of deep mauve-colored glass provide a whisper of curved ornament set between small open squares. Chair and space co-exist, the one because of the other: the chair defines and frames the space around it; the space, in turn, gives form to the chair.

Mackintosh created the chair as the high-backed centerpiece of an ensemble for Miss Catherine Cranston's music room in Hous'hill, her home in Glasgow, which he helped decorate between 1903 and 1919. He designed smaller, flanking chairs with low backs also formed by vertical slats. Stretching behind the chairs, a screen of vertical slats carried the design from wall to wall, creating the harmonious framework that separated the music room from the drawing room. Like musical notes, glass motifs embellished the entire ensemble with a simple refrain.

Mackintosh's Vision

Mackintosh's clear, uncluttered interiors reflect his unique vision: that the style and feeling of his dreamlike rooms, at once serene and sublime, could encourage higher levels of spirituality and states of being.

Miss Cranston and Her Tea Rooms

Famous for her turn-of-the-century Tea Rooms designed by Mackintosh in Glasgow (Willow Street, Argyle Street, Ingram Street, and Buchanon Street), Catherine Cranston was one of the architect's foremost patrons.

The Glasgow Four

Art Nouveau in Glasgow came to be defined by the group of "Four": Mackintosh, Herbert MacNair, and two sisters, Margaret and Frances Macdonald. As students of the Glasgow School of Art (whose new school was built between 1897 and 1909 according to Mackintosh's 1896 award-winning design), the foursome created rarified designs haunted by symbols of the imagination, mysticism, sexuality, and metamorphosis. These ghostly eccentricities earned the Macdonald sisters the nickname "Spook School" by critics setting eyes on Scottish Art Nouveau for the first time (see Margaret Macdonald's paintings of The Four Queens

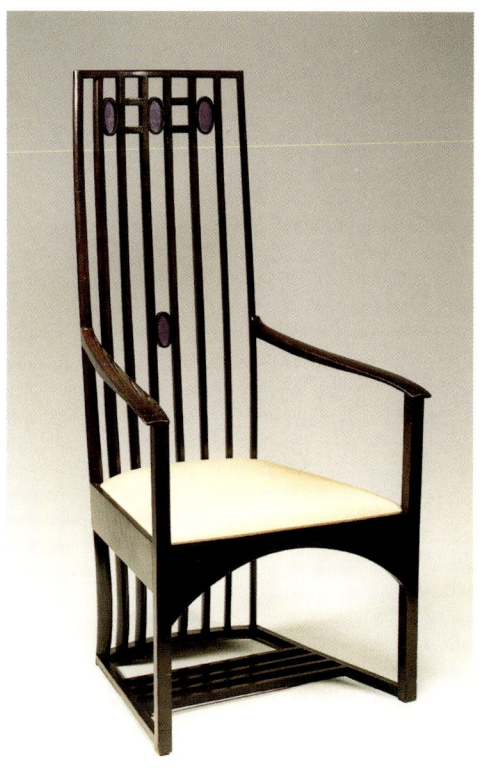

in the Virginia Museum's galleries). Designs by the Glasgow Four had a profound impact on the art of the Vienna Secession. Though the group of four eventually disbanded, Herbert and Frances married, as did Charles and Margaret, who shared a lifetime of design collaboration (furniture, graphic design, wall decoration, fabrics).

Armchair, circa 1904
Charles Rennie Mackintosh (Scottish, 1868–1928)
Stained wood, glass, upholstery; 47 by 24¼ by 25 inches
Virginia Museum of Fine Arts, Gift of Sydney and Frances Lewis, 85.145

Louis Comfort Tiffany, Punch Bowl

"Breaking waves," "foaming crests," "peacock-hued": these words first written in 1900 still capture the essence of Louis Comfort Tiffany's *Punch Bowl* today. When exhibited at the 1900 World's Fair in Paris, the *Punch Bowl* was considered to be the most outstanding piece in Tiffany's booth. It continues to provoke strong responses, ranging from "Tiffany's master-piece" and "exuberant" to "the weirdest" and "truly monstrous"! No matter how the viewer reacts to it, such a work of art might be admired for its wonderful power to inspire such emotion.

Reflecting the pinks, blues, and greens of a seascape at sunrise, the *Punch Bowl* conjures up images of froth, sea-foam, and sea creatures, true to its Art Nouveau style. Wildly curving lines assume forms borrowed from nature: shells, waves, tentacles. The bowl, made of iridescent glass, rests in a frame of gold-washed silver. The frame in turn is buoyed by six

tendril-like arms, curling into spirals at the tips. These glass arms rise in front of shimmering metal waves, which seem to splash and dissolve into a scalloped pool, so that the base of the *Punch Bowl* itself appears to ebb and flow. Around the top of the bowl, four metal-and-glass ladles hang from twists of glass, as though ready to be dipped into punch inside.

Tiffany devoted more than thirty years to his endless explorations of glass, believing "no effect or mood" to be beyond his artisans' reach. By the turn of the century, more than five-thousand colors and textures had been created by his studio. The *Punch Bowl* is made of handblown glass, called *favrile,* which Tiffany introduced in the 1890s, having registered the trademark in 1894. To attain the sea of soft colors, as many as seven hues might have been mixed. The hot glass was then exposed to metallic vapors, which deposited luster to the

surface and produced a satin finish. An eye-catching blend of opposites—energy and vibrancy, delicacy and fragility—Tiffany's favrile glass was much imitated in Europe after its debut.

Tiffany's History
Louis Comfort Tiffany, son of the jeweler who founded Tiffany & Co. on Fifth Avenue in New York City, became America's most prominent Art Nouveau artist by creating luxurious works in glass, beginning in the 1870s. For decades after, Tiffany's reputation as a master glassmaker and artist flourished. With his staff of chemists and artisans, he approached glassmaking as though painting or drawing, forever seeking new tones, textures, and expressive possibilities.

Tiffany's Lamps
It is said that Tiffany Studios cut glass left over from other projects to suit designs for lamps, often made in multiple copies. Many globes and shades that blossom from bronze, enameled, and stained glass bases took shape when glass sections were soldered together in colorful patterns. Immensely popular, the lamps offered buyers beautiful designs, impeccable workmanship, and several choices of illumination: by kerosene, oil, gas, or electricity. Many examples of Tiffany's lamps, treasures reflecting his comprehensive knowledge of light and his eye for color, now brighten the Virginia Museum's galleries.

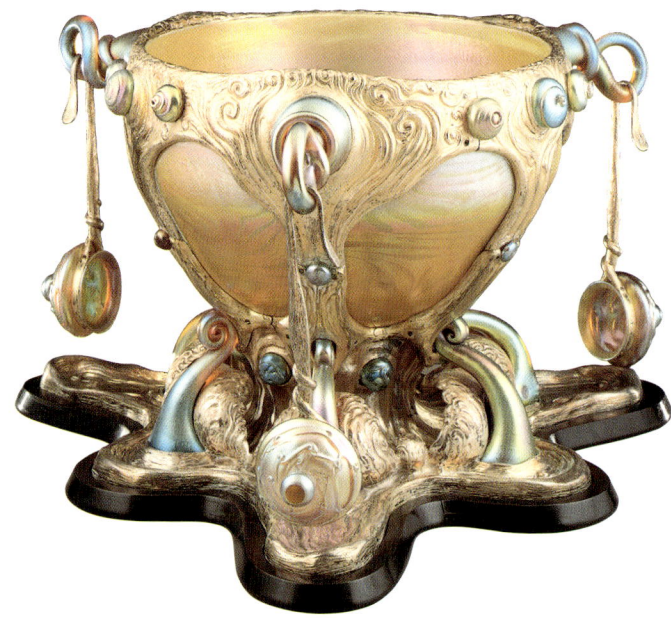

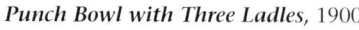

***Punch Bowl with Three Ladles**, 1900*
Louis Comfort Tiffany (American, 1848–1933)
  Tiffany Glass and Decorating Co.
Blown glass (favrile), silver gilt mounts; 14¼ by
  30 inches
Virginia Museum of Fine Arts Purchase, The Sydney
  and Frances Lewis Art Nouveau Fund, 74.16a/d

René Lalique, Brooch

René Lalique has been called the father of French jewelry. Enchanted creatures grew out of his artistic imagination into sinuous designs for gold, glass, and gemstones. His Art Nouveau jewelry took its inspiration from nature—poppies, dragonflies, grasshoppers, peacocks. Metamorphosis takes place before our very eyes. Here on this brooch, pink and green enamels form bony seahorses touched with gold. Above them, a fiery opal floats in a gold bezel, balanced playfully upon seahorse snouts. Below, the tips of seahorse tails curl on each side of a second opal. Still smaller opals rise like underwater bubbles through a pink and green sea, formed of translucent enamels set into a filigreed framework. Like a tiny stained-glass window, Lalique's *plîque-á-jour* brooch "lets in daylight," as the meaning of this phrase suggests. Below Lalique's translucent sea, a baroque pearl, so-called because of its irregular shape, anchors the brooch.

Lalique freely used glass, enamels, and semiprecious stones, bringing elements of surprise to traditional gold-and-diamond jewelry (see Fabergé, p. 95). Lalique's rows of diamonds turn into stems of plants; wild flowers and sylvan beings sprout from enameled vines. Colors and textures enhance his subject-matter—a seahorse brooch and a swan necklace cast in frothy opalescence; a brooch of flower petals formed of purple glass; a collar of leaping frogs fashioned in pale green enamel (see the Art Nouveau jewelry in the Virginia Museum's galleries). Lalique's jewelry charms the eye; at times it takes an eerie twist and an erotic turn. At the 1900 Exposition in Paris (Peter Carl Fabergé and Louis Comfort Tiffany were there too, see p. 95, and opposite), Lalique turned astonished visitors into admiring clients, who placed countless orders for his exotic creations.

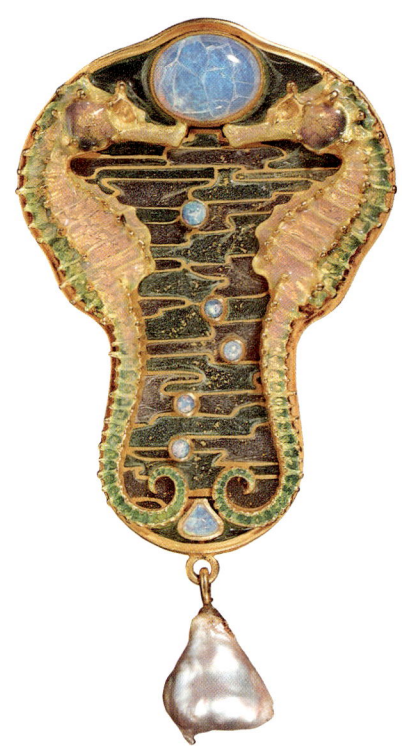

Lalique's Evolution

As a young man, Lalique was apprenticed to Parisian jeweler Louis Aucoq; he studied in London and returned to France to design for Cartier. In the mid 1880s, Lalique established his own jewelry shops and in 1898 he opened a glass workshop as well. Among Lalique's clients, Sarah Bernhardt commissioned stage jewels and other decorative objects; Coty and Guerlain sought his designs for perfume labels and bottles. After 1925, Lalique transformed his famous Art Nouveau style into Art Deco-based designs.

Style 1900

Art Nouveau carried the name of Siegfried Bing's shop, La Maison de L'Art Nouveau, *which opened in Paris in 1895 to feature new art emerging in a modern age. New design principles swept Europe and touched American shores: Lalique's jewelry in*

France, Tiffany's glass in North America and Europe (opposite), Hector Guimard's designs in Paris (see p. 98). Embracing architecture, glassworks, posters, prints, furniture, and fashion, the movement is sometimes known as *Style 1900 or* Style Nouille, *the "noodle" or "whiplash" style.* Japonisme *influenced Art Nouveau creations, with the delicate lines and asymmetrical patterns of Japanese prints and ornamental objects. Always lively, Art Nouveau takes its inspiration from nature—trees, birds, lilies, enchanted woodland creatures.*

Style 1925

Art Deco, also known as Style 1925, received its name from the Exposition Internationale des Arts Décoratifs et Industriels Moderne *held in Paris that year. Furniture, fashion, interior design, and architecture during the 1920s and 1930s became streamlined and angular (see Legrain, p. 105). Art Deco designers in Europe and the United States favored straight lines rather than curved ones, symmetry rather than asymmetry, and eastern influences from Egypt to Japan. King Tutankhamen's tomb (discovered, 1922), the Ballet Russe, the Jazz Age, and modern industrial materials—steel, concrete, plastics—inspired designs for silverware, screens, and skyscrapers alike. Art Deco imagery includes low furniture and high ceilings, plate-glass and glass-brick, chrome and silver surfaces, natural and lacquered wood (see Gray, p. 104).*

Brooch, 1902–05
René Lalique (French, 1860–1945)
Gold, opals, oriental pearl, enamel; 4 by 2½ inches
Virginia Museum of Fine Arts Purchase, The Sydney
  and Frances Lewis Art Nouveau Fund, 73.46.1

Frank Lloyd Wright, Windows

American architect Frank Lloyd Wright devoted a lifetime to exploring—and re-defining—spaces in which people live, work, and play. His designs reflect his genius for marrying his manmade buildings to their natural settings. They announce his sensitivity to the interaction between a given structure and the activities of its occupants. Inspired by nature in general and the American landscape in particular, Wright chose local brick, stone, clay, and wood for his building materials. For the glass panels and panes that played such an essential role as architectural decoration, he generally borrowed colors from autumn fields—amber, golden brown, olive green (see the *Tree of Life Window* in the Virginia Museum's galleries).

Glass windows and doors served as primary elements in Wright's architectural canon. He loved the way the shape and color of glass could affect the appearance of a room—its size, illumination, mood, focal points, vistas. Although far removed from the characteristically natural, neutral world of Wright's designs, the Coonley Playhouse Windows perfectly demonstrate Wright's talent for harmoniously integrating decorative glass—as well as furniture, carpet, and lighting—into its architectural setting.

Stained in bright, primary colors, these glass panes belonged to a larger set of playfully patterned windows for a kindergarten in Riverside, Illinois. As we see them now, out of context, we must imagine the vibrancy of the children's schoolroom with sunlight streaming through colorful clerestory windows above, floor-to-ceiling panels along the walls, and smaller square spaces set at eye level. Here, a circle floats like a red balloon above checkerboards of red, white, and blue. Now and then, small squares of black and green surprise the viewer, while butterscotch-colored bands attract the eye. Narrow metal strips connect the pieces of glass together, while understated wooden frames surround each panel. The windows' artful patterns create cheerful dancing rhythms as the eye moves from pane to pane. Wright himself thought that his festive playhouse windows evoked memories of lively parades, flags, balloons, and confetti.

The bright circles and squares may well have come from Wright's own childhood memories. Reminiscing about playtime with "gifts" from his mother—his "small fingers" grasping colorful maple blocks and cardboard cutouts of spheres, cubes, circles, and squares—he remarked in his autobiography that "all are in my fingers to this day." Created for children to see, by a man deeply attuned to the human need for sympathetic surroundings, such fun-filled shapes took on new life at the Coonley kindergarten. Perhaps the windows might even have inspired future architects.

The Avery Coonley House and Playhouse

Wright designed the Coonley Playhouse in 1912 for the grounds of Mr. and Mrs. Avery Coonley's home, built by the architect in 1908. Mrs. Coonley, like Wright's mother, was an advocate of progressive education. Both buildings, large and small, share Wright's innovative spirit: long, low, and fluid interior spaces; low-hipped or flat, cantilevered roofs; expansive garden walls and terraces.

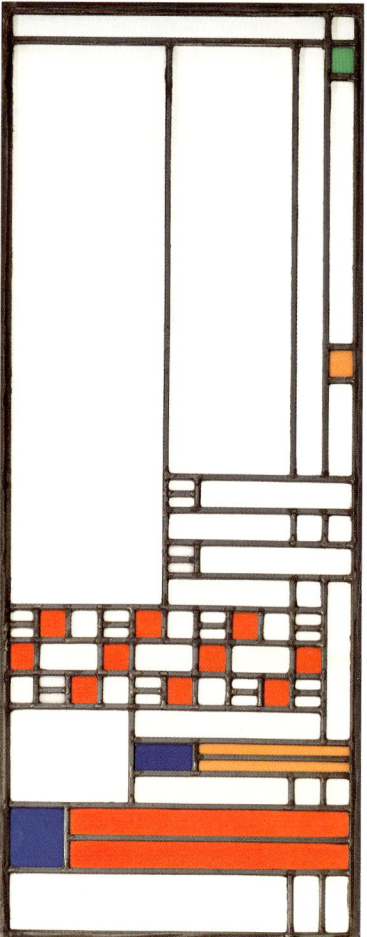

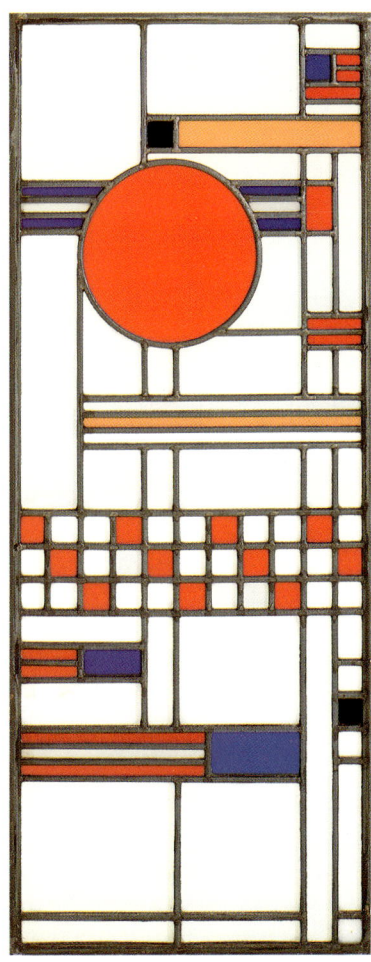

Wright's Architecture and Design

Wright grew up with Victorian architecture, yet abandoned the traditional boxlike house, composed of little boxlike rooms, for long, low houses of overlapping, intersecting spaces. Across the American landscape, Wright captured the Earth's beauty in houses that made him famous, such as Robie House (Chicago, 1909) and Fallingwater (Bear Run, central Pennsylvania, 1936). His houses fit the character of their settings: rocks, forests, and waterfalls; desert stone and sand; a prairie's vast expanses. His revolutionary plans inspired many suburban homes built between the 1930s and the 1960s.

Circles, Arcs, and Spirals

Wright first introduced the circle to his work in the Coonley Playhouse windows. The shape would eventually evolve into arcs, spheres, and spirals: Midway Gardens (Chicago, 1914), the circular rooms of the Ralph Jester house project (Palos Verdes, California, 1938), the Johnson's Wax Building (Racine, Wisconsin, 1936–39), the Solomon R. Guggenheim Museum (New York, 1956–59). As Wright himself recalled, he first learned the basics of order, proportion, and geometry from Frederick Froebel's kindergarten forms, the "gifts" that his mother had first discovered in an exhibition at the American Centennial Exposition in Philadelphia, 1876.

Wright's Glass

Wright designed vast quantities of glass in palettes of active and passive colors (examples of each type may be seen in the Virginia Museum's collection). His windows—sections of glass joined with strips of lead, copper, or brass in a process known as "caming"—took the shape of plant motifs and abstract patterns (see the Window with Two Roundels, *p. 47, and* Tiffany, *p. 100). Abstraction was indeed a novelty in the U.S. and Europe when Wright's geometric patterns appeared in the Coonley Playhouse windows.*

Pair of Windows, 1912
Frank Lloyd Wright (American, 1867–1959)
Stained and leaded glass; 30⅝ by 12⅜ by ⅜ inches
Virginia Museum of Fine Arts, Gift of Sydney and
  Frances Lewis, 85.348.1-2

Eileen Gray, Canoe Sofa

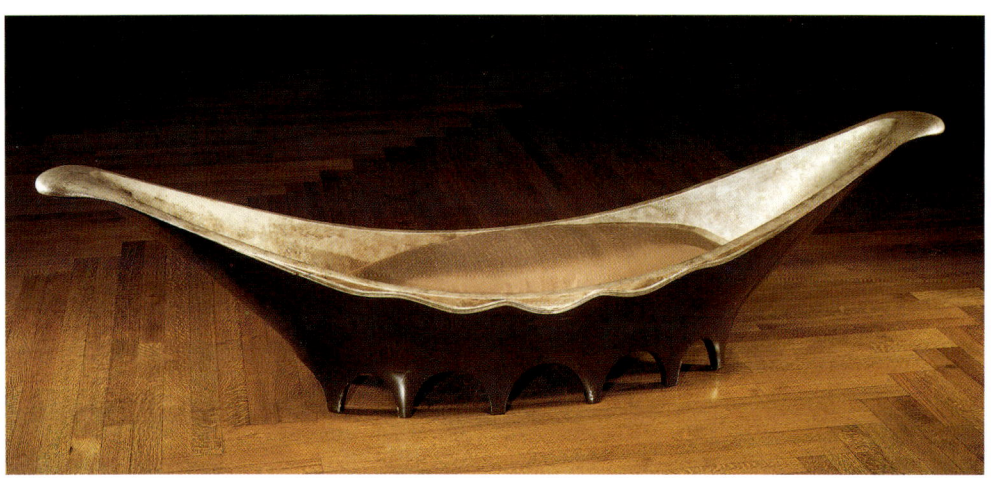

Independence and integrity define the far-sighted vision of furniture designer and decorator Eileen Gray. She was most productive during the early decades of this century (1900s–1930s), though her art found its broadest, most appreciative audience in later ones (1960s–1990s).

The *Canoe Sofa* represents one aspect of Gray's multifaceted career in design and architecture, then a man's world centered in Paris. At first she designed exotic and luxurious lacquered objects for the home; later, she created prototypes for contemporary furnishings forged from materials of the industrial age—tubular steel, celluloid, aluminum, mesh.

Gray's long, canoe-shaped divan was one of a pair created for a Paris apartment appointed with African carved figures, masks, and drums. In Paris in 1920, Gray's divan was called a *pirogue,* meaning "dugout canoe," or "boat bed" *(lit-de-bateau).* Like a canoe, this sofa is carved of wood. Graceful, tapering lines curve upward toward each end and downward to a base. Arches form the twelve legs, and the ends resemble a boat's prow and stern. The scalloped edges of the "hull" create a wavelike pattern, befitting

a boat. Gray finished the exterior in lacquer—her trademark—and the interior with silver leaf.

When filled with cushions, Gray's luxurious sofa became inviting. Gray celebrated the comforts of life—resting, sleeping, reading, eating, or simply being—in her designs for tables, screens, carpets, lamps, and, eventually, houses. She believed that art should be useful; she wanted to design, in her words, that "which was possible, but which no one was doing."

In many ways, she succeeded. And yet, by the time she retired in the late 1930s, the *Canoe Sofa* had become part of an exotic and theatrical world that she had left behind. Gray eventually renounced the modern movements of her era—Art Nouveau and Art Deco—as excessive. Trusting her instincts, she went on to develop her taste for objects of simple lines and planes. Gray's adventurous design and sharp-sighted style are often terse, geometric, abstract, experimental, and occasionally shocking or whimsical.

The Artist's Patron

Gray's Canoe Sofa *decorated the apartment of Madame Mathieu-Lévy, known by the name of her milliner's salon,* Suzanne Talbot. *Gray introduced walls of lacquered panels in Mme Lévy's entrance hall, an idea that she later modified into her freestanding screens, which she designed to divide space, admit light, and control interior views.*

The Art of Lacquer

Gray applied twenty to forty coats of lacquer to her objects and added color (often black, red-orange, or brown) to the last few layers (see the Japanese Ewer, *p. 31). Gray at first did much of the lacquer-work herself; the harsh liquid damaged the skin on her hands and arms. She also closely supervised a staff of artisans, many of whom remained with the reclusive artist for decades.*

Canoe Sofa, 1919–20
Eileen Gray (1879–1976; born Ireland, active France)
Lacquered wood, silver leaf; 28⅜ by 106⁵⁄₁₆ by 25⁹⁄₁₆ inches
Virginia Museum of Fine Arts, Gift of Sydney and Frances Lewis, 85.112

Pierre Legrain, Bird Cage on Stand

Pierre Legrain's striking black and red *Bird Cage* once stood in the entrance hall of Jacques Doucet's Studio St. James, a 1925 addition to his house in Neuilly, France. Photographs of the interior show state-of-the-art decor—chrome, enamel, and glass—that is now known as Style 1925 or Art Deco. Next to Legrain's *Bird Cage,* stylized metal peacocks guarded the metal banisters of the stairwell, while "modern" art adorned the walls. A prominent player in high fashion, Doucet hired an impressive list of designers to decorate his residences in Paris and Neuilly in the "modern style." Doing so, he became one of Legrain's most important patrons. Doucet's studio at Neuilly served as a showcase for his collection of contemporary art, including works by Rousseau (see p. 77) and Picasso (p. 108), and his commissioned collaborations in interior design, including furniture and sculpture now in the Virginia Museum (see Rose Adler, Gustave Miklos, and Marcel Coard in the galleries). Legrain directed the designers' efforts, which mirror his own love of textures—metal, glass, sharkskin, animal hide—and of richly colored lacquers and enamels. Although he is better known today for the art of bookbinding, Legrain displayed equal passions for furniture design and interior decoration.

For his *Bird Cage on Stand,* Legrain used the favorite materials of Art Deco artists: aluminum wires for the cage, and lacquered wood for the frame, perches, and stand. He selected parchment—traditionally used, like vellum, for books—to trim the cage, wrapping it around the feet, handles, and stretcher. The resulting design sings of Legrain's look—always creative and often described as energetic and architectural.

Pierre Legrain

As a young man in France, Legrain studied at the Germain Pilon School of Applied Arts. His work with artist and decorator Paul Iribe led to his meeting Jacques Doucet. In 1912, Legrain and Iribe collaborated with a design team, including Eileen Gray, to decorate Doucet's Paris apartment. Legrain acquired a reputation for word-of-mouth commissions— exclusive designs for exclusive clients, including Suzanne Talbot (see Gray, opposite).

Artistic Influences

Legrain's Bird Cage *shows the planar, geometric influence of Cubism. His* Stool *and* Tabouret, *also in the Virginia Museum's collection, reveal the direct impact of western and central African arts on his work. Legrain's furniture for his patron Jacques Doucet is strongly influenced by Ashanti designs for royal thrones, stools, and neck rests.*

Bookbinding

In 1917, Jacques Doucet commissioned Legrain to design bindings for his vast library. Legrain set up his studio in his patron's dining room and set about revolutionizing the art of bookbinding. Three-hundred sixty-five binding designs later, Legrain discovered that he had a viable way to support himself. He established a workshop and revitalized the art of bookbinding during the 1920s (see Rose Adler's binding design for Colette's Cheri *in the Virginia Museum's galleries).*

Commercial Enterprises

In addition to private commissions, Legrain also designed leather camera cases for Kodak and cigarette boxes for Lucky Strike and Camel.

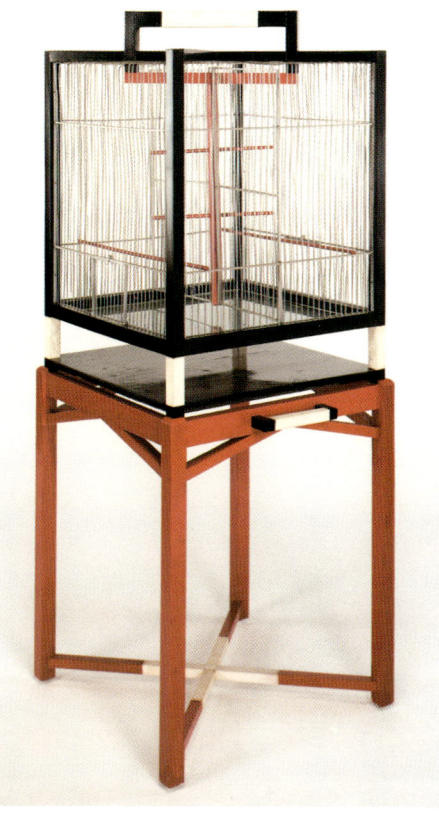

Jacques Doucet

Doucet's family business grew into a premier house of fashion in Paris. He amassed a formidable collection of art, including works by Fragonard (see p. 64) and Degas (p. 73). Selling this first collection in 1912, he began to collect contemporary art. Doucet is said to have financed the Surrealist movement; in 1921, the Surrealist poet André Breton helped him build his art collection and library.

Bird Cage on Stand, circa 1920
Pierre Legrain (French, 1889–1929)
Lacquer, wood, parchment, aluminum; 57½ by 22½ by 22½ inches
Virginia Museum of Fine Arts Purchase, The Sydney and Frances Lewis Endowment Fund, 89.23a/b

Frank Gehry, White Little Beaver Chair and Ottoman

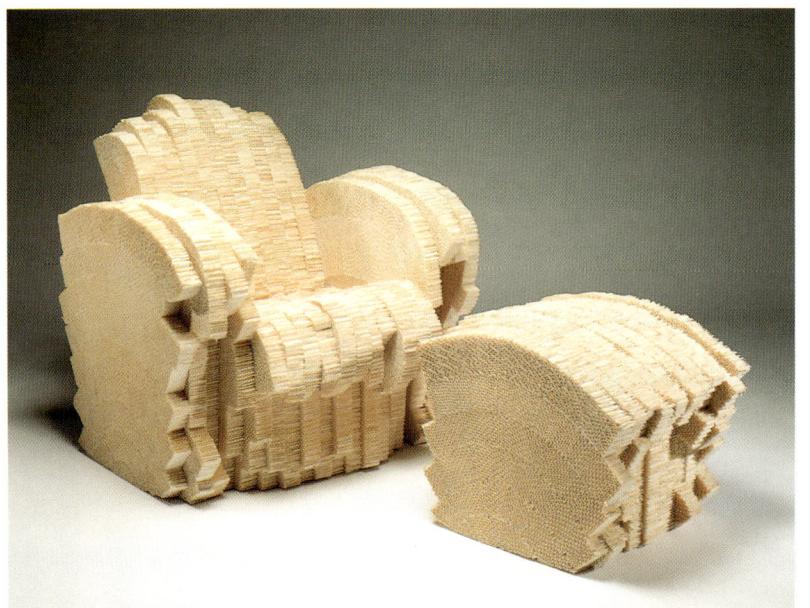

(see Guimard, p. 98, and Wright, pp. 102–103)

"Cardboard is a throwaway material." Frank Gehry is telling an interviewer that he likes the "homey" look of cardboard furniture. "I'm interested in things the culture denies yet uses in great quantities." The interior of his architectural firm in Santa Monica, California, is decorated with corrugated cardboard and laminated plastic. A photograph of his office shows him seated comfortably on a cardboard chair much like this one.

This chair and ottoman are part of a series that includes tables, lounges, and love seats designed by Gehry and exhibited in 1988 as *New Cardboard Furniture*. That exhibition followed *Easy Edges* in 1971, when Gehry introduced his first line of cardboard furniture and gained national attention with the question, "can a chair be art?" Each of Gehry's chairs expresses a personality as diverse as his production techniques. He crushes, rolls, glues, and stacks corrugated cardboard; he cross-laminates it. Here, he forms a chair and a footstool from rows of cardboard. When seen from different angles, the rows present a variety of patterns and textures, while giving the furniture its jigsaw contours.

From a long tradition of architect-designers (see Guimard, p. 98, and Wright, pp. 102–103), Gehry creates award-winning furniture and buildings that look like sculpture. He works with the materials of our industrial society—corrugated metal, chain-link fencing—because he believes that beauty can be made out of the inexpensive, often ugly, materials that surround us. He seeks surprising juxtapositions of shapes and materials, and pleasing asymmetry influenced by Japanese art (see Degas, p. 73; Cassatt, p. 90; and Lalique, p. 101). Gehry's chair and ottoman express his talent to bridge function and whimsy in designs that challenge and invite, equally at home in a commercial marketplace or in a museum gallery.

Designs in Context

Gehry designs his architecture and furniture in response to its setting. He created a twenty-two-meter fish to curl along the wharf outside the Fishdance Restaurant in Kobe, Japan, screening an unsightly view of a double-decker freeway. Gehry also added a jet fighter to the facade of the California Aerospace Museum in Los Angeles, transforming architecture into collage.

Gehry's "Carol" Chair

Gehry's White Little Beaver Chair *is related to his* Carol Chair, *named for Carol Burnett. The American comedienne, while sitting in her chair for an interview, remarked that the corrugated cardboard reminded her of childrens' cardboard playhouses and marveled at the chair's flexibility, to swell if wet but to shrink back into shape when dry. She also commented on the easy upkeep: "if it starts to come apart, you just put some glue on and it goes back together."*

Gehry's Architecture

The jury who awarded the Pritzker Prize to Gehry called his architecture "refreshingly original and totally American . . . refined, sophisticated and adventurous." Architects I. M. Pei and Philip Johnson have also received the prize. The firm, Frank O. Gehry and Associates, has designed buildings in Los Angeles, Dallas, and Japan. He has been called the guru of "deconstructivist" architecture, though he himself laughs at the term.

White Little Beaver Chair and Ottoman, **1988**
Frank Gehry (American, born in Canada, 1929)
Corrugated cardboard, edition 2/50; Chair: 40 by 34 by 33 inches; Ottoman: 21½ by 19¼ by 16½ inches
Virginia Museum of Fine Arts Purchase, The Council Good Design Fund, 88.65.1/2

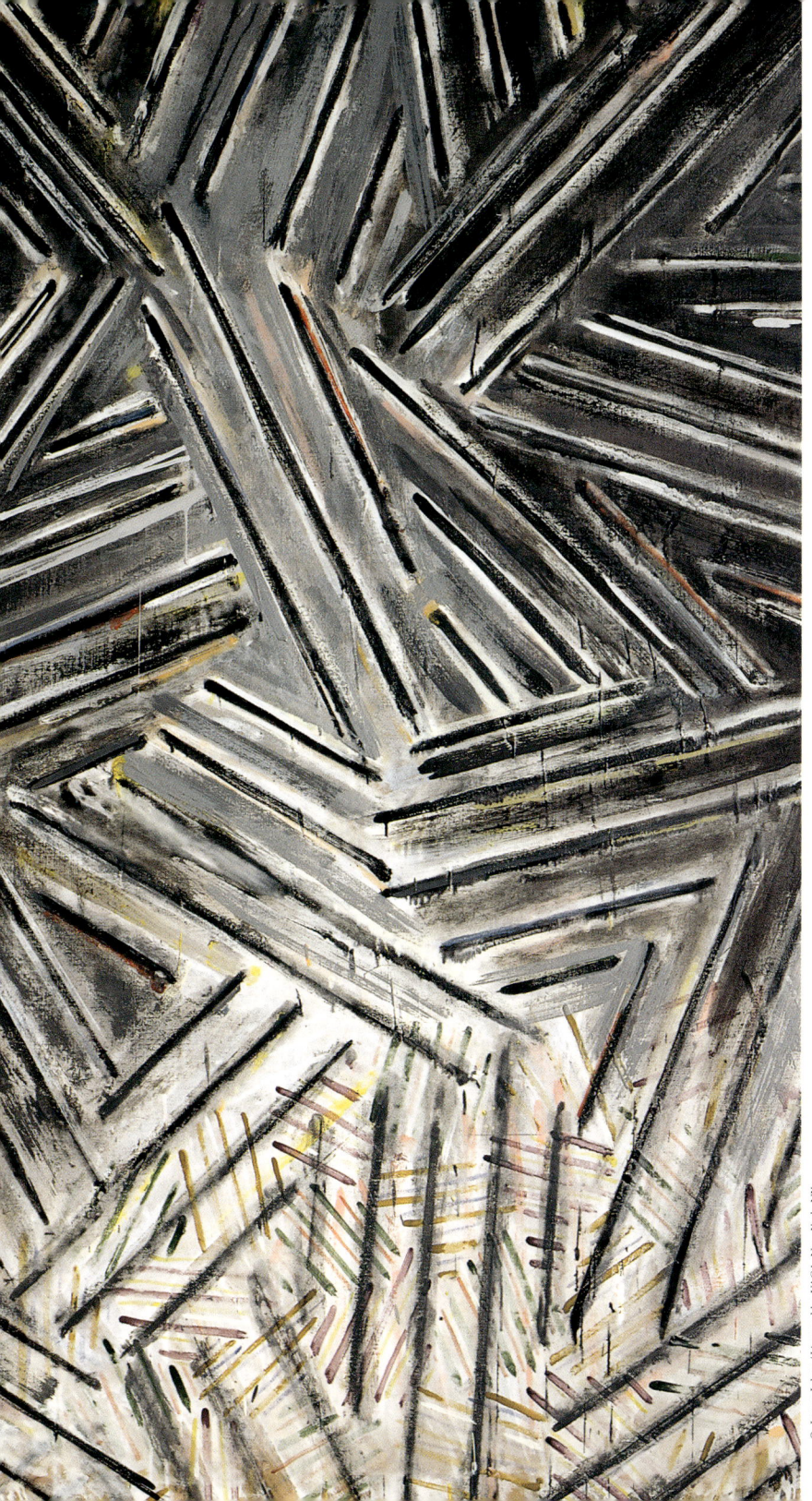

CHAPTER 9

European and American Twentieth-Century Art

1900s–1910s

1950s

1960s

1970s

1980s–1990s

Pablo Picasso, Jester on Horseback

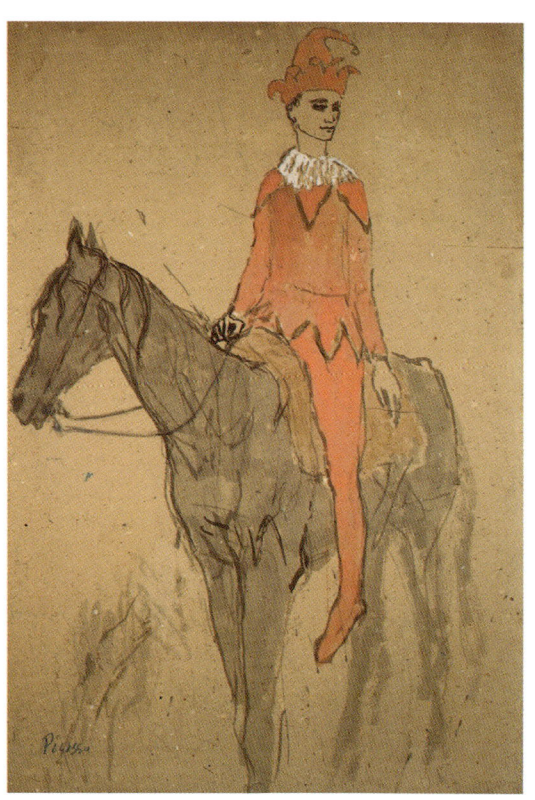

During his Rose Period (1904–06), Pablo Picasso painted harlequins and jesters. Deftly drawn and subtly modeled forms—tinted in a range of soft reds with occasional bursts of contrasting color—characterize Picasso's oils, watercolors, and pastels from this period. Here, Picasso's sketch reveals his artistic process: "To finish a picture? What nonsense!…The value of a work resides in what it is not." He once proclaimed, "The important thing is to create. Nothing else matters." Using a wash, Picasso first painted the forms of horse and jester, then outlined and defined the figures. Simple but assured strokes give expression to the jester's eyes and lips; strong lines form the contour of his jaw, neck, and stockinged foot; white paint highlights his collar, and rosy shades of red define his costume. With quick strokes, the artist sketched in the horse's head and torso, while suggesting the horse's legs in muted grays against the neutral background of the composition board.

In Paris at the Cirque Médrano, Picasso observed circus performers (in French, *saltimbanques*) and met some of them after-hours at cafés near his studio, *Bateau-Lavoir*, on Montmartre. He cast his circus models in quiet, isolated moments—alone or with their families, but never while performing. It has been said that in the introspective pictures of these itinerant acrobats and clowns living on society's periphery, Picasso found an alter ego. "Everyone wants to understand art," he lamented. "Why not try to understand the songs of a bird? Why does one love the night, flowers, everything around one, without trying to understand them? If only [people] would realize that above all an artist works of necessity, that he himself is only a trifling bit of the world."

Picasso saw the artist as "a receptacle for emotions that come from…the sky, from the earth, from a scrap of paper, from a passing shape, from a spider's web.…We must pick out what is good for us where we can find it."

At age seven, Picasso took his first art lesson from his father in Spain. A fully trained painter by age nineteen, he moved to France. His Blue Period of gaunt, melancholic figures preceded this picture. Still to come would be his invention of Cubism with George Braque (see examples in the Virginia Museum's galleries); his introduction of imagery from African art, particularly masks; his classical period; and his famous painting, *Guernica*. Devoting a lifetime to art, Picasso observed: "We all know that Art is not truth. Art is a lie that makes us realize truth, at least the truth that is given to us to understand."

Picasso on Abstract Art

"There is no abstract art. You must always start with something. Afterward you can remove all traces of reality.…the idea of the object will have left an indelible mark. It is what started the artist off, excited his ideas, and stirred up his emotions. Ideas and emotions will in the end be prisoners of his work.…They form an integral part of it, even when their presence is no longer discernible. Whether he likes it or not, man is the instrument of nature."

Picasso on the Creative Process

"In my case," Picasso once said, "a picture is a sum of destructions. I do a picture—then I destroy it. In the end though, nothing is lost; the red I took away from one place turns up somewhere else.…Destroy the thing, do it over several times. In each destroying of a beautiful discovery, the artist does not really suppress it, but rather transforms it, condenses it, makes it more substantial."

Jester on Horseback, 1905
Pablo Picasso (Spanish, 1881–1973)
Oil on composition board; 39⅜ by 27¼ inches
Virginia Museum of Fine Arts, Mr. and Mrs. Paul Mellon Collection, 84.2

Ernst Kirchner
Seated Woman with Wood Sculpture

A woman—hair bobbed, cigarette in hand, coffee cup before her—sits beside a figure carved of wood. Large areas of pink, green, yellow, and blue glow as they take the shape of simple forms, defined by lines that zig-zag their way across the canvas, defining dress, chair, and table. The creator of this work, German Expressionist Ernst Kirchner, co-founded *Die Brücke* (The Bridge), a group of artists dedicated to "modern" art. They expressed thought and feeling through the human figure—far removed from academic painting (see Poussin, pp. 60–61, and Van Loo, p. 63). They used simplified forms and angular lines: flat planes of color in painting, rough-hewn wood in sculpture, and hard, ragged contours in woodcuts, etchings, and lithographs. Forming a bridge to the past, the group revitalized medieval German printmaking and gave it new autonomy as an art form.

Kirchner borrowed imagery from African art, especially sculpture from Cameroon (see the *Buffalo Mask*, p. 41); from carvings by Pacific Island cultures; and from erotic art of ancient India. The wooden statue in this painting is the now-lost *Female Figure* carved by Kirchner. Her bent knees, prominent belly and breasts, and rough carving also appear in Kirchner's surviving sculpture *Dancing Woman* (Stedelijk Museum, Amsterdam). *Dancing Woman* and this painting share the same model: Erna Schilling, Kirchner's lifelong companion. A 1912 photograph shows the two sitting in the artist's Berlin studio filled with exotic, "primitive" objects of art. The photograph eerily sets the stage for this painting, as though Kirchner simply placed the wooden sculpture to Schilling's left, kept the coffee cup on the table, removed himself, and then tilted and compressed the space, harshening and exaggerating what he saw.

Expressionism

The term embraces avant-garde movements in art, music, literature, and theater that arose in modern Europe between 1905 and 1920. The psychological tension, intellectual unrest, and emotionalism before the first World War found expression in the arts, especially in Germany, promulgated by groups such as Die Brücke (The Bridge) and Der Blaue Reiter (The Blue Rider) which counted Wassily Kandinsky, Franz Marc, and Paul Klee among its numbers.

Die Brücke

Besides Kirchner, Die Brücke also included co-founders Fritz Bleyl, Erich Heckel, Karl Schmitt-Rottluff, and later, Max Pechstein, Otto Müller, and Emil Nolde (see Nolde's South Seas Landscape I and Müller's prints in the Virginia Museum's galleries). The group was formed in Dresden in 1905, the same year that Matisse and the Fauves (French for "wild beasts") exhibited in Paris and were so named by a critic appalled at their wild brushwork and arbitrary use of color. By 1911, most members of Die Brücke had moved to Berlin; by 1913, the identity of the group had dissolved, as the work of individual artists developed.

Modern Life, Modern Art

In their art, German Expressionists often responded to urban, industrial life and a shifting world order. Women and men take their places at the center of Kirchner's paintings and prints, seen in rooms and street scenes that reveal both the exciting and the dark, depressing sides of city life. As part of their campaign against modern artists and writers, Adolph Hitler's National Socialists confiscated much of the Expressionists' work in 1937 and placed it in their exhibition of "Degenerate Art."

***Seated Woman with Wood Sculpture (Sitzende Frau Mit Holzplastik)*, 1912**
Ernst Kirchner (German, 1880–1939)
Oil on canvas; 38½ by 38½ inches
Virginia Museum of Fine Art Purchase, The Adolph D. and Wilkins C. Williams Fund, 84.80

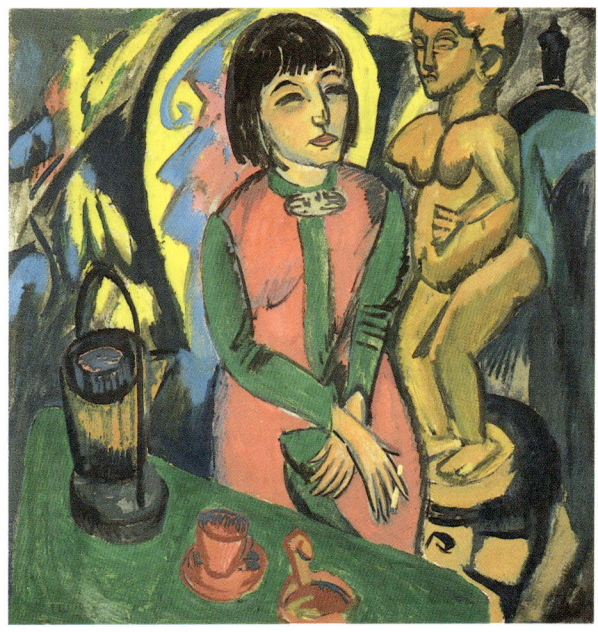

Franz Kline, Untitled

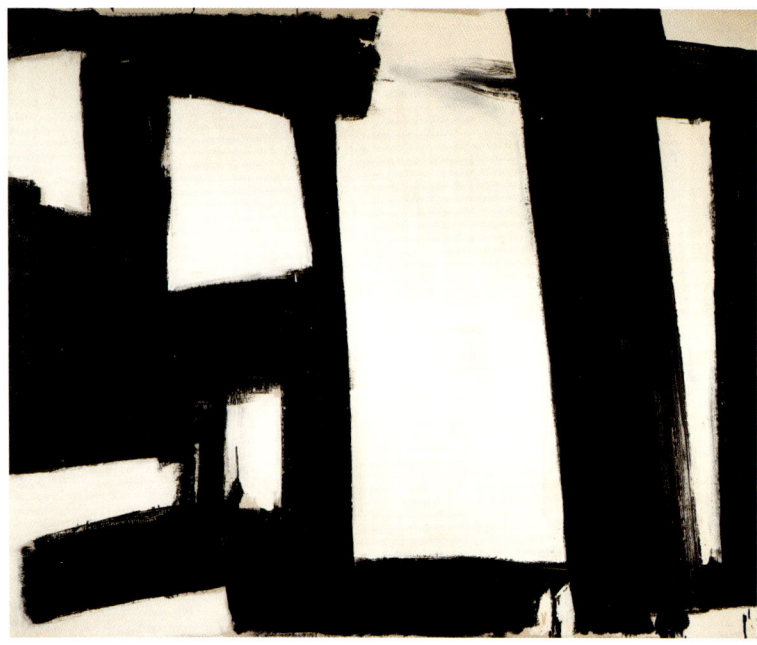

It has been said that Kline's canvases "seized the dynamism of contemporary urban life." This work suggests modern industry—large and heavy bridges or buildings—as well as memories, perhaps, of Wilkes-Barre, Pennsylvania, the coal-mining town where Kline was born and raised. Though he never admitted these associations, Kline built his compositions from a strong sense of balance and careful construction. He himself once said: "If you meant it enough when you [painted] it, it will mean that much." Kline's bare-boned words, enriched by his passion for painting, match the structure and simplicity of this work of art.

Black and White and Color
Kline's mature phase of paintings in black and white seems to have naturally evolved from his early linear and monochromatic figures and landscapes. In the late 1950s, Kline began to introduce color to his painting.

De Kooning and Kline in the Studio
A visit to Willem de Kooning's studio in 1950 changed Kline's art. That experience introduced Kline to the expressive potential of abstraction and to the Bell-Opticon projector. By projecting their small-scale drawings, the painters could experiment with compositions in a large format before actually beginning to paint on canvas.

Untitled, 1955
Franz Kline (American, 1910–1962)
Oil on canvas; 67½ by 83 inches
Virginia Museum of Fine Arts, Gift of Sydney and
  Frances Lewis, 85.415

The drama of Franz Kline's black-and-white painting—its stark contrast, dynamic brushwork, and physical presence—belies his subtle and traditional techniques. At first sight the viewer might notice only arresting scale and minimal color, yet careful consideration lies behind the composition. A closer look reveals that Kline did not simply place black paint on a white ground but that he worked with both black and white pigments (usually inexpensive house paint), pushing and pulling the shapes to create a balanced tension. Through this conflict, black and white areas assume equal importance in a controlled and deliberate structure. Kline made his brushstrokes seem effortless only after completing many smaller studies. His preparations do not show in the final painting, meant to exist simply in and of itself.

Like so many Abstract Expressionists, Kline had a background deeply rooted in European and American masters, especially Rembrandt and Goya (see p. 70). He began as a draftsman; during the 1930s, he painted mostly regional landscapes and murals for the Works Progress Administration. His art of the 1940s, focused on the human figure, changed after seeing the work of Willem de Kooning and Jackson Pollack, vanguard painters of Abstract Expressionism (in the Virginia Museum's galleries). Abstract Expressionists turned the form of painting—color and value, brushwork and surface—into its content. Painters' gestures as they applied paint to canvas became one focus of the art. Though other artists, particularly de Kooning and Robert Motherwell, sometimes painted in black and white, Franz Kline is best known for this style, which emerged in his art in 1950.

Andy Warhol, Triple Elvis

Straight out of a publicity shot from the 1960s Western, *Flaming Star,* Elvis is immortalized as singer-gunslinger in triplicate by Andy Warhol. The image is a portrait; a photograph, or rather, a reproduction of one; a silkscreen (ink pressed through a stencil), made to be replicated many times over. Its aluminum-painted background resembles the cinema's silver screen. It is an icon of two icons themselves, Warhol and Presley, artist and subject.

The celebrities in Warhol's images—Marilyn Monroe, Marlon Brando, Jackie Kennedy, Chairman Mao—have been called "secular saints," their portraits likened to venerated paintings of holy figures from centuries past. Warhol has been called a twentieth-century court painter, portraying "Who's Who" in modern society in an art form that is a product of its times. Neither unique nor hand-painted, most of Warhol's "paintings" have been manufactured in multiple copies, assembly-line style from a stencil, for a consumer-oriented society serviced by mass-markets: grocery stores stocked with frozen foods, discount chains featuring celebrity-endorsed clothing lines, multiple theaters showing movies simultaneously. Warhol's images—whether of Elvis or sensational tabloids—challenge us to notice what we sometimes overlook. He calls attention to mass-production with his images of Campbell's soup cans. He blurs the boundaries between art and life by using tragic headlines or tragic figures as subjects.

Warhol's Elvis—his eyes, sneer, and hips from the *Love-Me-Tender* years—still haunts us. Continued sightings of rock-and-roll's king and annual commemorations on the anniversary of his death merely underscore today what Warhol captured in 1964. We see Elvis—vulnerable, sexy, youthful, macho, portly, and debauched—all at the same time, everywhere, in multiples.

Trained as a designer for advertising, magazines, and clients such as Tiffany's, Warhol fashioned himself into the king of Pop Art in the 1960s, went on to avant-garde filmmaking, and by the 1970s had become *the* portraitist of high society. Interviews record the dead-pan, monosyllabic responses of an enigmatic man who distanced himself from his art, designed to be reproduced by others. On the one hand self-effacing and on the other self-promoting, Warhol brilliantly charted his course to be a star among stars, as much a celebrity as the sitters he portrayed. "I started as a commercial artist, and I want to finish as a business artist," he said in 1975.

Art as Social Time-Capsule

Warhol cast a cool eye upon society, making artistic time-capsules (see Brillo Box *in the Virginia Museum's galleries). He shared the limelight with his high-society patrons. As Sargent was to Madame X or Oscar Wilde (see p. 91), or Lalique to Sarah Bernhardt (p. 101), so Warhol was to the society that he depicted.*

Pop Art

Pop Art comments on the commercial and sometimes banal aspects of a consumer-oriented society. Objects from daily life— comic strips and clothespins (see Lichtenstein and Oldenburg in the galleries), typewriter erasers or Elvis Presley—become the subjects of Pop Art.

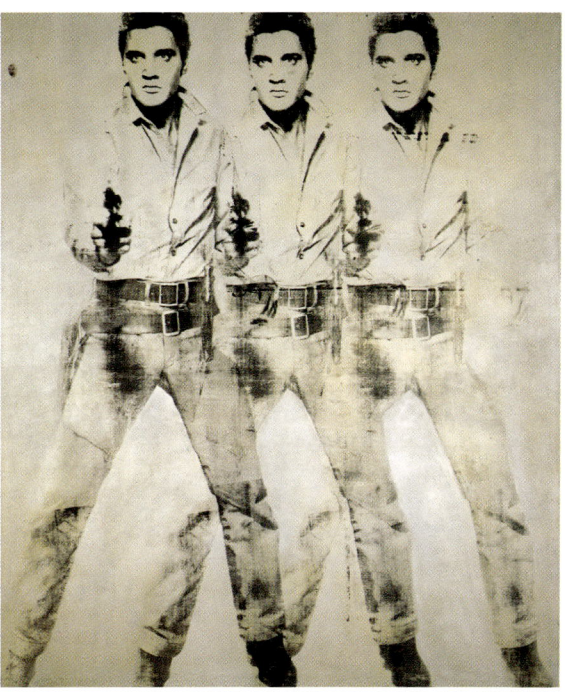

Making *Triple Elvis*

Gerard Malanga, a member of Warhol's entourage at the Factory, his New York studio, assisted Warhol with his images of Elvis. They cropped the head and boots, overlapped the figures, and graduated the values to imply depth.

Triple Elvis, 1964
Andy Warhol (American, 1930–1987)
Aluminum paint and silkscreened ink on canvas;
 82 by 71 inches
Virginia Museum of Fine Arts, The Sydney and
 Frances Lewis Collection, 85.453

George Segal
Blue Girl on Black Bed

George Segal's title aptly describes the scene, giving us a clue to its meaning. A woman, painted bright blue, sits on the edge of a bed. She lowers her head, as though deep in thought; her body seems fatigued, weighted down by her emotions. Her sleeping companion, a man painted black like the bed itself, almost blends into the background. The sculpture asks us to reflect on what we see: one figure lost in a world of her own, the other in dreams.

Children tend to respond instinctively to the sadness of the sculpture. Most comment on the loneliness of the figures. We see painful isolation and sense emotional distance between the couple. Segal himself used familiar American expressions to describe why he chose the colors that he did: a "blue funk," a "black mood." In the tradition of Adam and Eve expelled from Eden in art through the ages, the couple's naked, painted bodies seem an outer expression of an inner vulnerability.

Segal emerged during the era of Pop Art in the 1960s, observing human beings' places in the fast-paced world of popular culture. He cast his figures from life, using friends as models. Wrapping wet plaster bandages around them, he would ask them to hold a pose—twenty minutes or so—until the plaster dried. He then removed the casts, which he made into sculpture and placed in "real" settings. Segal's white-plaster figures sit at tables, ride buses and subways, eat in diners, and stand in doorways. His technique changed in the 1970s, when he created *Blue Girl on Black Bed*. Segal began to use the casts as molds, pouring plaster into them, peeling away the outer shell, and then painting the emergent figures in symbolic colors. On the surface, Segal's life-sized figures are chilly and

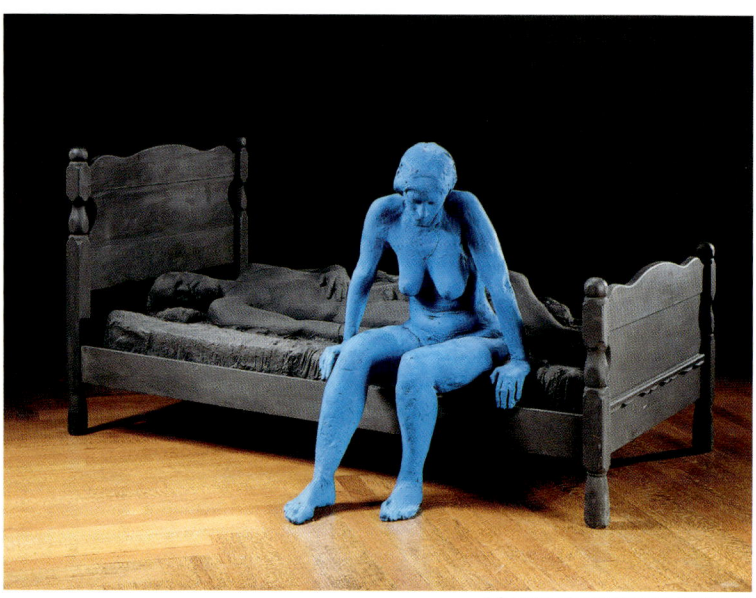

© George Segal / Licensed by VAGA, New York, NY

abstract, yet they have a human presence that disarms us. Segal's men and women—frozen, painted, immobilized—seem to be shells themselves, revealing, rather than protecting, sensitive inner lives.

George Segal, Edward Hopper, Edvard Munch

Edward Hopper's paintings of American cityscapes, landscapes, and silent, solitary figures influenced Segal's sculpture (see Hopper, p. 92). Segal's chilling art has also been linked to emotional paintings by Edvard Munch (Norwegian, 1863–1944)—whose anxious, despairing images elicit existential questions that affected early Expressionist artists (see Kirchner, p. 109) and later painters influenced by Expressionism (see Kiefer, p. 114, and Johns, p. 116).

If Sculpture Could Speak

Segal's models for this sculpture were his friends. The artist tells their story: "she was restless, twitchy, something seemed to be bothering her and he was in an oblivious state. I thought that it was important to catch this quality, and their moods, so separate from each other's."

Blue Girl on Black Bed, 1976
George Segal (American, born 1924)
Painted plaster, wood; 44 by 82 by 60 inches
Virginia Museum of Fine Arts, Gift of Sydney and
  Frances Lewis, 85.444a-b

Chuck Close, Jud

"Names are the essence of things." Chuck Close gives modern meaning to the ancient saying as he focuses on the big picture. Close creates looming portraits, so large that they have been called "landscapes of the face," showing every feature, flaw, or follicle. Close begins with a photograph; then, using a grid, he transfers the image to canvas or paper, transforming it into a meticulously hand-fashioned painting or collage. So enlarged, his portraits dissolve when seen up close and coalesce only when viewed at a distance. Here, *Jud* entices the viewer to examine it from both near and far.

Close made this portrait of artist Jud Nelson from circular pieces of paper applied with glue to a heavily primed canvas. Carefully modulated shades of gray, white, and black depict the moisture of eyes and the texture of lips. Jud looks directly at us, as he did at the camera lens. His neck, shoulders, and hair lose their sharpness around the edges, slipping from focus.

Close has often spoken of his profound respect for each individual mark placed by an artist on canvas or paper, like words in a novel. Called by turn a Photo-Realist and a Minimalist, he possesses vision and discipline that may defy artistic category. From priming the canvas, to drawing the grid, to finishing the last lower corner, each picture can take more than a year to complete.

Close uses friends and family members as models. While critics have commented on his sitters' strong egos to withstand the artist's scrutiny, it is their ability to renounce personal vanity that makes Close's work possible. Like Jud, many of his models are artists themselves, who are willing to explore larger issues of the artistic process. Close is clearly focused on technique and materials; his interviews reveal a pure appreciation of the act of creating. He has worked in oils, acrylics, and watercolor; he has airbrushed areas of color, layered to mimic the photomechanical printing process. He has applied his own inked fingerprints to the surface, instead of pieces of paper, to form dots across a grid that merge into a face.

While traditional portrait commissions do not interest him, Close acknowledges his artistic heritage: "That sense of continuity, of things passed on, is in fact one of the wonderful things about being an artist." His larger-than-life portraits are matched by a vision that transcends himself: "A work of art is not…complete until it's been returned by the viewer. There's something about that return that modifies the experience for the artist, and subtle changes occur. That's what happens in any communication."

Close vs. Warhol

Both artists revived portraiture in the 1960s using modern processes. While Warhol incorporated screen-printing, dots and all, to manufacture multiple images (see p. 111), Close finds its equivalents in painting and collage to make unique works of art. At one time he used only three colors to create his portraits—cyan, yellow, magenta (printer's inks based on primary colors)—layered, with black added, like four-color printing.

Magic, Spirit, Art, and Artist

Close talks about the magic of art: a photograph materializing in a bath; an image formed by paint sprayed with an airbrush that never touched the canvas. He also talks about discipline, to build a work of art from small steps. Early in his career, he learned to work long hours daily, to the background drone of daytime TV game shows. Facing the challenge of a paralyzing disability suffered in the late 1980s, Close continues to create. "Some people think I'm doing my best work now."

Jud, 1982
Chuck Close (American, born 1940)
Pulp-paper collage on canvas; 96 by 72 inches
Virginia Museum of Fine Arts, Gift of Sydney and Frances Lewis Foundation, 85.374

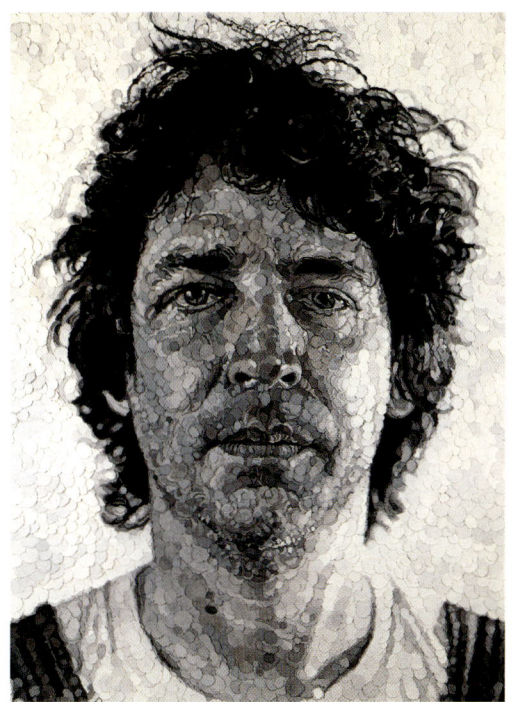

© 1982 Chuck Close

Anselm Kiefer, Landscape with Wing

Up close, Anselm Kiefer's work erupts with paint in carefully controlled and limited color. Black oil bubbles its way across the canvas; brushstrokes leave long ruts the color of flax and ash, interrupted by splashes of white and golden brown. Barbs of straw coarsen the surface, and an expanded wing hovers over the center. At a distance, the viewer has a bird's-eye perspective, as if soaring above huge plowed fields that stretch great distances to a strip of sky. From this viewpoint, a land of straw appears to lie charred and burnt, its magic and beauty trampled and vulnerable.

Kiefer is part of a generation of post-World-War-II Expressionist painters. His art often reflects upon history's horrifying lessons—about his native Germany in the twentieth century and about humanity through the ages. Primary elements—earth, air, water, fire—underlie his images of solitary figures, looming clouds, burning buildings, and the German countryside and cityscape.

Kiefer's painting is compelling, in part, because it is charged with positive and negative forces that counter one another. Though giant and powerful, *Landscape with Wing* is extremely fragile. A lively surface of texture, paint, and straw creates a grim, stark, and somber mood. Still, a landscape scorched and smoking after some unseen horror is touched with sunlight. A recurring motif, the wing—of a bird, mythical hero, or angel—offers the promise of earthly or spiritual hope, gliding high overhead, and yet fragmented and made of lead.

Kiefer's Art History

Kiefer's subjects have ranged from biblical tales and myth to 20th-century histories. This painting has a heritage in Netherlandish and German landscape paintings from the 1500s, which survey nature's majesty and human tragedy from high vantage points. Abstract Expressionism of the 1940s and 1950s underlies the networks of neutral color that record the artist's gestures as he paints (see Kline, p. 110, Johns, p. 116).

Kiefer's Art after 1990

The 1990s brought a change in Kiefer's art, less focused on the tragic past and more focused on global histories and hope. The reunification of Germany in 1991 marked a turning point: for an exhibition, Kiefer stacked his canvases, as though to discard them; he stopped painting for several years and traveled around the world before embarking in new artistic directions.

**Landscape with Wing
(Landschaft mit Flügel),** 1981
Anselm Kiefer (Germany, born 1945)
Oil, straw, lead on canvas; 130 by 218 inches
Virginia Museum of Fine Arts, Gift of the Sydney
  and Frances Lewis Foundation, 85.414

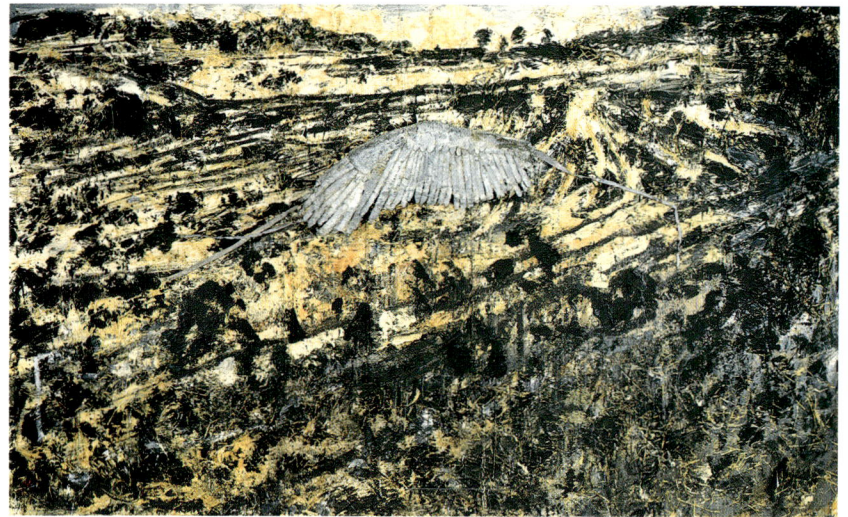

Romare Bearden, Autumn of the Red Hat

"Memories…direct experiences…my childhood…the present," so Romare Bearden positioned words in a short poem that describes his art. His paintings, prints, and collages express the experiences and memories of a lifetime: a collage itself of people and places from North Carolina to New York City, from Europe to the Caribbean. Here, Bearden positions paint and paper, cloth and string to fill a simple interior with color, texture, and light. A grandmotherly figure bends with dressmaker's tape and fabric in hand to measure a smaller, nude young woman. A threaded sewing machine stands ready with patterned piece-goods and small drawers for notions. A red hat tops a wardrobe, a guitar lies on the floor, a broom leans against the wall, and a lantern hangs at the open door. A rooster has wandered in; outside, someone feeds the chickens. A field unfolds to trees and mountains, and a sun (or a harvest moon?) shines through the window panes.

Autumn of the Red Hat belongs to Bearden's *Mecklenberg Autumn* series that evokes his boyhood experiences in Mecklenberg County, North Carolina. These domestic scenes—preparing meals, bathing, sitting on a porch at midnight—have been called "one of the great extended poems of postwar American art."

Bearden reinvented the collage in the early 1960s, combining found objects—wood, string, photographs, fabric—into images of rich color and texture. He often played upon a rectangular format with compositions made of smaller rectangles in green, blue, red, yellow, and orange. "Everything has a certain correspondence," he once said of art and life. In this image, the connections between paper, paint, and drawing are as strong as the family bond his subjects share. "Figures and foliage and objects are conceived as a continuum," he wrote in the margins of a sketch for a collage in the series.

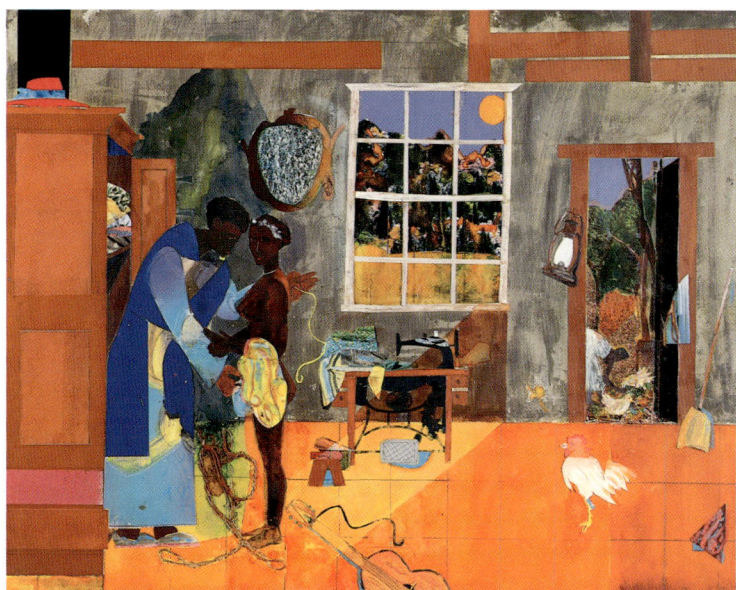

© Romare Bearden Foundation / Licensed by VAGA, New York, NY

Grandmothers, roosters, and red clay, urban life seen from Bearden's 125th Street studio in Harlem, the power of Benin masks and Manet's painting: all come from a family of memories forged into his fluid art. He punctuated interviews with references to Billy Holiday and Buddy Eckstine; Chinese landscape painting; Vermeer and Matisse; Charlotte in the '20s; Paris in the '40s. Bearden's guitar motif pays tribute to E. C. Johnson, a blues musician and town soothsayer, from childhood memories. Such memories figure as prominently in Bearden's art as the jazz of Duke Ellington, a patron. "What I tried to do in painting my people is to see in their everyday life the great classic themes common to all human existence."

Jazz Improvisations

Blues and jazz permeate Bearden's work (see Davis, p. 93). "It's like jazz," he said of making art, "you improvise." An assistant compared Bearden's artistic flexibility and freedom, from years of experience, to a musician who has "mastered his instrument and no longer feels the need for rules."

Feel Your Way on Faith

Bearden held a degree in mathematics and studied in Paris at the Sorbonne; he often quoted authors, painters, and philosophers. His lifelong pursuit to express specific experiences of African-American culture through universal art forms inspired his images of urban and rural life. Bearden found beautiful shapes in African sculpture and European icons: "So long as you can get everything in a nice shape, the picture will be all right…feel your way on faith."

Autumn of the Red Hat, 1982
Romare Bearden (American, 1911–1988)
Collage and watercolor on board; 30½ by 39⅝ inches
Virginia Museum of Fine Arts Purchase, National
  Endowment for the Arts Fund for American Art, 95.17

Jasper Johns
Between the Clock and the Bed

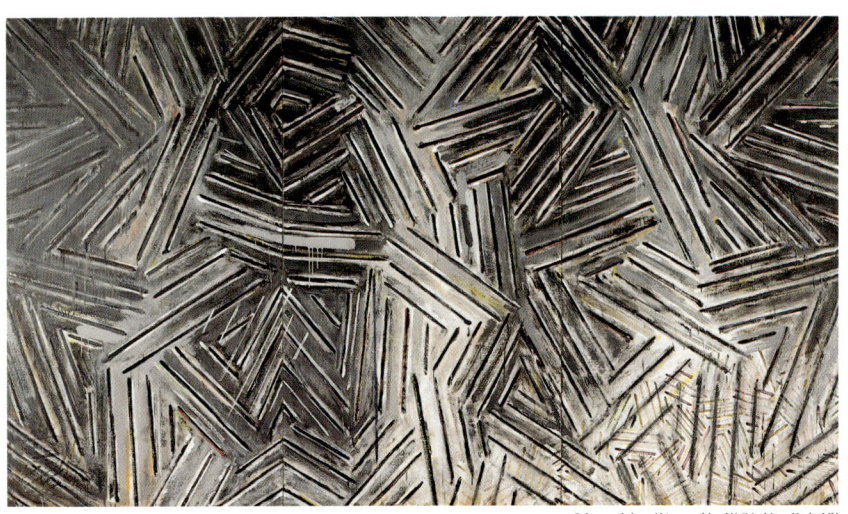

It is possible to see the history of painting in this image, although the picture may be puzzling at first. Jasper Johns' painting dances with elaborate cross-hatching but does not reveal the reason for its title.

Johns orchestrates fundamental elements of painting—light, shadow, line, space, and color—through his intricate patterns of thick and thin marks that intersect and overlap across the canvas. Artists since the dawn of painting have created value and dimension in their works by adding black and white to colors (see Kline, p. 110, and Close, p. 113). Johns reduces this process of shading and tinting to its essence. His simple lines of black, gray, and white either act as shadows and highlights themselves, or cast and reflect them, as they weave in and out of a shallow foreground and background. He enlivens his lines with red, blue, and yellow, primary hues.

Johns began experimenting with cross-hatching in the early 1970s. He explored issues of symmetry and asymmetry, sometimes painting mirror images of repeated and severed patterns on the left and right sides of a work. He altered Hindu and Buddhist imagery to study themes of life and death (see the Tibetan *Sacred Diagram of the Universe*, p. 24). A clue to this image, one of three paintings of the same title by Johns, may be found in a painting of the same name by Edvard Munch. In the early 1980s, Johns looked at Munch's self-portrait, made in the early 1940s. The isolated, aging artist, surrounded by his life's work, stands in his studio between a clock and a bed draped in a red-and-white crosshatched cover. Munch's crosshatching resembled the markings in Johns' paintings. The title intrigued him. Just as Johns pared down hue and value to their basics, so he transformed recognizable objects, like those in Munch's painting, into pure abstractions. Munch's ghost haunts Johns' image, just as Johns' picture nods to the elder artist.

Johns and the History of Painting

Johns trains his mind on the history of his art and casts an eye toward breaking its barriers. Emerging on the art scene in the 1950s, Johns ranks in the forefront of those who moved painting from Abstract Expressionism of the 1940s and 1950s (see Kline, p. 110) to Pop Art of the 1960s (Warhol, p. 111). Johns' series of American flags, targets, and numbers call attention to the actual paintings themselves as real objects, rather than as windows or mirrors to the visible world (see Poussin, pp. 60–61). Johns revived the ancient Mediterranean art of encaustic painting—pigments suspended in wax—to give richness and texture to works such as this one (see the Roman-Egyptian Funerary Image of a Woman, *p. 11).*

Between Abstract Expressionism and Pop Art

Abstract Expressionism is so named for the deep reaches of emotion, history, and myth expressed through pure color and brushwork rather than recognizable form (see Willem de Kooning, Mark Rothko, and Adolph Gottlieb in the Virginia Museum's collection; see also Anselm Kiefer, p. 114). Pop Art borrows from popular culture. In the early 1960s, Warhol painted Campbell's soup cans (p. 111), Johns sculptured cans of Ballantine Ale.

Between the Clock and the Bed, 1983

Jasper Johns (American, born 1930)
Encaustic on canvas; 72 by 126½ inches
Virginia Museum of Fine Arts, Gift of Sydney and Frances Lewis and the Sydney and Frances Lewis Foundation, 85.411

Alison Saar, Untitled

"I love the idea that materials have memory," Alison Saar says. She gathers discarded wood, tin, nails, scraps of iron, shards of glass, and bits of rubber, and then transforms "materials that have experienced more than I have" into sculpture. Her enigmatic figures have been called saints and shamans: born of ancient folklore, crossing many cultures, blending traditional and contemporary materials and meanings into their physical, and spiritual, beings. Uncompromising, made of grit not beauty, Saar's sculpture exudes a "refined savagery," in her words.

Here, ceiling tin covers a wooden figure, pierced with bits of blue glass and rusted iron. Nails puncture the surface of the entire body. Slightly smaller than life-sized, the figure stands rigidly, like statues of ancient Egypt or archaic Greece. One hand is extended—a Greek, and Buddhist, gesture of giving—and as Saar acknowledges, the other holds a piece of iron that curls like a whip.

Saar studies dualities: the potential of things to help or to harm humanity. Although some see pain and sadness in this sculpture, Saar reminds us that nails hammered into *nkisi* figures of Africa (see the Central African *Power Figures* in the Virginia Museum galleries) are meant to release medicines and healing spirits. She suggests that the scraps of iron at the figure's feet serve as food or fuel, and that pain can give way to enlightenment and hope.

This figure originally stood with three others in Saar's *Crossroads*. In this installation, the statues surrounded a cross on the floor with groups of stones, stacked like grave markers. The scene conjured thoughts about the cardinal directions (see the Nepalese *Ritual Crown,* p. 23), about making personal choices, about taking risks. Deities guard crossroads in many cultures, to help or hinder human beings: Eshu, the Yoruba god (p. 40), Ganesha, the Hindu god (p. 20). Saar's

depiction of "where the spirit world meets the material world" is part of her vision to incorporate "ancient religions into contemporary imagery" and her belief that ancient ideas are useful in modern life.

"Multivalence," "the human condition," "the soul"—so critics have interpreted Saar's work, rooted in the art and materials of Africa, the Mediterranean, the Caribbean, and Los Angeles. Saar hopes that her figures—transformations from folklore and found objects—might in turn transform the viewer, by posing questions about culture, race, gender,

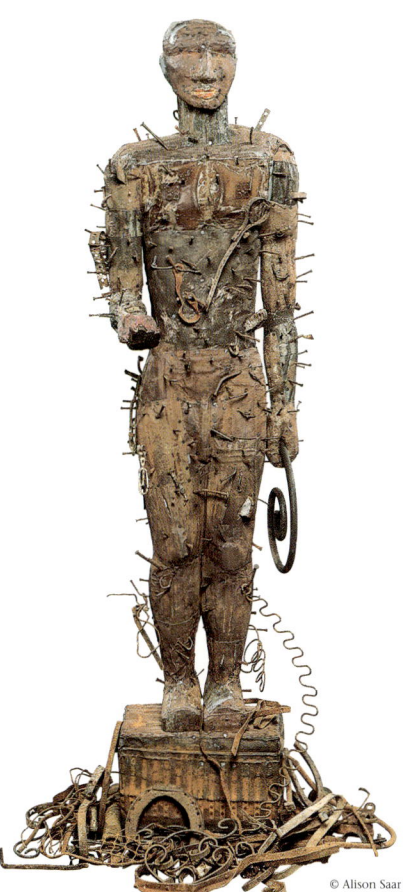

© Alison Saar

and spirituality. "What the viewer brings to it is the other half of the piece." She likens her silent and introspective characters to children, needing care and nurturing but having their own distinct natures: "Everything has a spirit to it and that spirit has to be recognized."

The Magic of Ritual

*Saar's collages, sculpture, and installations—*Sweet Thang, Medicine Man, Love Potion #9, Blue Boy, Salome, Dying Slave—*have an aura of magic about them. They hint at ancient ritual, connecting nature and spirit. They bear magical names:* JuJu Eugene, *a collage named for the African charm;* House of Gris Gris, *a collaboration with her artist mother, Betye Saar, evoking the French Creole tradition of grey magic, neither black nor white, good nor bad.*

Race, Gender, and Humanity

Issues of race and gender take a central position in Saar's often transcendental work about the human condition. She has found herself at the center of these issues since she rose to prominence in the mid 1980s. "We are all affected by the political," says Saar, describing her heritage as "floating between two worlds": African-American, Scottish and German, with a little Irish and Native American ancestry. She has been called "classically American," both black and white, though many cultures inspire her art. A student of African-American folk art, she shares her mother's interest in the African diaspora, Indian culture, spiritualism, and found objects, and her father's interest in ancient objects, especially African, MesoAmerican, Pacific.

Untitled, 1989
Alison Saar (American, born 1956)
Wood, mixed media; 72 by 18 by 16 inches
Virginia Museum of Fine Arts Purchase, The Sydney and Frances Lewis Endowment Fund, 92.233a-qqq

Further Reading

GENERAL

Cavendish, Richard, ed. *Mythology: An Illustrated Encyclopedia.* Little, Brown & Co., 1992.

Fleming, William. *Arts and Ideas.* 9th ed. Harcourt Brace College Publishers, 1995.

Gallery Guide. Virginia Museum of Fine Arts, 1985.

Hall, James. *Dictionary of Subjects and Symbols in Art.* Harper & Row, 1974.

———. *Illustrated Dictionary of Symbols in Eastern and Western Art.* Harper Collins, 1994.

Hartt, Frederick. *Art: A History of Painting, Sculpture, and Architecture,* 2 vols. Harry N. Abrams, 1976.

Henshaw, Julia P., ed. *The Detroit Institute of Arts: A Visitor's Guide.* 1995.

Willis, Roy, ed. *World Mythology.* Henry Holt, 1993.

ANCIENT MEDITERRANEAN ART

Ancient Art in the Virginia Museum. Virginia Museum of Fine Arts, 1973.

Arias, P. E. *A History of 1000 Years of Greek Vase Painting.* Harry N. Abrams, 1962.

Baratte, François. *"Deux Portraits d'Enfants Isiaques." Revue Archéologique* 1 (1993): 101–10.

Boardman, John. *Athenian Black Figure Vases.* Oxford Univ. Press, 1974.

Deppert-Lippitz, Barbara. *Ancient Gold Jewelry at the Dallas Museum of Art.* Dallas Museum of Art, 1996.

Getz-Preziosi, Pat. *Early Cycladic Art in North American Collections.* Virginia Museum of Fine Arts, 1987.

Hoffmann, Herbert. "Rhyta and Kantharoi in Greek Ritual." *Greek Vases in the J. Paul Getty Museum 4: Occasional Papers on Antiquities,* 5 (1989): 131–66.

Johansen, Flemming S. "The Sculpted Portraits of Caligula." In *Ancient Portraits in the J. Paul Getty Museum 1,* edited by Jiří Frel, Arthur Houghton, and Marion True. 87–106. J. Paul Getty Museum, 1987.

Jucker, Hans. "Caligula." *Arts in Virginia* 13, no. 2 (Winter 1973): 16–25.

Kleiner, Diana. *Roman Sculpture.* Yale Univ. Press, 1992.

Marshall, F. H. *Catalogue of the Jewellery, Greek, Etruscan, and Roman in the Departments of Antiquities, British Museum.* British Museum, 1969.

Mayo, Margaret Ellen, ed. *The Art of South Italy: Vases from Magna Graecia.* Virginia Museum of Fine Arts, 1982.

Peck, William H. *Mummy Portraits from Roman Egypt.* Detroit Institute of Arts, 1967.

Reeder, Ellen D. *Hellenistic Art in the Walters Gallery.* Walters Art Gallery, 1988.

Richter, Gisela M.A., and Marjorie J. Milne. *Shapes and Names of Athenian Vases.* Metropolitan Museum of Art, 1935.

Smith, W. Stevenson. *The Art and Architecture of Ancient Egypt.* Penguin Books, 1958.

Tait, Hugh, ed. *Jewelry 7000 Years: An International and Illustrated Survey from the Collections of the British Museum.* Harry N. Abrams, 1987.

Thompson, David L. *Mummy Portraits in the J. Paul Getty Museum.* 2d ed. J. Paul Getty Museum, 1982.

Von Bothmer, Dietrich. "Observations on the Subject Matter of South Italian Vases." *Arts in Virginia* 23, no. 3 (Spring 1983): 28–43.

Walker, Susan. "Aspects of Roman Funerary Art." In *Image and Mystery in the Roman World,* edited by J. Huskinson, M. Beard, and J. Reynolds, 22–44. Alan Sutton, 1988.

———. *Memorials to the Roman Dead.* British Museum, 1985.

Weitzmann, Kurt, ed. *Age of Spirituality: Late Antique and Early Christian Art, Third to Seventh Century.* Metropolitan Museum of Art, 1979.

Williams, Dyfri, and Jack Ogden. *Greek Gold: Jewelry of the Classical World.* Harry N. Abrams, 1994.

ANCIENT AMERICAN ART

Alva, Walter, and Christopher B. Donnan. *Royal Tombs of Sipan.* Fowler Museum of Cultural History, Univ. of California, 1993.

Benson, Elizabeth P. *The Mochica: A Culture of Peru.* Praeger, 1972.

Benson, Elizabeth P., and Beatriz de la Fuente, eds. *Olmec: Art of Ancient Mexico.* National Gallery of Art, 1996.

Berjonneau, Gérald, and Jean-Louis Sonnery. *Rediscovered Masterpieces of MesoAmerica.* Editions Arts, 1985.

Bernal, Ignacio. *The Olmec World.* Univ. of California Press, 1969.

Donnan, Christopher B. *Moche Art of Peru: Pre-Columbian Symbolic Communication.* Museum of Cultural History, Univ. of California, 1978.

Hagen, Victor W. von. *The Desert Kingdoms of Peru.* New York Graphic Society, 1964.

Lechtman, Heather. *Seven Matched Hollow Gold Jaguars from Peru's Early Horizon.* Dumbarton Oaks, 1975.

Sawyer, Alan R. *Ancient Peruvian Ceramics: The Nathan Cummings Collection.* Metropolitan Museum of Art, 1966.

Townsend, Richard F., ed. *The Ancient Americas: Art from Sacred Landscapes.* Art Institute of Chicago, 1992.

ASIAN ART

Cunningham, Michael R. *The Triumph of Japanese Style: 16th-Century Art in Japan.* Cleveland Museum of Art, 1991.

DelBanco, Dawn Ho. *Art from Ritual: Ancient Chinese Bronze Vessels from the Arthur M. Sackler Collections.* Arthur M. Sackler Foundation, 1983.

Dye, Joseph M. III. *The Art of India in the Virginia Museum of Fine Arts.* Forthcoming.

Fong, Wen, ed. *The Great Bronze Age of China: An Exhibition from the People's Republic of China.* Metropolitan Museum of Art, 1980.

Lee, Sherman. *A History of Far Eastern Art.* Harry N. Abrams, 1982.

Murase, Miyeko. *Jewel Rivers: Japanese Art from The Burke Collection.* Virginia Museum of Fine Arts, 1993.

Pal, Pratapaditya. *Art of Nepal.* Los Angeles County Museum of Art, 1985.

———. "Tibetan Religious Paintings in the Virginia Museum of Fine Arts, Part 1: 14th- and 15th-century Thankas." *Arts in Virginia* 27, nos. 1–3 (1987): 44–65.

———. "Tibetan Religious Paintings in the Virginia Museum of Fine Arts, Part 2: 1600–1900." *Arts in Virginia* 28, no. 2–3 (Winter/Spring 1988–89): 6–33.

Rhie, Marylin M., and Robert A. F. Thurman. *Wisdom and Compassion: The Sacred Art of Tibet.* Harry N. Abrams, 1991.

Rosenfield, John M. *Journey of the Three Jewels.* Asia Society, 1979.

Rosenfield, John M., and Shûjirō Suimada. *Traditions of Japanese Art.* Fogg Art Museum, 1970.

Shin'ichi, Miyajima, and Satō Yasuhiro. *Japanese Ink Painting.* Los Angeles County Museum of Art, 1985.

Yonemura, Ann. *Japanese Lacquer.* Freer Gallery of Art, 1979.

AFRICAN ART

Cole, Herbert M., and Doran H. Ross. *The Arts of Ghana. Museum of Cultural History,* Univ. of Calforica, 1977.

Kerchache, Jacques, Jean-Louis Paudrat, and Lucien Stephan. *L'Art Africain.* Mazenod, 1988.

Phillips, Tom, ed. *Africa: The Art of a Continent.* Prestel, 1995.

Preston, George Nelson. "People Making Portraits Making People: Living Icons of the Akan." *African Arts* 23 (July 1990): 70–76.

Ross, Doran H. "The Verbal Art of Akan Linguist Staffs." *African Arts* 16, no. 1 (November 1982): 56–66.

Woodward, Richard B. "A Buffalo Mask and Feather Costume from the Cameroon Grasslands." *Arts in Virginia* 29, no. 1 (1989): 40–43.

———. *African Art.* Virginia Museum of Fine Arts, 1994.

BYZANTINE and WESTERN MEDIEVAL SCULPTURE and DECORATIVE ARTS

Baxandall, Michael. *The Limewood Sculptors of Renaissance Germany.* Yale Univ. Press, 1980.

Caviness, Madeline H. "Canterbury Stained Glass." *Arts in Virginia* 13 (1973): A49–A60.

Forsyth, William H. "A Group of Fourteenth-Century Mosan Sculptures." *Metropolitan Museum Journal* 1 (1968): 41–59.

Gonosová, Anna, and Christine Kondoleon. *Art of Late Rome and Byzantium.* Technical entries by Lawrence Becker, Deborah Schorsch, Jane L. Williams, and Mark T. Wypyski. Virginia Museum of Fine Arts, 1994.

Kahn, Charles L. *German and Netherlandish Sculpture: 1280–1800.* Harvard Univ. Press, 1965.

Les Fastes du Gothique le Siècle de Charles V. Éditions de la Réunion des musées nationaux, 1981.

Muller, Theodor. *Sculpture in the Netherlands, Germany, France, and Spain 1400–1600.* Penquin Books, 1966.

Read, Herbert, and John Baker. *English Stained Glass.* Harry N. Abrams, N.D.

Weigert, Roger-Armand. *French Tapestry.* Faber & Faber, 1962.

EUROPEAN ART

Ashton, Dore. *Fragonard in the Universe of Painting.* Smithsonian Institution, 1988.

Bailey, Colin B. "The Comte de Vaudreuil: Aristocratic Collecting on the Eve of the Revolution." *Apollo* 130 (July–September 1989): 19–26, 68–69.

Baillio, Joseph. *Elisabeth Louise Vigée Le Brun, 1755–1842.* Kimbell Art Museum, 1982.

British Sporting Painting 1650–1850. Arts Council of Great Britain, 1974.

Cabanne, Pierre. *Edgar Degas.* Translated by Michel Lee Landa. Editions Pierre Tisné, 1958.

Campbell, Sara, and Daphne Bargour, Patricia Failing, Anne Pingeot, Theodore Reff. "Degas: The Sculptures." *Apollo* 142, no. 402 (August 1995).

Courthion, Pierre. *Édouard Manet.* Harry N. Abrams, 1962.

Egerton, Judy. *British Sporting and Animal Paintings 1655–1867.* Tate Gallery, 1978.

———. *British Sporting Paintings: The Paul Mellon Collection in the Virginia Museum of Fine Arts.* Virginia Museum of Fine Arts, 1985.

European Art in the Virginia Museum of Fine Arts. Virginia Museum of Fine Arts, 1966.

Evans, Siân, trans. *The Memoirs of Elisabeth Vigée-Lebrun.* Camden, 1989.

Friedlaender, Walter. *David to Delacroix.* Harvard Univ. Press, 1952.

Gassier, Pierre, and Juliet Wilson. *The Life and Complete Work of Francisco Goya.* William Morrow & Co., 1971.

Gopnik, Adam. "Love's Progress." *New Yorker* 64 (March 28, 1988): 84–87.

Gordon, Mary. "A Painter Who Found Drama in Home and Hearth: The Silent Drama In Vuillard's Rooms." *New York Times,* 13 May 1990.

Grasselli, Margaret Morgan, and Pierre Rosenberg. *Watteau 1684–1721.* National Gallery of Art, 1984.

Hanson, Anne Coffin. *Manet and the Modern Tradition.* Yale Univ. Press, 1977.

Hughes, Robert. "The Insider." *Time* 98 (November 22, 1971): 90–91.

Johnson, Lee. *The Paintings of Eugène Delacroix: A Critical Catalogue, 1832–1863.* Vol 3. Clarendon, 1986.

Kalnein, Wend Graf, and Michael Levey. *Art and Architecture of the Eighteenth Century in France.* Penguin Books, 1972.

Kendall, Richard. *Degas Landscapes.* Yale Univ. Press, 1993.

Kramer, Hilton. "Abundant in Visual Incident." *New York Times,* 26 September 1971.

Leiris, Alain de. "Manet: 'Sur la plage de Boulogne.'" *Gazette des Beaux-Arts* 57, no. 6 (January 1961): 53–62.

Levy, Jean. "Watteau's 'Le Lorngeur.'" *Burlington Magazine* 96, no. 616 (July 1954): 197–202.

Libin, Laurence. "Philip Reinagle's Extraordinary Musical Dog," Collections Archives of the Virginia Museum of Fine Arts.

Livingston-Learmonth, David. *The Horse in Art.* Studio Publications, 1958.

Meyer, Arline. "Wootton at Wimpole." *Apollo* 122 (September 1985): 212–19.

Moffett, Charles, S. *The New Painting: Impressionism 1874–1886.* National Gallery of Art, 1986.

Moxey, Keith. "A New Look at Netherlandish Landscape and Still-Life Painting." *Arts in Virginia* 26, no. 2 (1986): 18–31.

Muller, Priscilla E. "Goya's Portrait of General Guye." *Arts in Virginia* 12, no. 2 (Winter 1972): 2–11.

Near, Pinkney L. "Salvator Rosa: The Death of Regulus." *Arts in Virginia* 1, no. 1 (Fall 1960): 10–11.

———. A Turkish Fantasy. *Arts in Virginia* 8, no. 3 (Spring 1968): 22–23.

Near, Pinkney L. *Three Masters of Landscape: Fragonard, Robert, and Boucher.* Virginia Museum of Fine Arts, 1981.

———. "Carle Van Loo, A Pasha Having His Mistress' Portrait Painted." *Arts in Virginia* 23, no. 3 (1983): 18–27.

Os, Hendrik W. van. "Andrea di Bartolo's *Assumption of the Virgin.*" *Arts in Virginia* 11, no. 2 (Winter 1971): 3–11.

Prideaux, Tom, and the editors of Time-Life Books. *The World of Delacroix 1798–1863.* Time-Life Books, 1966.

Reau, Louis. "A Rediscovered Picture by Watteau: Le Lorgneur." *Burlington Magazine* 76 (March 1940): 92–93.

Richard, Paul. "Edouard Vuillard, Casting Color Out Of the Ordinary: At the Phillips Collection, 'Intimate Interiors.'" *Washington Post,* 18 February 1990.

Rosenberg, Pierre. *Fragonard.* Metropolitan Museum of Art, 1988.

———. *J. H. Fragonard e H. Robert a Roma.* Fratelli Palombi Editori, 1990.

Rosenblum, Robert. *The Dog in Art from Rococo to Post-Modernism.* Harry N. Abrams, 1988.

Roworth, Wendy Wassyng, ed. *Angelica Kauffman: A Continental Artist in Georgian England.* Reaktion Books, 1992.

Sanchez Perez, Alfonso E., and Eleanor A. Sayre. *Goya and The Spirit of Enlightenment.* Museum of Fine Arts Boston, 1989.

Shattuck, Roger, Henri Béhar, Michel Hoog, Carolyn Lancher, and William Rubin. *Henri Rousseau.* Museum of Modern Art, 1985.

Stabenow, Cornelia. "Artificial Paradise, Rousseau's Jungle Landscapes." *Arts in Virginia* 26, no. 1 (1986): 30–39.

———. *Henri Rousseau.* Benedikt Taschen Verlag, 1991.

Sutton, Denys. *Degas: Life and Work.* Artabras, 1986.

Thomson, Belinda. *Vuillard.* Phaidon, 1988.

Verdi, Richard, and Pierre Rosenberg. *Nicolas Poussin 1594–1665.* Royal Academy of London, 1995.

Walker, Stella A. *Sporting Art: England 1700–1900.* Clarkson N. Potter, 1972.

Wellington, Hubert, ed. *Journal of Eugène Delacroix.* Chronicle Books, 1980.

Wilhelm, Jacques. "Fragonard as Painter of Realistic Landscapes." *Art Quarterly* 11, no. 4 (Autumn 1948): 296–305.

AMERICAN ART

Ashton, Dore. *The New York School: A Cultural Reckoning.* Viking, 1973.

Boime, Albert. *The Art of Exclusion: Representing Blacks in the Nineteenth Century.* Smithsonian Institution, 1990.

Breeskin, Adelyn Dohyme. "Mary Cassatt: Her Life and Her Art." *Arts in Virginia* 21, no. 3 (Spring 1981): 2–15.

Catlin, George. *Letters and Notes on the Manners, Customs, and Conditions of the North American Indians.* Vols. 1 and 2. [London 1841] Ross & Haines, 1965.

Comstock, Helen. *American Furniture: Seventeenth, Eighteenth, and Nineteenth Century Styles.* Schiffer, 1962.

Cormack, Malcolm. *George Catlin's "Indian Gallery": Views of the American West.* Virginia Museum of Fine Arts, 1993.

Curry, David Park. "Shopping, Collecting, and Remembering: Some Turn-of-the-Century American Pictures," *The International Fine Art Fair.* (10–15 May 1996): 7–18.

Fairbanks, Jonathan L. *Paul Revere's Boston: 1735–1818.* Museum of Fine Arts Boston, 1975.

Fales, Dean A., Jr. "Boston Japanned Furniture." In *Boston Furniture of the Eighteenth Century.* Colonial Society of Massachusetts, 1972.

Fortune, Brandon Brame. "Charles Willson Peale's Portrait Gallery: Persuasion and the Plain Style." *Word and Image* 6, no. 4 (October–December 1990): 308–23.

———. "From the World Escaped: Peale's Portrait of William Smith and His Grandson." *Eighteenth Century Studies* 25, no. 4 (1992): 587–615.

Goossen, E. C. *Stuart Davis.* George Braziller, 1959.

Hills, Patricia. *Eastman Johnson.* Clarkson N. Potter, 1972.

———. *John Singer Sargent.* Whitney Museum of American Art, 1986.

Kelder, Diane, ed. *Stuart Davis.* Praeger, 1971.

McElroy, Guy C. *Facing History: The Black Image in American Art 1710–1940.* Bedford Arts, 1990.

Mendelowitz, Daniel M. *A History of American Art.* Holt, Rinehart & Winston, 1970.

Miller, Lillian B., ed. *The Peale Family: Creation of a Legacy 1170–1870.* Abbeville in assoc. with National Portrait Gallery and Trust for Museum Exhibitions, 1996.

Morningstar, Connie. "John Henry Belter: Father of Plywood Lived to See The Pirating of All His Designs." *The Antiques Journal* 25 (April 1970): 9–12.

O'Doherty, Brian. *American Masters: The Voice and the Myth.* Random House, 1973.

O'Leary, Elizabeth. *At Beck and Call: The Representation of Domestic Servants in Nineteenth-Century American Painting.* Smithsonian Institution, 1996.

Ormond, Richard. *John Singer Sargent: Paintings, Drawings, Watercolors.* Harper & Row, 1970.

Ormshee, Thomas Hamilton. *Field Guide to American Furniture.* Little, Brown, 1951.

Rasmussen, William. "Wild Gentlemen in the Simplicity of Nature." *Arts in Virginia* 26, no. 3 (1986): 14–39.

Schwartz, Marvin D., Edward J. Staneck, and Douglas K. True. *The Furniture of John Henry Belter and the Rococo Revival.* E. P. Dutton, 1980.

Sellers, Charles Coleman. "Monumentality with Love: Charles Willson Peale's Portrait of William Smith and his Grandson." *Arts in Virginia* 16, nos. 2–3 (Winter–Spring 1976): 14–21.

Simpson, Marc. *Uncanny Spectacle: The Public Career of the Young John Singer Sargent.* Yale Univ. Press, 1997.

Sims, Lowery Stokes. *Stuart Davis: American Painter.* Metropolitan Museum of Art, 1991.

Talbot, William S. *Jasper F. Cropsey, 1823–1900.* Smithsonian Institution, 1970.

Thistlethwaite, Mark. "Picturing the Past: Junius Brutus Stearns's Paintings of George Washington." *Arts in Virginia* 25, nos. 2/3 (Winter/Spring 1985): 12–23.

Voorsanger, Catherine Hoover. "Herter Brothers Furniture." In *Herter Brothers: Furniture and Interiors for a Gilded Age,* edited by Katherine S. Howe, and Alice Cooney Frelinghuysen. Harry N. Abrams, 1994: 105–24.

Ward, Barbara McLean, and Gerald W. R. Ward, eds. *Silver in American Life.* Yale Univ. Art Gallery, 1979.

19th and 20th CENTURY SCULPTURE and DECORATIVE ARTS

Adam, Peter. *Eileen Gray: Architect/Designer.* Harry N. Abrams, 1987.

Becker, Vivienne. *Art Nouveau Jewelery.* E. P. Dutton, 1985.

———. *The Jewellery of René Lalique.* Goldsmith's Company, 1987.

Billcliffe, Roger. "Mackintosh and Cranston: A Pioneering Partnership." *Arts in Virginia* 26, no. 1 (1986): 14–29.

Blondel, A. "Guimard, architecte de meubles." *L'Estampille* (May 1970): 40.

Borsi, Franco, and Ezio Gondoli. *Paris 1900.* Rizzoli, 1978.

Bouillon, Jean-Paul. *Art Deco 1903–1940.* Rizzoli, 1989.

Brandt, Frederick R. *Late 19th and Early 20th Century Decorative Arts.* Virginia Museum of Fine Arts, 1985.

Brunhammer, Yvonne. "Hector Guimard or the Obsession with Line." *Arts in Virginia* 20, no. 1 (1979): 38–47.

Cormack, Malcolm. *Champion Animals: Sculptures by Herbert Haseltine.* Virginia Museum of Fine Arts, 1996.

Culme, John. *Nineteenth-Century Silver.* Country Life Books, 1977.

Curry, David Park. *Fabergé.* Virginia Museum of Fine Arts, 1995.

Duncan, Alastair. *Art Deco Furniture: The French Designers.* Thames & Hudson, 1984.

———. *Louis Comfort Tiffany.* Harry N. Abrams in assoc. with the National Museum of American Art, 1992.

Garner, Phillipe. "Pierre Legrain-Decorateur," *The Connoisseur* 189 (June 1975): 130–37.

Hay, David. "Cardboard Chairs and Formica Fish," Collections Archives Virginia Museum of Fine Arts.

Heinz, Thomas A. *Frank Lloyd Wright: Glass Art.* Academy Editions, 1994.

Johnson, J. Stewart. "Eileen Gray at Richmond." *Arts in Virginia* 27, nos. 1–3 (1987): 34–43.

Kalec, Don. "Frank Lloyd Wright: An American Architect." In *Mackintosh and His Contemporaries in Europe and America,* edited by Patrick Nuttgens, 75–89. J. Murray, 1988.

Koch, Robert. "The Tiffany Exhibition Punch Bowl." *Arts in Virginia* 16, nos. 2/3 (Winter/Spring 1976): 32–39.

Lesley, Parker. *Fabergé.* Virginia Museum of Fine Arts, 1976.

Levy, Florence N. "Applied Arts at the Paris Exposition." *American Art Annual* 3 (1900): 21–22.

Meyer, C. James. "Masterpiece in Metal, René Lalique's Seahorse Brooch." *Metalsmith* (Winter 1981/82): 26–27.

Weisberg, Gabriel P. "L'Art Nouveau Bing." *Arts in Virginia* 20, no. 1 (Fall 1979): 2–15.

Wright, Frank Lloyd. *An Autobiography.* Dueil, Sloan & Pearce, 1943.

EUROPEAN and AMERICAN TWENTIETH-CENTURY ART

Arnason, H. H. *History of Modern Art.* Harry N. Abrams,1977.

Barron, Stephanie. *German Expressionist Sculpture.* Los Angeles County Museum of Art, 1983.

Betts, Susan. "Close to Paint, Close to Perfect," *Richmond Style Weekly,* 28 September 1993.

Brandt, Frederick R. *Late 20th Century Art: Selections from the Sydney and Frances Lewis Collection.* Virginia Museum of Fine Arts, 1985.

Brandt, Frederick R., and Eleanor M. Hight. *German Expressionist Art: The Ludwig and Rosy Fischer Collection.* Virginia Museum of Fine Arts, 1987.

Chipp, Herschel B. *Theories of Modern Art: A Source Book by Artists and Critics.* Univ. of California Press, 1968.

Crichton, Michael. *Jasper Johns.* Harry N. Abrams in assoc. with the Whitney Museum of American Art, 1994.

Francis, Richard. *Jasper Johns.* Abbeville, 1984.

Friedman, Martin, and Graham W. J. Beal. *George Segal: Sculptures.* Walker Art Center, 1978.

Gordon, Donald E. *Ernst Ludwig Kirchner.* Harvard Univ. Press, 1968.

Harshman, Barbara. "An Interview with Chuck Close." *Arts Magazine* 52 (June 1978): 142–45.

Kramer, Hilton. "Chuck Close—In Flight From the Realist Impulse," *New York Times,* 4 November 1979.

Kuspit, Donald B. "George Segal: On the Verge of Tragic Vision." *Art in America* 65 (May 1977): 84–5.

Lawrence, Sidney. *Directions: Alison Saar.* Hirshhorn Museum and Sculpture Garden, 1993. Brochure.

———. "The Color of Art." *American Art* 11 (Spring 1997): 2–9.

Livingstone, Marco. *Andy Warhol: A Retrospective.* Hayward Gallery, 1989. Brochure.

Lyons, Lisa, and Martin Friedman. *Close Portraits.* Walker Art Center, 1980.

Lyons, Lisa, and Robert Storr. *Chuck Close.* Rizzoli, 1987.

McCully, Marilyn, ed. *Picasso: The Early Years 1892–1906.* National Gallery of Art, 1997.

Paoletti, John T. "Contemporary German Art in the Virgina Museum of Fine Arts." *Arts in Virginia* 29, nos. 2–3 (1991): 35–43.

Rose, Barbara. *American Art Since 1900.* Praeger Publishers, 1975.

Rosenblum, Robert. In *Andy Warhol: Portraits of the 1970s.* Edited by David Whitney. Whitney Museum of American Art, 1979.

Rubin, William, ed. *"Primitivism" in 20th Century Art: Affinity of the Tribal and the Modern.* Vol. 2. Museum of Modern Art, 1984: 369–403.

Sandler, Irving. *The Triumph of American Painting: A History of Abstract Expressionism.* Harper & Row, 1970.

Schwartzman, Myron. *Romare Bearden: His Life and Art.* Harry N. Abrams, 1990.

Sprout, Francis. "Alison Saar: Inside Looking In." Neuberger Museum of Art, 1992. Brochure.

Varnedoe, Kirk. *Jasper Johns: A Retrospective.* Museum of Modern Art, 1996.

———. *Artist's Choice: Chuck Close Head-on/The Modern Portrait.* Museum of Modern Art, 1991. Brochure.

Washington, M. Bunch. *The Art of Romare Bearden: The Prevalence of Ritual.* Harry N. Abrams, N.D.

THE DICTIONARY OF ART, the 1996 Macmillan publication edited by Jane Turner, served as an invaluable resource. Refer to the following entries from the *Dictionary of Art* for further reading about the works of art and the artists in this handbook.

Ancient Mediterranean Art

VOL. 13: *Hellenistic Art* Reynold Higgins, 598–99; Andrew F. Stewart, 464–67. VOL. 27: *Roman Art* Ann Thomas Wilkins, 32–34; Henning Wrede, 34–35; Richard Brilliant, 8–12; Elizabeth Bautman, 20–23.

Ancient American Art

VOL. 21: *Moche* Christopher B. Donnan, 749–50; Izumi Shimada, 750–52; Theresa Lange Topic, 752–54. VOL. 23: *Olmec* David C. Grove, 416–19.

Asian Art

VOL. 15: *Indian Art* Michael D. Rabe, 506–21; Dipak Chandra Bhattacharyya, 213–24; Daniel J. Ehnbom and J. P. Losty, 543–51. VOL. 22: *Nepalese Art* Ian Alsop, 774–78. VOL. 30: *Tibetan Art* Deborah E. Kimburg-Salter, N. G. Ronge, V. Ronge, 809–11.

African Art

VOL. 1: *Akan* Doran H. Ross, 503–04. VOL. 5: *Cameroon Grasslands* Gloria J. Umlauft-Thielicke, 523–24. VOL. 18: *Kuba* Jan Vansina, 484–89. VOL. 33: *Yoruba* H. J. Drewal, 553–60.

Byzantine and Western Medieval Sculpture and Decorative Arts

VOL. 1: *Altarpieces* Alexander Nagel, 707–13. VOL. 11: *French Sculpture* Anne Prache, 553–56. VOL. 29: *Stained Glass* Carola Hicks, Virginia Chieffo Raguin, M.B. Shepard, 497–509; 514–17. VOL. 30: *Tapestry* Caroline Clark, Scot Mckendrick, and Catherine R. Joslyn, 307–31.

European Art

VOL. 8: *Delacroix* Colin Harrison, 637–48. VOL. 11: *Fragonard* Colin Harrison, 366–70. VOL. 13: *Goya* Priscilla E. Muller, 240–54. VOL. 17: *Kauffman* Peter Walch, 850–53. VOL. 20: *Manet* Beatrice Farwell, 254–62. VOL. 21: *Molenaer* Dennis P. Weller, 813–15; *Poussin* Hugh Brigstocke, 385–97. VOL. 22: *Moroni* Francesco Frangi, 132–35. VOL. 26: *Robert* Jean De Cayeux, 447–50. VOL. 27: *Rosa* Helen Langdon, 149–55; *Rubens* Hans Vlieghe, 287–303. VOL. 19: *Van Loo* Laurie G. Winters, 645–47. VOL. 32: *Vigée-Lebrun* Kathleen Nicholson, 494–97; *Vuillard* Belinda Thomson, 738–43; *Watteau* Humphrey Wine, 913–20. VOL. 33: *Wootton* Stephen Deuchar, 375–77.

American Art

VOL. 28: *Silver* John K. D. Cooper, 737–41.

19th and 20th Century Decorative Arts

VOL. 9: *Doucet* Malcolm Gee, 195–96. VOL. 12: *Gehry* Michael Spens, 236. VOL. 18: *Lalique* Catherine Brisac, 659–60.

European and American Twentieth-Century Art

VOL. 7: *Close* 461. VOL. 17: *Johns* Michael Crichton, 613–15. VOL. 18: *Kiefer* Stephan Mann, 31–32; *Kirchner* Lucius Grisebach, 77–82; *Kline* David Anfam, 132–33. VOL. 24: *Picasso* Melissa McQuillan, 712–30. VOL. 28: *Segal* Kristine Stiles, 353–54. VOL. 32: *Warhol* Marco Livingstone, 862–63.

Photography Credits

Ronald Jennings: 22, 24, 45, 46, 56, 59, 65, 69, 70, 73, 76, 77, 85, 88, 92, 96, 98, 113.

Ann Hutchison: 1, 27, 55, 57, 67, 83, 111, 117.

Grace Wen Hwa Ts'ao: 26, 32, 33, 86, 90, 91.

Linda Loughran: 11, 93.

Joseph Szasfai: 68.

Virginia Museum Photography Staff & Others: 34, 35, 47, 58, 80, 84, 87, 90, 109, 114.

All other objects reproduced in this book were photographed by Katherine Wetzel, Richmond, Virginia.

Index